AJ Taylor has a degree in fire safety engineering and a masters in mathematical computer modelling. Having served for thirty years, he retired from the London Fire Brigade in 2010. In addition to fire command, one of his last roles was as a chartered fire engineer where he assessed fire prevention measures in buildings including the London Shard and the O2 Arena. However, he would assure you that his best years were the first fifteen as a firefighter on Lambeth Red Watch.

In memory of Andrew 'Baldy' Baldock, 1958–2015.

For Phillip 'Pip' Dwyer, who was there at the inception and coined the phrase 'That's got to go in the book'.

Lambeth Red Watch circa 1980–1995. (None of whom are characters in this work.)

Firefighters everywhere.

AJ Taylor

FIREFIGHTING: BETTER THAN WORKING FOR A LIVING

AUSTIN MACAULEY PUBLISHERS™

LONDON * CAMBRIDGE * NEW YORK * SHARJAH

A CIP catalogue record for this title is available from the British Library.

ISBN 9781035808649 (Paperback)
ISBN 9781035808656 (Hardback)
ISBN 9781035808663 (ePub e-book)

www.austinmacauley.com

First Published 2023
Austin Macauley Publishers Ltd®
1 Canada Square
Canary Wharf
London
E14 5AA

Always in my heart is my dear and patient wife. Thank you, Bernadette, for the advice, criticism, and most of all the encouragement to actually turn my thoughts and scribblings into this piece of work.

1

September 2019…June 1983
Persons Reported

There are two types of people who visit a nudist beach, the exhibitionist and the voyeur. The first of these will strip off whilst still standing and then lather themselves up with sun oil. They will manage to bend their body more than is necessary and spend far too long reaching intimate parts before either, strolling up and down the shore or prostrating themselves in all sorts of poses to ensure that all over tan. The second, a somewhat partner of the first, for without someone to watch what would be the point of the display, they need further tools. Having applied their lotions in the privacy of the hotel, they squat and sit to surreptitiously remove their clothes. Generally, they will be armed with a paperback but most definitely with sunglasses, the darker the better. This will allow hours of pretending to read whilst spotting the best exhibitionists and keeping a watch on the other voyeurs.

There are no innocent bystanders.

After spending a couple of days in both of these roles, I lost my book. I lay back, exhausted by the sheer dilemma that ensued. I spent some hours doing the inevitable hot sand dash, heading for the crystal waters of the Mediterranean only to aid in its continual dilution with urine and factor-thirty. And although I would recommend skinny dipping to anyone, it does involve a constant stress. There is always a fear that the cooling plunge will leave you less of a man than on entry, when the *bespectacled readers,* who saw only your arse, will now get a full frontal. My wife's part in this drama is betrayed by her creamy skin and fiery red hair, streaked now by the occasional silver thread. Moved from unlikely sun worship by one so fair, she feigns sleep of an almost professional quality, and captures some unsuspecting new arrivals.

I actually managed to close my eyes, not both at once, and drift off into recollections of my once more active and harrowing career as a firefighter. The next day, having found a notepad and pen, I started to scribble some anecdotes. I found each memory bred another and was soon spending most of my day engrossed in some sort of creative flow. As each cathartic line provided another use for my *Reactolites*, I did a sunbed shuffle to provide other interest and deflect from the strange appearance of moisture in my eyes. The raucous memories meandered but finally fell on previously secreted traumas; I was suddenly aware of my nakedness. The silent words leapt from the page, and I was afraid again, exposed.

I have to admit here that the authors gaze into the far distance, seemingly for inspiration, was not only a time of panic, but also a resumption of a former beach occupation that suited my narrative far better.

However…

Distant bell (tele-printer), click (electrical circuit made), LOUD BELLS (fire call bells ring), lights come on.

My arse had hardly hit the seat when the tele-printer bell rang, I had a quick slurp of my lukewarm tea, groaned audibly and rose from the now lukewarm chair. Before I got up and back out of the Mess doors, the bells dropped. We all knew; the electrical connection needed for this to happen had given us its pre-warning. The station came alive, every light glared and the bells immediately reached their deafening pitch. This was accompanied by a loud watch cheer, 'Go on Tom, go on Tomato!' My brothers were howling, sending me on my way back to the Watchroom.

There are all sorts of bells at a fire station, a relic of a nautical past. Historically, firefighters were ex-seamen, being more able to deal with long shifts, consequently we still have many naval terms and practices; not Tomato though, that's me. A bell sounds when the tele-printer actuates, this could just be a message, but it is often followed by the Fire Call Bells. These are much louder and accompanied by all the station lights; the electrical connection is just an unplanned, intuitive simulating by-product.

The route back to the Watchroom, or Box as we called it, is much straighter than my very recent journey from there to the Mess; it is my turn to go and retrieve the call slip. A long corridor runs right through our first-floor accommodation, the length of the station. Normally only lit by internal windows from our dormitory and the window at the end locker room, it was now ablaze with the station call lights. I couldn't have been further away from my target pole house. I leapt straight into a sprint, flying along the dark, shiny, wooden floorboards, like a winger with a ball in hand and accelerating towards the try line. My audience, if I had one, would see me stop with yards still to go.

I slid the final few feet grasping out with my left hand for a purchase to stop my progression and at the same time reaching above the pole house doors for the release mechanism with my right hand. If the doors had eyes, they would think I was John Travolta, straight out of Saturday Night Fever. I loved this, we were so full of energy we needed the release, but it didn't really work; the exertion kicked in adrenaline and only served to increase my excitement. I could hear the rest of the crews already sliding down the main poles to the awaiting fire engines. I threw myself at the pole and let gravity have a brief share of the journey.

This was also long due to the excessive height of the appliance bay. I had to use my shoes as a brake; we all have burnt leather patches on our shoes. Apart from being a hole in the floor with its obvious dangers, any use of the fire pole needs attention, it can be the most dangerous place on the fire station. You could easily burn your hands or even worse, break your ankles, we settled for burnt shoes.

Even with my rapid flight, the ancient printer had already finished typing the call out instructions and was sitting contrarily, waiting for acknowledgement.

The first word was FIRE.

It often was.

Most of us had been on the beer the night before, a late night at The Lion, a less than salubrious establishment in downtown Walworth. The sort of place where an entrance fee gave you a ticket for sausage and chips, and importantly a late-night lager, albeit in a plastic beaker. We had stayed at the station rather than going home. From the noise they were making now you could be mistaken for thinking they were still at the party, they weren't, it was normal. We had only been on duty about twenty minutes and for some reason I knew we were about to pick up a job.

I'd already had to deal with the flak from gate crashing the White Watch's night duty. H was their dutyman, I was his relief. He was in rather relaxed dress for Watchroom duties, but they'd had a busy night; and that wasn't considering

11

us interrupting their shift! He looked like he could do with a few hours more bedtime.

'Did you have a good one last night then? Where did you end up? You made a bloody racket getting in.' He might have been drowsy, but he was still smiley, his thick dark hair pointing to the distant ceiling and everywhere else.

'What us, we were like little mice.' I went for the dishonest denial routine, hands outspread. My collar and tie, the correct Dutyman attire, somehow enforcing the obvious falsehood.

'Yeah, mice with their fire boots on,' Patty, normally the White Watch spokesperson, came shouting into the Box and added his analysis. He was shorter than H but made up for it in character. The Box, normally bland and unimpressive, can get quite busy at change of watch.

'Sorry guys, you know how it is,' I changed tack.

'Yeah, but you nicked my bed; bloody Tomato,' said Patty, who was now trying to tuck his t-shirt into his trousers. I don't look like a tomato, but unfortunately the day I got a bit sunburnt a new advert came on the TV. I can't remember what it was for, but it involved children dressed as tomatoes with a prisoner dressed as a carrot. The carrots catch phrase was, 'I want to be a tomato.' I didn't stand a chance.

'But you was already akip, when we got back,' I said, confused.

Patty tried to explain, 'Yeah, but then we had a shout and when we came back you was sending them up…in my pit.'

'Shit Pat, I'm sorry, I must have got up for a piss and got back in the wrong bed,' it was slowly dawning on me. 'Pat, where did you sleep then?'

'Well in your bed, init.'

'Oh, okay.' I gazed into the distance, 'Did I really?'

'Yeah really.' Patti had given up on the attempt to hide his t-shirt and his porch; he was crouching and now scratching his back on the radiator.

'But I was in my pit this morning.'

'We had more than one shout, init.'

'H?'

'Really Tom, you're a bloody nuisance, they even had to open your bedding locker for you,' answered H. I was starting to remember things now, like almost getting into bed and realising it wasn't my duvet, I'd long since dumped the old grey issue blankets for my own bedding but so had everyone. It was time to change the subject, I didn't get a chance.

'At least we didn't have to push you out of the machine!' Patty said, who had again moved and was sitting on the desk.

'What do you mean?' I asked.

'What were you lot on last night, you were worse than usual and that's bad enough,' said H, he hadn't moved throughout this whole encounter apart from balancing on the back legs of the only chair.

'What? Nothing it must be the weather or something,' I was starting to wish I had some support. My watch were all getting ready for Roll Call; I propped myself up against the Tele-printer, a subconscious position of power.

'Too much falling over juice,' laughed Patty.

'But who tried to get on the fire engine?' I said, the change of focus removing any need for defence.

'Bloody Toby, it was 'horrible, he had nothing on but his socks, we thought we'd find him wandering the Embankment when we got back, scaring the locals,' said H. Fortunately there aren't many residential premises that near the front of the station but there was always a dribble of traffic, even in the early hours. I shuddered thinking of Toby sleepwalking alongside the Thames.

'But he was in his pit, *his own pit*, when we got back and sending up the zeds,' Patty finished off the story with another little personal dig.

'I can't believe it; he definitely likes a snore, but we have trouble getting him up when he's actually on duty.'

Lambeth is in Central London so it's far easier to stay than go home, and considering it's the Head Quarters of the London Fire Brigade it is surprisingly easy to break-in. A well-placed kick of the third appliance door from the Watchroom normally springs it open; in fact, none of the doors are that secure. Then there is the wall by the front gate, well within easy climbing height. However, we all have our own key to the rear wicket gate, keys similar to the, *not to be copied key*, kept on the fire engine; they normally allow us back in during night hours without disturbing anyone.

The over packed taxi had dropped us at the front of the station and before we could think about walking around the back, someone had kicked the bay door open. That was when H would have first known we had returned, he was sleeping in the Box. At that time of night, it is a lonely, remote and exposed room, especially when someone starts kicking at the appliance doors. H might not have appreciated the convenience at that moment but apart from the lack of a decent doorman, it was our inner London hotel, complete with a river front and views of the Houses of Parliament, our second home.

Patti and H were long gone now, and it was time for us to make a more dramatic exit. I hit the appliance indicator lights for both land appliances, an initial sign for my boys that this was probably some sort of fire call. I ran from the Watchroom, handing a call slip to our Guvnor and another to Bones, our Leading-Hand who was in charge of the Turntable Ladder. I dived into the back of the Pump Ladder. I would normally have had time to put my boots on before we left the station but for some reason, they were ready to roll; I would have to struggle to rig in the rear cab.

The Guvnor pulled the rope to open the appliance bay doors and we roared out into the expectant street. That was our moment, no matter where we were going, fire or rubbish, I dreamt of the public gratitude, perhaps hero worship; little did they know. The Embankment was at a pause, the lights were red, holding this part of London at a standstill; all eyes were waiting on us. I allowed myself a sigh of relief, I was sure I had forgotten to hit the button that controlled the lights, and the traffic would still be in full flow. We screeched a left out of the doors, then sharp left back down the side of the station, the Turntable Ladder following us along Black Prince Rd. The two-tones blasted a warning and a thank-you to the patient polluting limousines.

Rocking about in the chicane that was the main route to the centre of our ground, we all expertly avoided elbows and arms as we fought to completely rig. As we got to the end of Black Prince Rd., the air held a faint waft of burning, Frankie said, 'I think we've got one.' We all knew something was alight and it wasn't far away. Frankie held his crooked nose sideways in the air, as if to demonstrate; he was a great driver, but I still wished he'd keep both his eyes on the road. He turned back, almost bouncing into his seat, he was in his element. Lambeth's ground isn't that big and if we pick up a job you can often smell the smoke from right outside the station. I wondered if I could have smelt it earlier and that was the cause of my intuition; that was normally Granny's job.

Nod, our new boy, was sitting between Toby and me on the back of the machine, his face was pure horror; I could virtually hear his heart thumping. I made a mental note to try and ease his obvious apprehensions but there was a more pressing issue.

'Where's Granny?' I asked Toby. Granny was our resident giant and I'd only just missed his great lump.

'Out-duty,' he answered, more interested in something or some-her in the street. We would occasionally have to go to another station to make up their numbers. Although this can be a pleasant change of scenery, I always found it an inconvenience, preferring to stay with my brothers.

'Someone could have told me, I'm only the dutyman!' That meant all my bookings were wrong, there would be some alterations to do when we got back. 'Pass me the Nominal Roll Board, please Guv.' I still had him written down as riding our machine.

'I'll do it Tom,' shouted Frankie, aware of everything. When Frankie drove, he was the machine, its fourteen tons becoming part of his normally wiry physic; it didn't make him any prettier though. We slid around the back seat as he threw us around another corner. The journey to an incident is often more dangerous than the arrival, we'd had our near misses, we would have more.

The increasing scent of the fire brought me back from this brief distraction to the anticipation of something much more exciting. I glanced at Noddy trying to remember my first job and realised he was grasping the BA board for all it was worth and struggling for composure. I wondered how to tell him that it never completely goes away, it just becomes easier to control and much more addictive. There is a thrill just sitting in the back of a speeding lorry, hearing the muted two-tones from the inside and not quite seeing where you are going as you're being thrown about. On top of that we were now expecting to *get to work*, we'd been out a few times yesterday, Nod's first day with us, but it was looking like he was about to experience his first job, his first fire. He was old for a Junior Buck, he had at least a few years on me and Toby, but he was still the new boy and needed looking after.

We all had one ear on the radio and the other on the Guvnor. Whilst the machine blared and weaved around braking vehicles and staring public, Tobe and I checked each other subconsciously, a glance and a smile, we'd done this before. We had both slipped into the harnesses of our Breathing Apparatus Sets.

'You okay Noddy?' Toby asked, 'You gonna take that board and get a line?'

'Yep, no worries.' I thought his bloody head will come off one day if he keeps on wobbling it up and down like that. We sent him an invite to training school, so he'd be prepared for our little soiree the night before. It went something like:

You are cordially invited to after duty refreshments on Friday, the first day with your fabulous new watch. Please ensure you have eveningwear and the appropriate remuneration…'cause we're going down the pub and you're buying the beer.

Apparently, his squad instructor read it out at roll call.

Noddy was christened almost immediately he arrived. 'Are you with us?' Frankie asked him.

'Yes, Fireman Buckwood,' he replied, nodding his head at the same time. It was almost imperceptible, just three or four short nods. I thought it might have been nerves, apparently not.

'More importantly did you get our invite?' I asked.

His head was nodding before he even answered. 'And what's your real name?' Frankie said.

He didn't get a chance to reply, 'Okay, Noddy,' said Gran, 'welcome aboard.' And that was it, first day, well first few minutes really, a new moniker.

'Got your tally, Tobe?' I said as I slipped mine into the board. Toby slid his yellow bit of plastic into the board beneath mine.

Then we heard it, our call sign on the radio, 'Bravo two-two-one.' The Guvnor told them to go ahead, and we all listened silently, swinging from handgrips, as Frankie continued to swerve the Machine around. 'Bravo two-two-one, for your information, we have received several further calls to this address…' the rest of the message was lost to us in the rear cab, we now knew that this was no false alarm.

The Guvnor looked over his shoulder from the front seat and said, through his thick moustache, 'You got that chaps.'

That's all, just four words. He managed to look right at me to be sure I'd heard, he did the same to Toby and Nod. He was on top of his game, he could have been ordering a cup of tea; I could have done with one.

I always imagined him as a Wing Commander and was dying to ask him if he ever twirled the ends of his whiskers; I never would though, he commanded too much respect. According to Rodney, our old hand, he'd never flown a Spitfire in his life and used to be a waiter. I preferred my image.

We had a set of on-arrival tactics to which we'd added, *keeping an eye on Nod.* Toby and I would be going in; I tightened my straps and turned the set on to standby mode. We had fought many fires together, we had that sixth sense that binds brothers, the way you can laugh without even saying a word, a mutual knowledge grown over time and activated by facial expressions. Except he wasn't my brother, and his name wasn't Toby, but he did have big ears (Toby jug, lugholes, ears, it's a Cockney Rhyming thing, probably had Frankie to thank).

I could feel the excitement oozing from our new junior buck, touched with a fair bit of nervousness, I could feel my heart racing too. It didn't take long to get anywhere on our small patch of South London, but we were ready and there were just a few spare moments to reflect. A few moments to realise what we were about to do. I decided to distract Noddy to stop him over-thinking the following brief minutes; I reached for my route book in my inside pocket.

'You'll need one of these, Nod,' I said, gaining his curiosity as I turned to Braganza St. and pointed out the handwritten directions. He glanced up from the page expectantly as I put the tatty book away. 'See me later. We're here.' I pointed out the front windscreen as we turned the corner, and the smell finally became a vision. Not for long, we soon got too close to see anything from inside the back cab.

Frankie was stretching forward and looking up whilst still driving, he shouted, 'Third floor, pulling past.' He was calculating the best place to stop, in seconds he had considered: ladders, hose, water supply, access and, knowing Frankie, where he would look the best. The machine slowed, our doors opened, and we were out.

The Guvnor was immediately accosted by a screaming woman, he took a breath away from her and shouted, 'PERSONS,' over his shoulder; as ever a man of many words. It is an abbreviation of a fireground message; we knew it meant there could be someone in the fire. I took a quick glance up, saw the clouds of black and grey smoke bellowing out of the third floor and thought to myself, *not another stiff*. Not many people survive a fire, not in these small dwellings and not with that much smoke. Most are dead before we even leave the station.

Noddy, with Long Line over his shoulder and the B.A. Board in hand, sprinted up the stairs; Toby and I followed but slightly slower.

'Go on Nod, we'll be there when we've got a minute,' I cried. Firegear and BA sets do tend to slow you down, even Toby couldn't keep up with Nod who was fresh from Training School. We raced behind him as best we could, one hand on the rail and one hand protecting our facemasks. They are our link to normal air, our buffer against burning toxins and the poisonous world that we were about to inhabit. We were going to need them soon.

We were at Harcott House, an early nineteen-twenty style tenement block with open stairways and communal balconies that lead to the front doors. Our ground and those around us are full of housing estates, built at various stages in the twentieth century, they range from sixties tower blocks to these classic older builds. These were easier to deal with, unenclosed and nearer to the ground. The staircases normally had rubbish chutes with bin rooms at the ground floor, these often caught alight, but not today. That was our general work, that and people stuck in lifts; today was what we called, *a proper job*. The whole event had attracted plenty of attention and people were watching from other balconies and across the street. We were only vaguely aware of their scrutiny, to an extent we had gone into automatic mode; this is what we practised for, this is what we lived for.

The possibility of someone being involved elevated our response, if there was going to be any chance of their survival, we had to cut a few corners and get in quick. There is no such thing as a good building fire, they all hurt someone. But we loved them, except a fatal, which could always ruin your day. We were high, everything was occurring instinctively, everyone knew their part, and it was all happening fast. Even Noddy, fresh from training school knew what to do, as long as he got a confirmation from one of us.

We arrived at the third floor, fortunately a light breeze was keeping the smoke away from the front door. Noddy was shouting at the top of his voice, 'Stand from under.' He turned to us desperately, 'The old bill won't get out of the way.' He was poised, the green canvas bag full of rope that we called a Long Line, balanced on the balcony, the end already under his foot as a back-up, just as we'd taught him.

'Try, *get out of the fucking way*, Nod, they won't understand fire brigade talk,' said Toby. It was good advice, but they still didn't move. The line needed to be thrown down so our fire hose could be hauled back up.

'Just throw it Nod,' I said. We all peered over the balcony and saw a local PC almost get a haircut.

'That'll learn 'im,' said Toby. Below, Frankie had laid out the uncharged hose while the TL crew were trying to find a hydrant. They were helped now as the police finally got out of the way.

Nod got on with pulling the hose up the front of the building as Toby and I put our arms around each other for balance and attempted to both kick down the front door. It was putting up a battle. Just then one of Brixton's crew turned the corner with a fourteen-pound sledgehammer in one hand; he held it like you or I would hold a rolled-up newspaper.

'I've got it boys,' he said. As we watched, Granny appeared through the billowing smoke. Before I could ask what he was doing, he said, 'I got there just in time.'

'You got there bloody quick Gran,' I said, surprised, 'I haven't even booked you out.'

'The Brixton boys phoned up, they wanted to get away sharp for something or another; I left early. Stand back.'

'You're a Saint, Gran,' said Toby. Granny swung the hammer in the confined space of the balcony and the door gave up its last attempt at security. He really was built like a brick shithouse and my mind flashed back to the night before and the *not so young beauty*, half his size and twice his age.

'Granny, where's your mum?' I asked, I wouldn't normally be that brave, but Toby was standing between us.

'Get in that fire bold boy, I'll deal with you later,' he grinned. Toby was putting on his facemask and starting up his breathing apparatus set, I followed suit; he looked at me quizzically.

'What's that all about Tom?' he said, his last coherent words before the restrictions of the, not so perfect, speech diaphragm.

'Didn't he tell you about his sultry encounter last night,' I said, holding back a second before I too disappeared behind the rubber mask.

'Tomato!' Granny's voice had gone up an octave. I was always the full Tomato when I'd gone too far.

'Alright, just starting up here, ready Tobe?' I mumbled. I'd got over the shock of seeing Granny and realised that back-up must have arrived, which would mean that Frankie would have help downstairs and today we could be confident of our water supply.

Toby and I were changing, notching down the excitement and switching into a more furtive mode. We were getting ready to enter our *third home*, that blind heated world that should have you running the other way. We normally loved nothing more than the chance to get to work, except today the Guvnor had shouted, *Persons*. We both knew subconsciously, if not actually, that there was

19

too much black smoke coming out of this flat for anyone to survive. If we were quick, there just might be a chance.

Noddy had the hose secured, charged and ready, he handed me the branch and I tested it again, out of habit. With our faces covered, Toby and I could only be vaguely differentiated now, apart from his blond locks which provided a fringe around the rubber seal of his mask. 'Ready Tobe,' I said, he was talking to Granny. I could see the shaft of his axe sticking out uncomfortably between him and his BA set. Toby was the only single guy on the watch, although a couple of those with partners seemed to forget that sometimes. He was lithe to the point of skinny, as fit as hell, and always had a cold.

I looked at our bizarre threshold, clouds of smoke were pumping out, threatening our admission. Toby turned to face me, we stared at each other with imperceptible grins, 'Let's go,' he said. With one pace we were swallowed by unbreathable fire fumes, and we disappeared through the recently vacated doorframe.

Once inside a heavy, straw-grey shadow dropped over our visors and existence was transformed. The everyday, unnoticed noise from outside softened, became muffled and even quieter with every crouched step forward. We naturally bowed as we moved on, a show of respect for the obscurity and increasing warmth. Now I could only hear the rasping of my exhalation valve, reminding me I was alive, and Toby, shuffling behind, reminding me I wasn't alone. Our lives reliant on a cylinder of air and, above all else, each other. I turned behind to check he was alright, his speech diaphragm vibrated a muted, 'Okay.'

The hose and branch were still light, being carried by us both and fed by those left safely behind. The further into the flat we crept the more we were cozied by the enveloping smoke, embraced by the entrapment of a wicked comfort blanket. We were now detached from the outside world, physically and mentally. Their only awareness of our progress was the slow movement of the hose as it was seemingly sucked further into the flat. We were making sense of the alien environment by touch, feeling our way along with the back of our hands and testing the floors integrity with a size nine boot. Faintly, through the tingling, rising temperature, I thought I could hear the cackle of combustion.

We knew the rough layout of these flats, we'd been in enough, we would be in many more; we expected the kitchen to be close. We were right, there was thicker smoke and more heat up ahead than in there, so we dropped the hose outside and both entered the kitchenette. This was our last hope of finding anyone remotely alive; we hadn't fully worked that out, we were still full of hope. We circled the room; I went left and Toby took the right although we could virtually reach each other across the small space. Technically we should have stayed together, providing support and back-up for each other; that would also slow the search. I stumbled upon a tiny table and chair in the murky invisibility, they seemed to be incongruous in such a little room. There was an unfinished plate on the surface which, with a sweep from my hand, almost became floor scraps. In a matter of seconds, we had kicked all the furniture and disturbed all the surfaces enough to prove to ourselves that it was vacant. We were thorough but quick, a person wouldn't last long in these conditions. The kitchen was empty, there was no one to be found, just soot and grease. We met somewhere on the far side and returned together, across the centre for a final sweep.

Our hose was where we left it but playing hide and seek among the thickening fire gasses, I groped the floor outside the kitchen and we were reunited. In buildings bigger than this there is a constant fear of getting lost and running out of air before you find your way out. It's easy to become disorientated, even in a cramped smoky room, even in a Lambeth flat. A line of hose can show you the way out, as long as you remember which way the couplings are laid. It's also handy for putting out fires.

With a lounge, one or two bedrooms and a bathroom to go, our quarry could be anywhere. His chances of survival vanishing, we slowed in subconscious realisation. We knew, in our hearts, that we were the only living things in this flat. It was smoky black and too hot for anything else to be alive. The transfer from would be rescuers to body searchers was imperceptible. Unknowingly we relaxed a little, urgency had dissipated and we now focused on finding the fire. We were on our knees, our thin plastic leggings trying desperately to stay in one piece. The hose was like an over inflated tyre, stretched out and laying heavily snaked along the passageway. It felt like it would have preferred to stay right there for all the extra effort it took to drag it to the end of the hall. We found a room we thought should be the lounge; it was currently an incinerator. We carried out a mutual check to make sure we both had enough air, an action we continually repeated, almost sub-consciously.

'What you on Tobe?' I turned, sat and shone my torch at my air gauge.

'One-thirty,' was his muted reply, one hundred and thirty bar pressure. I had a little less, but we both had plenty of air left in our cylinders.

At the same time, we realised we were wrong, two more life forms in the shape of Brixton's crew had entered the flat behind us. They hauled some hose, temporarily releasing it from the grasp of the corridor walls and giving us a decent bight to take to the fire. Toby pointed them towards the bedrooms while we manoeuvred the hose towards the lounge, it was still fighting us, refusing to fit in the narrow passageway and impatient for release. We managed to creep surreptitiously towards the fireroom, feigning not to hide from the erupting furnace. At the door I took a glance into the frenzy. The dark scorching fumes failed to conceal a rapidly growing beacon at the far end of the room. We hid at the side of the door like scared children, afraid of the monster.

The fire had now broken the window and was venting out the back of the flat; it must have looked quite spectacular from outside. It was also flashing over, long disproportionate flames laughed above our heads, licking out of the chamber. This is what happens when you try to restrict a fire under a ceiling, when you confine the vertical plume. With nowhere to go the heat builds up and soon gets so hot the whole place ignites. We both got down even lower, trying to become an invisible part of the skirting board and avoid the searing heat that would follow my attack. I could feel the sweat on my face running down and pooling, sloshing about my chin, the rest of my body was scalding inside my itchy tunic.

I turned the jet skywards, hoping this would dislodge any loose, burning embers before we entered, better under our boots than down our backs. Large pieces of plaster crashed to the floor. Whilst still sheltering outside the doorway, away from the flaming intensity, I poked the jet around the door again to give what looked like the seat of the fire a drink. I could feel the rise in temperature on my exposed ears and hands, probably from super-heated steam; a return volley to answer our barrage. On our knees we moved into the room, sweeping the jet around to quickly knock down the rest of the fire. I turned off the branch but, as always, the place was already soaked.

It was still uncomfortably hot but the fire was virtually out and venting from the broken windows; I could make out steam issuing from the now precariously plastered, blackened walls. With the heat now dissipating, we managed to stand-up into a crouch and inspect our triumph. A lot of the ceiling was laid over the floor and everywhere was wet; fire runoff squelched and sloshed under our boots.

There was no one alive in this room, there was never going to be, not once the fire had moved in with its poisonous burning gases. There were no dead bodies either. Only the debris of someone's lost life, their possessions and curiosities stolen by the blaze. The furniture was arranged to view the fire corner, just as it had been before the TV became a memory. Now there was only a mound of plastics and glass, covered in lumps of spent wall and soggy ceiling. We kicked the debris about and gave a few of the hot spots a drink.

With the fire out and the windows gone I could feel the welcome breeze of the third-floor location. The whole flat started to clear and vision improved. Brixton's crew hadn't found the missing occupier either. We carried out another search of the whole place before we felt happy enough to leave the flat.

And that was that, just fifteen minutes ago I needed a cup of tea bad, now I was gagging. I was relieved as well, fighting fire can be great fun but finding bodies is not the best part of our job. I was also exhilarated, a strange feeling I got at having just successfully extinguished a fire; it's a sort of guilty pleasure. There is an elation at having fought the beast and won but it has to be supressed, after all, this is someone else's tragedy. For Noddy, it was the first of many and from what we'd seen he was going to do alright.

The screaming woman quietened when her Dad, the flat occupier, had returned from the shops with a pint of milk in one hand and a newspaper under his arm. They had disappeared into a neighbour's place. The Guys were busy putting all the gear away and the Guvnor wanted us to tell him what we had found.

That's when it happened, you didn't need attuned senses to hear it, although the first chink was faint.

'Any of you boys want a cuppa,' an angel had just emerged from a nearby flat and I was first there. There wasn't enough to go around.

'Most important lesson of the day Nod,' I slurped.

'Don't be last!' the Guvnor said.

2

September 1983
Cats and Bears

Frankie had asked me round while we were on our days off, he lived in Grove Park with his wife and two young boys. Well, that's not quite all, there was the Doberman and five, three-week-old kittens. The mother cat must have been around somewhere but she remained aloof. He said he had something for me but had kept it secret. That didn't matter, it was nice to pop in for a coffee.

At work Frankie was a bit of a poser, well a lot of a poser really, his comb would often be sliding through his hair as he spoke, and he had a lot to say. It was like he needed to frame each sentence with the sweep of his quiff. We reckoned he thought he was something big in the movie business, just because he'd done some work as an extra, but he was no film star. He wasn't the prettiest guy on the watch either, we all have our faults but Frankie could have done with a straighter nose and less crooked eyes. However, he had one of those infectious sort of smiles; I always wondered if I had missed the joke, but it couldn't help put you in a good mood. Maybe that's what made him a success with the ladies, although I thought that was more in Frankie's mind than in reality.

Frankie's mum called him Frankie or Frank, it was his name after all, he was just in the enviable position of it also being his nickname. To us he'd recently graduated from Frank to Frankie, as in the Band, *Frankie Goes to Hollywood*, it was more of an endorsement. He was also very laid back, relaxed.

He had an excessive pride in the uniform, shiny shoes, well pressed trousers, even his firegear looked just a little too manicured. I couldn't put my finger on it but I wouldn't be surprised if he had his tunics tailored. Once, when preening himself, the Chief Officer walked across the yard, which was an occupational hazard when your fire station was housed below Head Quarters. I was still quite

24

new at the time and I guess I was being trained in how to wash the Fire Engine, I hadn't had a chance to clean myself from the fire the night before.

'Morning Guv, have you seen the state of our new boy,' Frankie was pointing directly at me. I guess I must have looked frightened to death as well as filthy.

The Chief walked straight up to me and held out his hand to shake, 'Nice to meet someone who does all the work,' he smiled, cast Frankie a contemptuous glance and was gone.

'He's a nice bloke,' I smirked at Frankie.

Frankie was much more casual at home, an old sweater and jeans, even a pair of slippers. He'd put the Doberman out in the garden and plopped a kitten in my lap as he poured the coffee. I sat at a tiny table, squeezed into the corner of a small kitchen, crammed with gadgets, the work surfaces were like a showroom for sandwich makers, food mixers and of course a cafetière which was now cast into the sink. He saw me looking, 'All courtesy of Rodney, most of them don't work properly, you've probably got the same.' I didn't, but I didn't get time to say, Bruce, the dog, came bounding back in through the bottom panel of the back door. I protectively cradled the baby cat; the whole episode could have been stage managed to start a kitten/Tomato bond. He was sent straight out again, thankfully, but not before he managed to give me a friendly slobber.

'He probably won't bite you but he's messy,' laughed Frankie. Frankie could do that to you, make you comfortable and disturbed at the same time. I was glad Bruce was back out in the garden but not quite convinced he wouldn't be back.

'Great idea, the Dog flap.' I took one of the biscuits on offer. 'Did it take long to train him?'

'He virtually made it himself.' Frankie was laughing even more now and passed me another kitten. 'We came home from the shops and there he was running around the garden with the bottom panel of the door round his neck. We reckon he was chasing Misty; she went through the cat-flap and he must have tried to follow. So, we made a dog flap, with a cat flap in it; good ain't it.' I was getting giddy myself, I kept one eye on the huge dog doing laps of the garden. 'They look after themselves you know, what are you going to call them?' Straight back onto the kittens, was Frankie trying to catch me off guard? I now had two bundles of bony fur in my lap, one all black and a tabby.

'They're tiny. Where's Mum?'

'She won't be far, they can't leave her yet, you'll have to wait another couple of weeks.'

'I can't. They are gorgeous but we're not at home enough.' I considered the possibility of new arrivals saving my marriage and quickly gave it up as unfair on the felines.

'Two are promised already, I didn't want you to be disappointed. That one's taken to you she's one of the girls. They look after themselves you know.'

'Don't you worry about burglars with that great big hole in the door?' I was trying to change the subject, again.

'Naw, Bruce loves burglars.' At that moment Frankie looked extremely comfortable, a natural part of the surrounding domestication, his tall frame leaning against the sink with a coffee in his skinny hand. It was the total opposite to how he acted at work; I guess we all enjoyed the escape from one life to the other. Barbara, his wife was as absent as Misty.

Frankie was one of those people that could make you think his idea was your idea; I knew if I stayed there much longer, I might end up with all the kittens and probably a Doberman to boot. I made my excuses and checked my coat pockets on the way out, just to make sure I wouldn't need to buy cat food on the way home.

I didn't do much else on those four days off: there was no part time work, there was a cold snap putting everyone off of golf, and any chance of getting on my allotment was eventually scuppered by the rain. It had got to a point where I didn't like being at home. We all called the Fire Station our second home, it was becoming my first. I'd got to know the nightly routines of the Blues and Greens as well as the White Watch, they were much the same as ours. They gathered in the late evening in different locker rooms, talked a similar amount of rubbish, and there was always a spare bed, as long as I could remember which one it was. The Whites loved to play cards, I never got involved in that, the pot got too big.

My wife and I have a small, terraced house in the Blackheath end of Lewisham, that's meant to be the posh bit. She called it Blackheath, I called it Lewisham, the Estate Agent agreed with her. It was an old place, built at the turn of the century, known as a *Two Up, Two Down*. I'd got to the point where I would physically slow down as I got closer and closer to my front door. A hard thing to do without falling off my bike. I don't know why, she was home less than me, often away for days on a job she wasn't allowed to talk about. I didn't want to know; I'd stopped asking about her days long ago. Sometimes it felt like her rota was designed to run opposite to mine.

She was out again tonight, according to the scribbled note left sloppily on the table. I occasionally thought of taking down my shift calendar but I never did, I don't think she understood it anyway. I guess I didn't mind her not being there, perhaps we both felt the same? I looked at the lonely vegetables, going wrinkly in the rack, and sighed; they would be going back to the allotment for composting. I was really looking forward our next tour.

As normal we were sitting around the dormitory in various stages of putting on our uniforms, Granny was telling us about his last game of rugby. I always needed a shower after my cycle and was drying myself off when Toby said, 'Who's going for a beer tonight?'

'You okay, Toby? It's a bit early for pub talk,' asked Granny.

'I'm great, I just wanted to be first to ask, someone always beats me to it.'

It wasn't even nine o'clock and we weren't even on duty. There always seemed to be an appropriate time during the day when someone suggested a drink after work, it didn't have to be a tragedy but the moment had to be perfectly timed for a maximum affirmative response. It had become a bit of a charade and apparently a competition, but we didn't really need an excuse.

'Oh, all right then, if you twist my arm,' we all said at once. And that was it, we were set up for the day. Nothing could touch us now. Although we could have done without the news at Roll Call that we had a BA drill and were supposed to be there by 10.00.

'We'll never make it; don't they know how far away we live?' Frankie was talking out loud but the Guv made it clear.

'Have your tea whilst you're doing your checks. We leave at 09.30.' We'd still be late but at least we weren't going to miss the first cuppa of the day.

Breathing Apparatus or BA is a fundamental part of our job, without it we just wouldn't be able to get in and extinguish the fire. So, we were on our way to one of the many purpose-built facilities for BA training; apparently, we have to practice. It was also good for Nod, who couldn't wear operationally until he'd finished his first six months.

Noddy, our Junior Buck, was turning out to be quite a nice guy, he had joined the Brigade after some years as a Postman. Toby and I have got used to the idea that he was older than us, even though he was the JB. He has a beautiful wife and two young kids, consequently he is continually looking for extra work; a fireman's wage doesn't go far if you have a mortgage and a family. We all have second jobs, we called them our *part-time* or our *fiddle*, but Noddy seemed to have more than all of us. I suppose in his previous life as a Postie, he was well qualified in this area and must have carried a few over. He wouldn't say no to anything, building, driving, he was currently trying to sell showers. It was a constant source of entertainment, discovering his latest adventure.

One morning he proudly showed us some business cards he'd had printed to push his new plumbing business. He couldn't work out why we found them so funny. Granny read it back to him, 'Twenty-four-hour plumber, phone after 6pm…' He still didn't get it; he didn't get much work either. His greatest claim was the occasional Punch and Judy show, something we didn't really believe until we caught him practicing in the shower. He must have been waiting for Toby and me to walk in.

Two socks appeared above a shower curtain and he began his routine, 'Where's the baby? What you done with me sausages? That's the way to do it,' and then the sound of a Swazzle. Toby and I got drenched attacking the shower curtain.

The BA chamber can be altered internally to make the layout different and is littered with old furniture and the occasional hazard, just to make things interesting. Unfortunately for the instructors, we have been in them so often they no longer hold much curiosity, and that can only lead to mischief.

The instructors fill them with cosmetic smoke and send us in to play, or as they prefer to put it, to train. There is a control room where they sit to monitor how we are progressing with their latest scenario. This is achieved by a series of strategically placed, weight sensitive panels in the floor. We know exactly where these are located.

Granny and I followed a few minutes behind Nod and Frank, through one of the side doors. We were searching for two training dummies, or missing persons for the purposes of the drill. These dummies live outside the chamber on a specially designed bit of concrete floor in a corner of the yard. Actually, they just lay about in a pile anywhere, we sometimes find that they have wandered up a drill tower and can't get down on their own. Luckily, they never manage to get very high, probably due of a combination of their spineless nature and horrendous weight problem. Today two of them have left the comfort of their companions and have got lost in the drill chamber.

On our way in I overheard one of the instructors saying that the panel indicators were playing up. Granny heard too; he was grinning under his facemask. You'd think they would have worked it out by now; we'd planned not to tread on every panel to keep them guessing where we were. Toby took our tallies with a wink; he'd landed the job of Entry Control. The first sensor is in sight of the door so we stepped on it in case they were watching. We stomped and groped our way around, quickly catching up with the other two. The smoke wasn't very thick today, 'They must be running out of smoke bombs, it's getting quite clear,' I said.

It is bizarre how flippant we are about a very important part of our profession. Maybe we just didn't want to admit to the real risks. Toby said it was because it just didn't compare with a *proper job*; he may be right.

Frankie was sitting on an old sofa with his arm around an unsuspecting dummy. 'Your new girlfriends prettier than most of them,' said Gran. As if I'd been heard, more smoke entered the chamber.

'Yours is behind me, taking a nap on the floor,' said Frankie.

'How's your air Gran,' I said, 'I'm a bit low.' We reckoned we'd wasted enough time and should be on our way out, get out too quickly and they might find you something else to do. We all checked our air and decided that Gran and I should go back first. Granny lent over and grabbed the dummy behind the sofa, he is strong but it was still an effort.

'Shall we two it?' I said.

'Naw, it'll be easier once I get him on my back.' I held him up and Gran slipped him onto his shoulders in a firefighter's lift. Off we went, stepping over all the sensors, an easy job for Gran even with his load; I had to almost jump to clear them. We burst back out of the doors to the instructors' surprise. They were both glued to the indicator panel, for some reason expecting it to be accurate. Granny threw the dummy on top of the pile with the rest of her family.

'Well done guys, close down and do your sets. Cylinders are over in the charging room,' the instructor seemed happy enough. Frank and Nod came out with a casualty that was identical to ours and to those lying in the corner. Frank let Noddy drag him the rest of the way. He still had his set on as he came back from laying the final dummy to rest.

'You can close down now,' I said, 'it's all done.' Walking back towards the control room, Noddy looked to the instructor for confirmation. As he removed his helmet to take off his mask his whistle began to sound. The once friendly drill organiser was on him like a shot.

'You should have been out already, that was your whistle, don't they teach you anything at training school.' He obviously knew he was the new boy and had decided to give his own self-appointed importance an airing. He was doing a good job of making himself look like a pratt. The whistle is there to give you an audible warning that your air supply has gone into the safety margin, you should be out of any incident, or drill, before it sounds.

'But I was out,' said Noddy.

'That was too close, what if something had gone wrong?' Nod decided not to argue, I didn't, especially as I may have caused his delay.

'How much air should we have when we get out then? Surely that's just good management of supply.'

'I'll have to put it in my report, whatever you say Tommy.' Granny stood up; he had been kneeling down sorting out his set. It was easy to forget how big he was until times like this.

He looked at Nod, 'Good drill Nod, well done for finding that other stiff and especially for pointing the way out. I reckon you almost led from the back.' He turned to the instructor, 'Can you put all that in your report and make sure the whistle incident is after exit when the drill was over, after moving your dummy and after coming back to talk to you.' Granny wasn't threatening, it all sounded quite reasonable. He turned his back on the instructor, 'There's a full cylinder here for you Nod.' Gran had a way with words!

'Thanks Gran,' Nod answered.

On the way home the Guvnor turned to us all, 'Good drill chaps, they said you all did well.' I just nudged Nod with my eyebrows raised.

Bravo two-two-one, priority, over

We were not quite on our ground but the Guvnor had already booked us available. We were called almost as soon as he put the radio hand set down. It was to a bin room alight, we all relaxed to just another load of rubbish, so we thought, and an extended ride on the bell.

It was most definitely alight; clouds of smoke were surging from the open doors at the base of the concrete tower block. We dived in and started to wheel out all the paladins, crammed, empty, hot, and cold, they were all as full of smoke as the bin room itself. We really should have been wearing our breathing apparatus but we never did for trash; just in case we got a *proper job*. Somewhere, in the deep recess of my brain, I knew that burning refuse contains excessive amounts of toxins, but we all chose to ignore this. We could deal with waste by holding our breath or standing upwind, but we could never enter a flat that was alight without a BA set. The introduction of man-made materials into modern furnishings in the seventies, had turned most dwelling fires into deadly poisonous environments. So, knowing best, we continued to cough and splutter around anything that wasn't a flat or bigger. The image of the brave, handsome fireman emerging from a burning building with a child in his arms, just wouldn't happen today; we look more like spacemen in our BA facemasks. This image was about to be proved completely wrong.

The bin room was still full of smoke, taking a long time to vent and in our rush to pull out all the giant dustbins we had forgotten to mark the one currently in use, the one most likely to be alight. The Guvnor was shaking his head, he just looked on as we danced around trying to locate the target. Frankie laid out the hose reel for us to douse the fire when our pantomime had finally stopped. Undaunted, he disappeared into the cloudy lair, just to have a check around. With the vast clouds of expanding smut, it must have looked like a more serious incident; two police officers had even turned up to see what was going on. They must have been having a quiet day as they didn't seem in any hurry to leave; preferring to watch us unsuccessfully try to flood a bin that had far too many holes at the bottom.

'We're going to have to tip it,' said Gran. We don't like to turn them over because of the mess it creates, that and the fact that we have to clear them up. This one just wouldn't go out so we noisily threw it over the pavement.

'Go and get the shovel Nod,' said the Guv, but he was already on his way.

Then we heard Frankie shout, something muffled from deep inside the grotty den. Toby and I were both looking at each other and, like me, he must have thought he heard the words, *still alive*. The police heard it too, one of them was already on his radio' probably trying to raise the alarm before we had a chance. Suddenly my heart started to race, we had grabbed the bins with our eyes closed unable to see anyway. We must have missed something more important than garbage. Even the Guvnors normal composure was being stretched.

The entrance revealed nothing but an obscure fug, meanwhile we were frozen in uncertainty, staring at the shrouded doorway. The shouts and hurried footsteps got louder and we snapped into action. Something was amiss and we were going to be needed, each one of us getting ready to maybe save a life. Frankie emerged from the bin room like a rock star breaking through dry ice. There was urgency in his voice as he now shouted, 'I think he's still alive.' We were stunned by the poor creature in his arms.

Our pile of drowned, domestic leftovers now forgotten, we converged on this apparition, ready to help. Frankie dived dramatically onto the floor, being more careful of his firegear than the casualty, even in this critical situation. He started mouth-to-mouth resuscitation and I jumped in with cardiac massage. It was no good, our attempt to save his life was knocking the stuffing out of him.

All over the sidewalk.

'I don't think he'll make it,' cried Granny.

'Oh, save him, save him, save the baby,' Toby took on the role of Mum, worthy of any Punch and Judy routine, his arms flailing in the air.

If we carried on you wouldn't be able to tell where the trash ended and the casualty began. Frankie had rescued a huge, but definitely dying, Teddy Bear. For a time, it was touch and go but we eventually brought him back from the edge.

The two police officers scowled, if it hadn't been for the laughter from the rest of our crew, I think we might have got arrested. 'Keep it professional boys,' said the Guv, 'Nod, get some bandages, Gran, go and ask for an ambulance, now.'

'I've already done that!' said an angry constable, as they finally left the scene.

Teddy was more than the worse for wear, he was wet, filthy, torn, and at least one arm was in need of surgical attention. Noddy immediately adopted him, I thought, *surely he's not taking him home for his kids.*

We just sat down to a cuppa when the bells dropped. I'm sure Granny was responding before any bell rang. We'd only been back long enough for a driver change around.

Distant bell, click, LOUD BELLS, lights come on.

Rod was mad, not at the bells, although as Mess Manager we all preferred him to stay in the kitchen and cook the meal. He was mad because he was now driving the PL. Rod was sane until you put him behind the wheel of a fire engine, a sort of occupational hazard. Rod was driving us now; he and Frankie took turns on the PL and TL and had switched for the duration of the drill. We were short of drivers; Granny was waiting for a course but he wasn't really that keen.

I have an awkward relationship with Rod, I think my vegetarian diet puts him in a bit of a spin. I like to eat with the rest of the watch as much as possible, so I try to have a similar meal. I'm sure he isn't that bad, we just don't hit it off, I don't get him and he doesn't let me in. Although the more I thought about it, the less I could find to fault him. He has a sharp tongue, everyone knows that; I just felt it more often than the rest, I thought.

Rodney lets me have a sort of half mess, I guess it is a bit awkward. I make up for it when they have a roast joint that needs carving, then it's, *Get the Tomato to do it*; Rodney reckons I'm the only one who won't nick any. I suppose I expected a hippy cook to understand a vegetarian, but he really wasn't much of a hippy, that was just an image. He was more of a cross between Wyatt Earp and Andy Williams, a sort of gun toting firefighter in an apron. He thought Flower Power was something you added to make a cake rise. Although flour can be quite dangerous in the wrong hands, as we would find out. But not today, today was going to be hair raising.

It would be nice here to say that Rod was a really great driver and never hit anything, but that would be unfair to all the wing mirrors and bumpers of the cars along Black Prince Rd., the main route to the rest of our ground. He seemed to get into his stride by the end of the road though, and then nothing was safe. He was forever filling in accident reports, not that you would have noticed from the Fire Engines, they were so tatty anyway. Most of the time he managed to hit things that were moving unnecessarily, leaping out from open spaces, you know the sort of stuff, bollards, lampposts, parked cars. I shouldn't criticise, being a driver was a bit of a thankless task and I had failed my driving course. It is expected though, if you do something wrong and no one says a word, you start to think you've really messed up.

We did have some spectacular close shaves, but all the time they were only glancing, they didn't seem to matter. They just joined the reverie of later drinking sessions; everything was brought to court in the pub. Today, Rod nearly wiped out Brixton's Pump.

We were haring down Camberwell New Rd., having been called to smell of burning on the edge of our ground. Toby shouted, 'Crash positions,' and we flung ourselves all over the rear cab with arms and legs everywhere, mimicking the film *Airplane*; it is good practice for the real thing. We had no idea how close we were about to come.

We approached the crossroad, needing to turn left, it was blocked with traffic. Without even a passing thought for the brakes, Rodney swung into the oncoming lane, sirens blaring. Brixton raced from our right, sirens blaring. They couldn't see us and we couldn't see them, both two-tones now mystically synchronised. Traffic had slowed in hesitant anticipation and we were on the wrong side of the road, trying to make the corner with more than two wheels on the tarmac. All the heads of people in the street were fixated, lost in the probable disaster that we must be rushing to reach, wondering who needed our help and staring at the comfort only we could bring.

I remember hearing our Guvnor say, 'Easy.' I actually found time to hold on to some part of the cab, we all did, anticipating the left swing. There was a frightened silence in the rear cab, noticeable compared to the clamour of our sirens outside and compared to the inevitable crescendo that should follow. Rodney finally opted for a lower gear.

Blindly, Brixton raced from the west, a red beast coming directly into the glare of the late summer sun, they didn't need to slow down; they were going straight on. All other traffic had stopped, probably confused as to where all the noise was coming from. In the fire engine we weren't aware of the other two-tones, they were the same as ours. Neither machine knew the other was even there. We did know that we were breaking the sound barrier, although Rodney still refused to believe we had any brakes at all. I was seated directly behind Rod, braced and looking out of my side window. I always reckoned that the closer you could get to him the safer you might be, a synopsis I have since changed.

There was an audible gasp, loud, and now etched in my brain. It was a group intake of breath accompanied by the requisite unexaggerated dose of fear. It wasn't an absence of noise, it was a refusal to listen, just in case. I hadn't seen it; I must somehow have been momentarily distracted. I took a chance and opened my eyes, expecting a view of the junction, expecting sun, and traffic lights, and cars, and houses, all lined up as we careered by. They weren't there, they were replaced by lips of fire engine red, a flash of metal which almost kissed our machine. So close I could see the fillings of Brixton's crew, as they screamed in terror.

Then it was gone, so quickly I thought it didn't really happen. I tentatively put my head out of the window and could see the squeezed rear of the other appliance disappear ahead. I looked behind, sure of devastation. I saw wide-eyed faces of people staring, retreating into our distance as the dust and feathers settled softly to the ground. Time had shifted for them; they couldn't understand why they weren't looking at piles of blood and metal; nor could I. There just wasn't enough room for two fire engines around that corner, we must have got very thin or tall or just passed right through one another. The only loss was a few cat's lives in each machine. We started to breathe again but still no one spoke. I wondered if I had accepted one of Frankie's kittens, I would be any safer, would I have been able to transfer some of its supposed spiritual fortune.

We got to the address on the call slip which was just a bit further along the road. Whilst some of the crew went with the Guv to investigate, I hung back. I was starting to feel the trauma; I had just seen death, in all his dentistry, scrape past my window.

The two drivers both got out of their cabs and were pacing towards each other, gunslingers in a dusty old town, they stopped face to face. For a moment I thought it was all going to kick off, but they just threw their arms around each other. After a brief moment of silent, mutual respect they separated, 'Fucking 'ell,' they both shouted at once and then broke into frightened laughter.

It was just a false alarm, no fire, not even a sniff.

After some time with everyone talking about our near annihilation, we got back on board to return home. Then what did we do on the way? We broke into song,

'We Nearly Wiped out Brixton's Pump, Do Dar, Do Dar,
We Nearly Wiped out Brixton's Pump, Do Dar, Do Dar, Day.'

We had all calmed down from what we in the fire brigade call a near miss incident, except we didn't report it; that would mean far too much paperwork. Lunch was over and Bones was taking us for some topography when one bell rang, our promise of an easy afternoon was about to be rudely interrupted by a visit from the group Assistant Divisional Officer. Senior Officers have to announce themselves like this, they can't just walk on the station.

LOUD BELL.

'Dutyman,' shouted Bones.

35

'Who the bloody hell is that,' said Granny. Our Guvnor poked his head around the door.

'Good, carry on,' he said, and disappeared. It's very convenient having a warning before being turned over, but we were actually testing our knowledge of the ground and how to get to different streets. We didn't need to invent something to look busy. Unfortunately, all senior officers must think we do a lot of topography, it's the easiest and quickest to feign on their arrival. We were devastated that we were actually deep in street navigation when he arrived, it was a waste of a subterfuge.

'I bet he turns us out for drill, the bastard,' said Bones.

'What's that?' Noddy asked.

'Yeah, what's that?' I said. Before Bones could answer the call bells actuated.

LOUD BELLS, lights come on.

'Just pretend it's a shout,' said Bones as 'we piled out of the TV room and ran for the poles.'

As soon as we pulled across the threshold the Guv said, 'Right, stop there, reverse up.'

'What's that all about?' Granny said.

'Turn out drill,' said Rodney, 'we stopped doing them years ago.'

'Looks like we started again,' I said as I took off my Fire Gear.

'Leave it on everyone, line up for inspection,' called the ADO. It was Assistant Divisional Officer Farmer, *Fatty* to us minions. We considered him a disgrace to the uniform, in which he waddled around full of last week's breakfast. What's more we had to endure an inspection from what we thought of as an embarrassment. I wondered if he wanted to compare fried eggs. After this brief foray of incompetence from management we were back in the TV room, this time for a friendly chat with Fatty himself. Bones, who now looked slim, got us all together before he arrived.

'He's bloody sharp, I only saw the order this morning,' said Bones. Apparently *Turn-out Drill* had been re-introduced.

'He's many things, but sharp isn't one of them,' said Frankie.

'Won't last long,' said Granny, 'about until the first accident, wait and see.' Granny had a healthy disregard for senior officers, *they're just here to mess up your day*, he would say. I tended to agree.

I don't know what the ADO was going on about, I'd got bored and was staring out of the window. I heard Granny's voice, 'I treat this job as my life's vacation.'

'That's very commendable but I think you mean vocation,' said Fatty.

'I know exactly what I mean Guv,' said Granny. By the look on his face, the Senior Officer couldn't work out whether Granny was taking the piss or just stupid.

He looked at the Guv, 'Anyway, you've been caught napping, literally. A member of the public has put in a complaint that you must be sleeping during the day because she could see the curtains had been pulled. What have you got to say Station Officer?' I could smell a rat, and not Rodrick our pet, more than likely another Officer from HQ had seen the curtains and this was their way of getting someone from our Division to give us a bollocking. It didn't matter, they should have used someone with a little more savvy. I wondered why he was trying to show up our Guv in front of his team, not a very polite move and one he was about to regret.

'I actually encourage the boys to have a snooze during their lunch break,' said the Guvnor, we all looked at each other, it was the first we'd heard of his approval. 'I get greater productivity throughout the afternoon when they have satisfied their natural circadian rhythm. I'll get you the research, an American fellow.' The Guv was in full flow, every word hanging heavier on the ADO's now drooping jaw. 'There is a natural low around midday that it's best not to fight against. All over America, offices are designating quiet areas next to their canteens. I'm surprised you haven't heard.'

Distant bell, click, LOUD BELLS, lights come on.

I got the impression that our Guv could have gone on forever, Fatty's open mouth returned to a faint smile as relief spread visibly through his body. He was as pleased we had a shout as we were. I'm sure I also detected a larger than usual smile beneath the Guv's moustache as we all piled out of the TV room, forgetting the ADO was even there.

We were off to St. Thomas Hospital and a smell of burning, one of our regular haunts, even the fireboat attended as riverside cover. Our station was left empty and Fatty all alone. Hopefully, with no one around to witness his pretence at being a real officer, he might bugger off.

Toby and I were fully rigged, including Breathing Apparatus which was starting to get heavy. The incident was taking longer than usual to resolve as there was no obvious fire. We were following a senior nurse and a maintenance crew around a ward, practicing our sniffing skills; I couldn't smell anything other than the cosmetic smoke from this morning.

'The hospital could have burnt down by now,' Toby said to one side. We were holding our helmets in our hands and slouching against a counter.

'How much do you think we weigh in all this clobber then Tobe?' I said.

'You can find out if you want, those scales look like a proper job,' he said. There was a platform and a balance system screaming *get on Tommy*.

'Yeah, I was looking at them,' I stepped up and started playing with the weights.

'Hope you haven't broken my scales,' I jumped, nearly falling off, and turned to see where the voice had come from.

'Oops, no they must have been broken already,' I stuttered. She came straight over.

'Stay there,' she slid the weights around. I noticed her smooth skin and delicate perfume, subtle but enticing. 'There you go, fifteen and a half stone, you're a big boy.' I avoided the obvious innuendo reply but there was enough of a pause to make us both grin.

'It's the kit, I'm only twelve stone stark naked,' I insisted.

'Now, I wouldn't know about that, would I?' I could feel myself getting warmer.

'There's only one way to be sure,' I sounded like Frankie, I couldn't believe what I was saying.

'You two finished over there,' the Guv was calling, 'we're on our way, if you can spare the time.'

'I thought we shouldn't get back too quick Guv, we don't want our visitor to still be around,' I said. He didn't answer, he just gave one of those looks to remind me who was in charge. As we walked away, I turned back but the pretty nurse had vanished. Well, I wouldn't have taken it any further I tried to tell myself, it was just a playful impulse. Then there was that seductive aroma again and I felt a hand push some paper into mine. She held a finger to her lips as she disappeared once more. Toby had caught the whole thing.

'Your face is about as red as her hair; does she know you're a tomato?' he said.

'Toby! Toby! What me?' Any act of innocence was really a waste of time.

It was nearly the end of the watch. 'I think Rodney owes us a pint tonight,' said Granny, 'after nearly killing us earlier.'

'He doesn't drink though,' I said.

'I don't see how that makes a difference,' said Toby, 'I did ask everyone earlier, if you remember.' That seemed a long time ago. It had been an eventful day, there was no way we could go straight home, whoever had done the asking.

Rodney didn't get to the pub but that didn't stop us singing his song. Between renditions Toby couldn't hold himself back, 'So Tom have you phoned her up yet?'

'Who Tobe?' I said, maintaining some pretence. I didn't know what I was going to do with that phone number but I couldn't get the whole affair out of my mind. Granny started again,

'We Nearly Wiped out Brixton's Pump, Do Dar, Do Dar,
We Nearly Wiped out Brixton's Pump, Do Dar, Do Dar Day.'

If a cat has nine lives, we must have about ninety-nine each.

3

January 1984
The Little Green Troll

'Where 'bouts do you two work then?' asked the relatively new barmaid. Toby and I looked at each other, nonplussed. Her name was Anne and after two weeks we assumed she knew who we were.

'Next door, in the fire station,' I said, as if it should be obvious.

'Oh,' she said as she moved to serve one of the suited crowd in the other bar. I couldn't tell whether she was disappointed or uninterested. We were quickly distracted as Granny squeezed through the door.

'What you doing here Gran, it's Friday you know?' Toby seemed to be pointing out the obvious but Gran never came out when he had a rugby match the next day.

'Just a quickie, I had to be here for the show. Nice to see you've smartened yourselves up for the occasion.' We weren't exactly dressed to go out for a beer, we were ready to cycle home. Our kit was a mixture of shorts, cycle shorts and tatty old shirts over tatty old t-shirts, we hoped the holes wouldn't line up in an attempt to exclude any draughts. Toby even had a Sam Browne, although I classed that as specialist equipment. We stood at the bar as if we had every right to be there, however we were dressed, just like when we blocked a road with the fire engine.

'What are you on about – *the show*? Usual?' I said. The barmaid had come back over before he could answer either question.

'Lager please love,' said Granny, 'he's paying,' he cast a thumb at Toby. I wondered how he knew it was actually Toby's round.

'Didn't you know we were firemen?' I resumed our previous conversation with Anne.

'What real firemen? I thought you were fitness instructors,' she said, casting a surreptitious glance at our outfits.

'You're wrong on all counts there,' Granny screamed whilst grabbing for his pint.

As we were trying to calm down from our hysterics I remembered Gran's earlier remark, Toby beat me to it and asked, 'What show are you talking about anyway?'

'Bones is on his way, he cycled in this morning.' This was news to us but I still didn't understand. We moved from our regular pitch by the bar to our regular table by the door, Toby and I attempting to get far away from the new comedienne behind the bar.

Bones eventually arrived, as he walked in the pub, he was momentarily silhouetted, back lit by the evening glare. We didn't realise it was Bones until he stepped out of the light. He was sporting a one piece, leotard-type, cycle outfit, and it wasn't hiding anything! Bones didn't have the best figure but he'd walked in looking like a model, only it was a model of the Cotswolds. If you know your geography, or even if you don't, there was one bump that certainly shouldn't be in our *Green and Pleasant Land*.

'Was that the only one left?' Granny jibed.

'I didn't know you could get them with all those lumps in 'em,' I added.

'Aww, give us a break lads, I had to wear it, Julie bought it,' he pleaded. We were shifting around to find him a seat. Bones was always moaning about his wife: *Julie won't let me come out tonight, Julie says I can't do this, I've got to get home.* We were expecting a dragon but when we eventually met her, she couldn't have been sweeter. The kids, on the other hand, were feral; five of the most uncontrollable little angels I've ever met.

I was thinking *she's got quite a sense of humour*, when Toby said, 'I don't think she wanted you to wear it out in public, probably just wanted you to show off that lump down there.' Bones looked down, we all did, most of the Pub did.

Bones muttered, 'Bastards,' as he turned and walked straight back out onto the seemingly inappropriately named, Lambeth High St.

'I just bought him a beer,' said Granny, returning from the bar.

Bones was a couple of stones over-weight, just enough to make the rest of us look good. Originally, he'd been christened because his name was McCoy, like Star Trek's doctor, that had long since been forgotten and it now was more about his physique. He was proud to say that after three months on a diet he'd managed to only gain two pounds. We told him that if he ever got skinny, we would change his name to Roly.

He was also one of those people that no matter how much they try, they just can't look smart. His tie was always crooked, his shirts never really fitted, there always seemed to be a button missing from his tunic and his leggings were always crinkly, crumpled up around his ankles as if he'd borrowed Gran's. But this outfit, this was a whole new level.

'Beer will never go to waste.' I said, 'Have you ever seen a cycle kit in that shade of green before? It goes well with his ginger locks.'

'Are you kidding, he must think he's Robin Hood,' Granny answered. We didn't have to wait long for Bones to return, the pub is right next door to the fire station. He'd found a long t-shirt to put over what we'd decided was a dressing up outfit.

'Look, the Little Green Troll has got a disguise,' I said.

'Not so little, depending where you're looking,' Toby joined in.

'Bastards, give me that beer,' he strode into the pub with his arm outstretched. Of course, we stayed for more than one beer, and Bones was soon taking the piss out of himself. We never did see that kit again though.

'I'll sort you lot out on nights,' Bones was smiling now, 'the Guv's off you know.'

'Yeah, I know, and Subby's sick, they'll just send someone in, won't they?' I said, already suspicious.

'Nope, no one available,' said Bones.

'Don't tell me your acting-up?' As ever my tongue leaping ahead of my brain. Bones didn't seem to take any offence. I knew, as well as we all did, he'd not done it before. It's a big step, there's a lot more responsibility being in charge of the station and, if we were to pick up a job, being in charge of the first attendance. Bones had only ever been number two.

'What are you going to do if you pick up something big?' Granny asked, he looked disturbed, but that might have been because he'd nearly finished his pint.

'No worries, me and the Leading Hand will sort it out,' said Bones with an air of unjustified confidence.

'Oh, okay, who's that?' I said, and then I noticed he was looking straight at Toby. Toby managed to look over his beer, sip it and grin at the same time.

'I'll drink to that,' I said, and ordered another round, the third, *only one beer*, of the night.

'Yeah, and we can call it the Little Green Troll meets Big Ears and They Take on the World,' Granny laughed. I nearly spat my beer out; the others weren't that successful.

The machine was parked up on Fitzalan St, it probably looked like we were hiding. Granny and I were sitting on a low wall under a streetlamp, whilst the rest of the crew had draped themselves inside the cab. He was watching me make an outline drawing of one of the estates on our ground. Bones was pretty laid back about being in charge and we were out on the Station's ground, killing time before supper. We were ignoring the inner-city grime and enjoying a pleasant, but fresh, early evening.

There was even a patch of tired grass in front of the apartment windows; for Lambeth it was almost the countryside. I was the only one doing any real work, continuing my job of making a flats book by copying an estate map from the street board. I'm sure some passers-by wondered what we were up to, but nobody asked, all we got was our normal friendly, *good evening*. The footprint of our ground, B22 Lambeth, isn't that big but everywhere you look is another block of flats. This book, when I eventually finish it, will stay on the appliance and make it easier to navigate the confusing layout that never seems to bear any resemblance to the addresses we are given.

'Good game today, Gran?' I asked. He played wing forward for his old school team and despite his size could beat most of us in a sprint, except Toby, of course, who thought running was the new walking. Granny's hair was short and spikey, and a colour my Mum would call mousey. He hated it being touched, although it was a stretch to get that high. If you were brave enough you could catch him sitting but I was too easily captured to take the risk.

'Top banana Tommy, twenty-one, three.'

'Is that good, then?' I tried a wind-up but should have known there was little point, not when his team had won.

'I thought you was trying to get the night off,' he said, having totally ignored my play, 'aren't you meant to be going out with Maria?'

'Naw, I'm letting her go to this one on her own.'

'Do you think she's up to something Tom?' he said.

'Aww, nothing probably, just work, I suppose.' I showed him the sketch, 'What do you think?'

'I think you're worried.' Granny was on the button but I didn't want to go into it out on the street, I didn't really want to talk about it at all. It is my other life and keeping it separate allows a release when I'm on duty. It works both ways, we are always guarded when we get home to avoid sharing the burden of experienced tragedy; not that my wife was ever around to listen.

My wife is a detective sergeant in the Met. Our shifts seem to continually keep us apart; the trouble is that it suits me more and more every day. I tried not to mix my home life with my Brigade life but the guys all seemed to have picked up that something was wrong. Being in the fire service isn't just a matter of having two homes it's more like having two families. I probably spent more time with these guys than I ever did with my wife.

We'd been married about two years, after meeting and tying the knot within three months. It was a classic case of being attracted by the uniform, but she'd long since hung that up for the plain-clothes job. I think we were both regretting that initial crush, where I had certainly mistaken lust for love. It was a bad decision, we just needed to get around to sorting it out.

The rest of the crew were sitting in the machine on the other side of the road, well out of earshot. Bones was giving Nod another new boy talk, I could remember it, *your probation tests will be here before you know it, let the Guvnor see you studying.* Frankie was reading something, with one eye on the road in case anything female came anywhere near.

'No, what do you think of the drawing?' I said, trying to bring Granny back to the fire brigade. Although my mind had wandered to the little scrap of paper that was a nurse's phone number and was now pinned to the back of my locker.

'I think you've missed all three of those blocks, there,' he pointed to the right of the large static board.

'I was going to add those on this next bit of paper; just seeing if you were awake.' I don't know how I'd missed them; my mind certainly wasn't on the job tonight.

'So, what, you told her you couldn't get the night off.'

'Yeah, I hate her works get-togethers, I always feel like I'm being interrogated. There's always a little hesitation when they find out I'm a fireman and not old bill. She wasn't that bothered anyway, I got the idea it pleased her, she knows I'm not that keen...' I'd almost started to let go, to say what was troubling me, but I guess I was saved by the bell.

Do, Dah (appliance two-tones sound).

The two-tones beeped and as I looked over to the machine, I could see Bones on the radio.

'Looks like we've got one,' said Granny. They could have shouted out of the window but the two-tones removed any room for misunderstanding. I closed my pad, there wasn't much hope for any more artwork.

'Just rubbish guys,' said Frankie as we got back on the appliance, 'Cardboard City.'

I groaned; we have several regular locations of bonfires set by the homeless. Cardboard city, or Waterloo Underpass to give it its real name, was one of these. A maze of tunnels to keep out of the rain and make a den out of old boxes. We would have liked to let them keep their transient warmth and leave the small fires burning, but they always managed to annoy someone with the smoke. Occasionally that someone was another cardboard occupier so we had to put them out.

'We can leave you here Rembrandt, if it's going to interfere with your creative flow,' shouted Frankie from up front.

'I think I'll come along, you never know you might even need me,' I answered. Frankie was already accelerating and the machine had picked up a sway that was strangely in time with the two-tones.

'Don't be too quick Frankie, we're still rigging in the back here,' said Granny. Nod was ready, he'd had a brief head start when we were first called up over the radio. He was now trying to make himself disappear and avoid our arses and elbows as we pulled on our leggings and tunics, he shuffled closer to me. Gran needed much more room to get dressed, he needed more room than everyone.

Frankie pulled up on the roundabout near one of the pedestrian entrances, it was going to be a leap over the railing for us. It turned out to be a false alarm, or it was already out, you could never really tell. There was quite an encampment in the tunnels that were meant to be pedestrian walkways. We sauntered about, sniffing and kicking the odd pile of vacant boxes; nothing was alight, well not yet. I'm sure that sometimes the sight of us walking around gave them an idea and we'd soon be back. The homeless problem in London has got worse in the few years that I've been at Lambeth. These days it was unusual to find an empty doorway and this encampment got bigger every day.

'So how are you coping with your new responsibility, Sir?' Gran asked Bones as we returned to the machine.

'Aw, you know, just another shift.' I thought there was a slight nervousness in his tone, I wondered what Granny thought.

'Nothing you can't cope with Bonesy,' I said, although I hadn't factored us into the equation; maybe he had.

'You finished your scribbling for tonight Tom?' he said and without waiting for an answer, 'Back home then, Frankie.'

I was about to say I needed to go back just briefly but I could see the whole crew staring at me, 'Yeah, all done,' I said.

Supper was late, as usual, it was nearly 21.00. Not too bad, officially we should eat at eight; it was often much later.

'SCOFF IT AND HOP IT,' came the distant shout from Rodney in the Mess, loud enough to reach the whole station, the first floor anyway. His scream was followed by a herd of firefighters pounding the floorboards, crashing into each other as we met coming through doorways, emerging from corners and hiding places all over the station and eventually bottlenecking at the Mess room.

'What's this then Rodders?' Noddy asked, once we were seated and most were devouring his creation.

'It's bloody mince D, and don't be so fucking cheeky,' said Rod. His grey ponytail and wispy tufts of whiskers, that he insisted were within regulation guidelines, managed to display displeasure.

'Sorry Rod, I mean it looks lovely.' Nod was trying to backtrack, he wasn't being rude, that was Rodney's standard response however nicely you spoke to him. Mince was the staple ingredient for Mess dinners, Rodney had an amazing repertoire of different ways to camouflage it into a culinary delight. It looked to me that the only difference was the carbohydrate. Tonight, it was Chilli, he occasionally brought individual pies (dead tortoises, always served upside down), accompanied by lumpy mash and peas; that was about the lot. Sometimes Abbey, our day cook, made one of her chicken and mushroom pies and left it for Rod to bung in the oven.

Going on the cacophony of oohs and aahs, I would have to say it was legendary even though I'd never tasted it myself. It was the only time that the slurping was louder than the banter. Unfortunately, it was also about to be history; the Brigade in their wisdom had decided it was time for her to retire. This meal plan was cyclical and a background to the occasional experimental treat. It's enough, the boy's only want to be full and all Rodney wants is the ultimate compliment, 'That was shit,' accompanied with an empty plate, of course.

'I'll have yours, if you don't want it,' said Toby. Toby was our resident dustbin; nothing went to waste when he was around.

'Careful Nod, if he doesn't eat it, he'll take it home, he'll be building himself up for another marathon,' I said.

Distant bell, click, LOUD BELLS, lights come on.

We'd only just sat down; I took a quick second mouthful. 'Lend us your China, Tom,' said Toby. I threw him my little stub of Chinagraph pencil to write his name on the side of his plate.

'You can have that, a Leading Hand needs all his own tools Tobe,' I said, trying not to spit Chilli Con Veggie all over him whilst having a dig at his brief authority. We have to say something, it's in our blood; he would think there really was a problem if we didn't.

'Alright, alright,' he said, as we threw our plates on the serving hatch and embraced before racing down the corridor.

'One or two of the floaties always put the dinners away; on the rare occasions that they actually had a shout they could still get across the road to the pontoon by the time the rest of the crew were ready to let the lines go and motor away. Whenever we got back our carefully prepared meals would be waiting in the hot plate, identified by our Chinagraphed initials.' If we were lucky, they would even have an aluminium lid and if we were really lucky, they wouldn't be too cremated. They were always eaten, even if not quite edible; it's too long a shift to go without. This shout didn't include the Fireboat, it was near the centre of our ground, away from the river; they didn't turn out that often.

In fact, if they got a shout at night, we'd have to put the bells down a second time, just to make sure they got out of bed. They always got a cheer from the rest of us on those occasions. The fireboat was our river appliance, moored against a small pontoon across the road from the station. The land machines, the Pump Ladder and the Turntable Ladder, are parked and lonely in the seven bay appliance room; when it was built in the 1930s, the station was much more crowded. Now we didn't even have a Pump at Lambeth, which left our Pump

Ladder to deal with our densely populated suburb. We average 3600 shouts a year.

At most stations the Pump is the workhorse while the Pump ladder is the rescue machine; we had to do both. The Fireboat and Turntable are specialist appliances; the boat goes out on anything with a river front and the TL whenever there are high-rise buildings nearby. Occasionally we get to ride these machines, but only as an extra pair of untrained hands, *the gofer*. It makes a change but most of the time we ride the PL, which we prefer, at least I do, there's more chance of getting to work. More chance of playing with fire.

We jumped into our boots, strategically left around the machine, and pulled up our scrunched plastic leggings holding each other for balance. Noddy called out as he ran from the Watchroom, 'Rubbish, Wincott St.'

'Not more good old shit and rubbish,' said Toby.

'You'll be okay Tobe, you're in charge of the TL,' said Granny.

'Oh, yeah,' he smiled, realising that he wasn't going. We screamed out of the station.

'I'm bloody hungry, I hadn't even taken my first mouthful,' said Granny.

'It's not real scran if it's not burnt up a bit,' shouted Frankie while negotiating a red light. Bones gave him a look that was pure worry. The hot plate would be doing its slow job of adding a crispy edge to all our meals.

'You'll just have to stir it up a bit,' I added.

Rubbish is still an emergency call, we never really know what's alight until we arrive, so on went the blues and twos as we raced through the traffic.

It was just garbage, already piled on the pavement, perhaps someone had decided it was a good way for it to disappear. It had also attracted a crowd of youngsters as an audience, or more likely, a group of budding arsonists. We wasted no time dealing with the burning trash, our favourite. We often thought we were another branch of the Dust, a bin lorry with privileges. It wouldn't go out without some help so we were having to turn it over, wet it and then sweep up the debris into a smaller more satisfying pile.

Whilst all this was going on, I saw two tiny boys sidle up to Bones, they can only have been about four or five years old. They certainly should have been tucked up at home but the kids on the estates around Lambeth didn't seem to have a bedtime, they were often roaming around well into the night. The set of *Oliver* would have been more appropriate for them, except the smaller guy had what looked like his big brothers trainers on his feet. I thought they would wear out long before he grows into them. Their faces were full of filth and cheekiness.

The taller lad, the bolder of the two, tugged at Bones' sleeve, 'Oy, mister,' he said, 'are you the Guvnor?' I nudged Gran and pointed. Bones didn't realise that we were watching this little charade; he grew taller, his chest puffed out and he even seemed to lose a bit of stomach.

'I am, son,' he proudly announced, lost in the glory of his elevated position.

The lad turned to his buddy, his hand covering his mouth, unsuccessfully trying to keep their secret, 'See, told ya.'

Bones was obviously feeling elated by this perceived adulation, he should have left it there but he wanted more. 'How did you know that young man?' he asked. I thought, *if he tousles his hair, he'll get his hand bit.*

The child turned back from his friend, looked Bones in the eye, and without pausing for breath he said loudly, ''Cause you ain't doing nufin.' Then they both scampered away, giggling like only kids, and firefighters can, their mischief slowly fading into the estate. Bones looked around to see us leaning on our respective broom, shovel and each other.

'Did they know you was a Little Green Troll?' Granny asked.

'They thought I was the Guvnor,' he muttered, but he knew he'd been caught.

We rode back to the station asking each other, 'What are you doing?'

'I ain't doing nufin.'

'What are you doing?'

'I ain't doing nufin either.'

Bones kept quiet; he knew we'd get bored if he didn't bite.

4

January 1984
Bones Nemesis

Bones first night in charge went without a hitch, despite our antics. Unusually, he declined a game of golf in between our night duties. I caught him sneaking away as I was sorting out my clubs in the covered wash. 'Oy, oy, Bones, you're looking almost dapper, got a date or something?'

'No, that wouldn't be worth my skin, I'm off to price a job.'

'Must be for the Ritz! See you in the Windmill tonight?'

'Have a good un.' He disappeared; something wasn't normal.

Granny came around the corner, 'What's he up to, then?'

'Just his fiddle. Are we going in your motor Gran?' Just then it started to rain.

'That will have stopped by the time we get there,' Toby turned up, as enthusiastic as ever.

'It's just us three, Bones isn't coming. Did you see him though? He almost looked posh,' Granny brought Toby up to speed.

'What, not in his green porno outfit?'

'No, but it didn't look like our Bonesy,' I chipped into the group gossip.

We all liked Bones. The thing we all loved most, selfishly I suppose, was that he was a fixer. Anything extra you needed or just wanted, he could get, he was forever on the phone, networking, I guess. He was a listener too, he always had time for you. He took us for most of our lectures as our Sub Officer was always ensconced on the fireboat. He was also helping Toby and Nod with their promotion exams, something in which I'd agreed to take part. I've no idea why, I intend to spend all my career riding the back of fire engines; it's far too much fun to give up. The leading firefighter rank is often a bit blurred, we all treated

Bones as one of the boys but tonight I was finding it hard to remember he was a Sub. Officer and the Officer in Charge.

Bones hadn't changed desks, our Guvnors seat remained vacant. Even if the office was empty, you could still tell where Bones sat, there was a little added disruption, just to make him comfortable. Even the typewriter relaxed its ribbon when Bones typed, just to add a well-placed smudge here and there. He hung-up the phone as I entered the office, writing something at the same time.

'Frankie wants the board, the Blues didn't take it down,' I said. Tonight's runners and riders were on the Roll Call Board and it should have been in the Watchroom. He put his hand out and picked it up. 'How do you know where anything is?' I asked.

'I can't help it, I've got anti-OCD, a place for everything and nothing in its place.'

'Did you get that job?'

'What's that Tom?'

'You was off to price a job. You didn't miss much; it was far too wet for a decent Round anyway.'

'That's normal for you Tom, how did the other two get on?' Unfortunately, my golfing prowess was no secret, I did occasionally hit a good shot, at least one that stayed on the fairway. Generally, whenever I picked up a club, my brothers stayed un-politely out of the way. I decided it was time to take the board downstairs.

I had suggested to the guys that we should make a special effort tonight.

'He won't notice you know; we'll just make him look scruffier than ever,' said Granny. We were having a good clean up before duty.

'It won't hurt, we are pretty filthy from last night,' I said, as I got the yard broom out of a locker and started trying to clean my tunic. Our dress for entering a burning building was a sad mix of inappropriateness and folklore. The only good thing about our firegear was that you knew when it was getting too hot. It wasn't a protective kit, just a uniform. We wore it, cleaned it and tried to look good, some making a better job at that than others. It leaves bits of you exposed, hands and ears mostly. We do have red-oxide coated, cotton Debris Gloves, we keep them in the bucket; I don't really know what they are for but it's not firefighting. There is nothing to protect our ears; Toby is sure they are picking on him.

Our woollen Tunics were designed in the mid-nineteenth century, totally inappropriate for modern firefighting, or any firefighting come to that, but I think we appreciated the traditional edge. They were like hoodless, double-breasted, duffel coats with faux silver buttons. They are also our Dress Uniform so we all tried to purloin an extra one to keep clean, for funerals mostly. There was nothing comfortable about them, they itched, they rubbed your neck and they weighed a ton when wet. However, we were issued with black neckerchiefs as protection from falling embers, they also helped soften the tunic collars. Frankie somehow managed to make his look like a dashing cravat.

Noddy mumbled to himself, 'I'd forgotten how good a match they were.'

'What is Nod?' I said. He was actually talking about our uniform and a little surprise he had planned; he didn't mean to be overheard.

'I might need a new pair of leggings, what do you think?' asked Granny, changing the subject or not having heard Noddy's comment.

'You'll be sorry,' said Toby. In an effort to embrace the times and modern materials, we wore yellow plastic over-trousers. That's over our everyday working trousers, the ones Rodney thought were also for going down the pub. They had integral braces which we had to pull as tight as possible to enable easier crawling through burning buildings. It would take a couple of good hot jobs before the plastic became malleable enough to be easily wearable and to fit around us and our fire-boots. Until then they were stiff and uncomfortable.

'That will be a special order, for a pair your size,' said Frankie.

'Yeah, it will, and I'll ask for another pair with a crease down the front just for you Frankie,' said Granny, 'or do you iron them yourself?'

Noddy was now polishing his boots. 'When the Brigade bothers to give us back our leather boots Nod, that's when we'll polish them,' said Rodney. He took it personally that we only had steel toe-capped rubber wellingtons.

'They made us polish them in training school,' answered Nod.

'Come on, it's nearly time for Roll Call,' I said. We finished rigging, canvas belts with axe and polymer yellow helmets. All shiny for inspection and ready to crawl into anyone's inferno.

Six bells rang and we were on duty. Toby was reading out the runners and riders when he made a little addition. I was lucky to notice it, I always read the rider board before Roll Call and normally didn't pay much attention. We had an extra rider on the Pump Ladder, Fm Ted was on duty. We all broke ranks and said, 'Where is he then?'

'Hold on,' said Toby, 'you're not dismissed yet.'

'Okay,' said Bones, knowing it was not worth making a stand.

Well, there was Teddy, and what a transformation, he was clean for a start, and he was wearing a cosy, knitted Fire Uniform of yellow leggings, helmet and navy tunic. A proud Noddy took him to the appliance and showed him his riding position. We must have all looked about five years old, each having a touch just to confirm he was there. Probably only to dirty his pristine appearance with our sweaty paws. 'I don't remember him only having one eye,' I said.

'Yeah, I know, it must have come off in the washing machine,' said Noddy, 'we couldn't find it anywhere.'

'Don't tell us you've got a machine big enough to get him in,' said Frankie.

'We haven't, we took him to the launderette.' I had an instant image of the Noddy family watching him go around and around, lined up on the bench in front of the washer.

'Wow,' Granny looked genuinely amazed, 'I'd forgotten all about him. Thank the Misses Nod, from all of us.' I'm sure it was last year that we'd found him, I wondered if his kids had got fed up with their rescued toy.

Distant bell, click, LOUD BELLS, lights come on.

Jake from the Blue Watch ran excitedly back out of the gear room, his kit falling from both his arms, 'Is it us, is it us?' he panted.

'Five minutes past. Go home,' shouted Granny. He turned back quickly, trying to avoid the sound of our jeers, but we would have done the same for a bit of overtime.

The call was to a flat alight near the Kennington Oval and there was plenty of evening traffic around. The ride through the streets on the bell is always quite exhilarating, tonight it felt like Frankie was playing dodgems.

'Easy Frank,' I shouted, 'we've got a Granny rolling around back here.' Nod and I slipped into our BA set harnesses. Fm Ted was a star, even squashed against the window he was leaving the concerned public with a smile.

As we got closer Bones turned to us in the rear cab, 'Kitchen, I think,' he said. There is a distinct, acrid aroma to pots left unattended on a stove and it's way beyond an enticing cooking perfume. I could smell it myself now, a pungency that you could taste filled the street. We were waved down, although there really was no need, we could see remnants of smoke still coming from the ground floor flat. Frankie stopped and we blocked the narrow street.

'Sout mate, sall out, don't need yer,' an old gentleman, complete with cardigan and slippers, came coughing and spluttering to my window. He was pointing to his little front garden, more a patch of weeds and wind-strewn rubbish, I couldn't see anything culinary. He coughed some more.

'The pan,' he waggled his finger about as if that made it easier to see. I could make out a pot among the other rubbish that littered his doorstep.

'Okay mate, we'll have a quick look while we're here,' I answered. I caught Nod's eye and we dumped our sets. Our adrenaline regretfully seeping away.

'What did he say?' Bones called out from the front. Guvnors hate this, and that obviously included Bones tonight, they expect members of the public to go straight to them. I don't know why they think everyone should know the officer in charge sits in the front.

'He said he's put it out,' I called back.

'Go and have a look and ventilate, it still looks a bit smoky to me, take the reel, just in case.' I resisted the urge to say that's what we were planning, remembering I was trying to give him an easier ride tonight. It also occurred to me that I wouldn't dream of talking back to the Guv.

Frankie took the old man to one side to stop him walking back into his own flat. Nod grabbed the hose reel; he was dying to squirt some water at something other than the drill tower; he was allowed to wear BA in a working job now but we'd been surprisingly quiet. Granny and I followed him in. We have a drum of high-pressure hose reel on each side of the back of the appliance but the nozzles aren't up to much and they certainly don't supply enough water to tackle a decent size fire. It should be fine tonight, especially if it was *sout*, and besides, the hose reel is much easier to put away afterwards.

'Remember this smell Nod,' I said, 'we get it a lot, someone's left a pot on the stove. It'll give you an idea where the fire could be,' I was giving Nod the benefit of my scant knowledge. The three of us, Gran, Nod and me, walked straight into the billowing front door as if it was the most natural thing. It wasn't, I immediately had to crouch and put my hand over my mouth. My eyes started streaming. All the evidence that we needed was there, the smell was unmistakeable, the pot was on the doorstep and, according to the occupier, it was *sout*. It didn't feel like it though, but it didn't feel bad enough to go back and put on our sets. I knew when I got back to the station I would have black nostrils, schoolboy smudges only more sinister. We take far too many liberties with our lungs, but I can wash my face and get rid of all the worry.

'Let's get some windows open,' spluttered Granny. We had a wander around the little home, ventilating as much as possible; it helped and the stinging fumes started to clear. It wasn't a big place but it was someone's haven. I forget sometimes that for the gentleman outside this is a great trauma, because for us it is just another job. We have to maintain our respect and keep our opinions for the ride home. We also have to be professional at all times; well, we try.

Nothing was alight but it was going to take a good while to get rid of the new pungent smell throughout his flat. Bones came in and asked, 'You got it boys?'

'All done in here Bones,' I insisted. He turned around and headed back out, comfortable with the apparent result.

'He's gone to send the Stop,' I reminded Noddy, who was looking a bit confused. We were back in the kitchen and making sure everything was turned off.

'It's a bit smoky still,' said Nod. He was getting very good at stating the obvious.

'Yeah, but it's clearing and nothing's really alight,' I said. Then, as if the fire had heard me, I opened the oven just to check, and it was there, teetering on ferocity. 'Give it a quick drink Nod,' I said, my face alight and urgency dripping from the sudden radiance. We performed a last dance of the night, trying to squeeze round, so he could get to the oven, but Granny was in the way and this wasn't a very big kitchen. Nod was reluctant to relinquish the branch, gripping it in a lover's clinch, meanwhile the ovens ardour was rapidly rising.

'Pass me the fucking reel Nod, it only needs a squirt.' I couldn't have been more wrong.

As the spray from the hose reel hit the fervent oven walls, years of grease flashed in a minor eruption, lit up the rest of the cooker and sent flames briefly into the kitchen. Only then did it dawn on me that the pot in the front garden, the pot that was *sout*, was a casserole pot. It had come from this witch's cauldron. We fell back from the blast of heat, Granny and I also finding it highly amusing, even Nod got caught up in the ridiculous drama and joined in the belly laughter.

Our new temporary Guv came back in just as we had completely lost it. Bones, having sent the stop message to cancel any further help, opened the kitchen door with perfect timing and was confronted with a wall of candescence.

It must have looked like the whole kitchen was alight, and whatever had happened had taken out his three bravest firefighters.

'What the fuck,' he shouted. I recovered and quickly knocked down the flames with a proper drowning before they did any real damage. I don't know what was funnier, the oven debacle or the look on Bones face? 'I thought you said you'd got it.'

'It's just the oven, Bones,' I said.

'It looked like just my career. Bloody Tomato.' As he walked away, I'm sure I could hear him muttering, 'Bastards.' I wasn't doing a very good job of making this second night any easier.

Noddy said to me, 'Are you going to show me anymore great firefighting tips tonight, Tommy?'

'Oy, gratitude Nod, gratitude, that could have been you holding the branch.'

We took a long route home just to give Ted a view of the ground. We saw Brixton's Pump who had been on our shout and were also out cruising. They were amused until Ted gave them a Moon as our machines passed. He was keeping us entertained; it wouldn't last.

On the way home Bones turned around to speak, he looked at me and I'm sure he was about to say something about our recent firefighting debacle.

'Sorry Bones, but Granny and Nod made me do it,' I said.

Hopefully he would act up again, we'd all enjoyed his two nights in charge.

5

February 1984
Door and Gate

I cycled into the yard; it was our first day duty. I was feeling great as I usually do when I get back to work, despite all the extra layers of clothing for this cold February morning. The Green Watch were washing down an old Denis Fire Engine. 'What's that about?' I asked.

'It's the best they could do, we broke ours,' said Curly, who had the straightest hair you could ever imagine.

'What, that old thing is on the run?' It glinted in the morning sun but only where it had been dented so many times. Even the red paint that had been used to cover up many previous disasters was different shades and the rare bit of original colour was going pink.

'You betcha.' Suddenly Curly got a broadside from the hose reel as they started squirting each other as well as the machine. It was definitely the wrong time for a water fight on every level. Apart from being nearly change of watch, it was bloody freezing. I quickly got out of the way, took my bike to its resting place on the balcony and headed for a nice hot shower. I was missing Toby who was off in Austria learning to ski. We were both going in March so he'd got a last-minute deal to take some lessons. I'd made the mistake of letting him know that I'd been twice before, on school trips.

At role call the Guvnor said we would be going out for a ride first thing so the drivers could familiarise themselves with the replacement appliance. He seemed almost excited that we would be touring the ground in a bit of Brigade history. Apparently, this machine had a *crash* gearbox.

'What's a crash box when it's at home?' I asked Rodney who was slopping the dutyman's cup of tea all over the place.

'You'll find out, Frankie's driving yer, ain't he?'

'Do you want to have a go then?' Frankie asked Rodney.

'No, no, you'll be fine,' he laughed, even Rodney was chipper this morning.

Noddy leant over and pretended to whisper in my ear, 'There's no synchromesh, the driver has to rev the engine to change gear.'

'Is that hard then?' I declared.

'On yer bike Tomato,' said Rodney, back to his old form, the smirk now also a part of history.

This must have been the oldest machine in the fleet, it only looked good from a distance; a closer inspection revealed all the wrinkles that belong to retirement. It even had a hole in the roof above the Guvnor, a design feature where a plaited length of cord was attached to an Emergency Bell.

'Fucking 'ell, where's the two-tones,' I shouted.

'Stick your head out of the window Tommy, everyone will know we're coming,' Granny responded in a truly Rodney fashion.

I'm sure it had a few other holes, I was amazed it was still in service, but it did look the part, even with its multiple shades of red. Our new, but now broken machine was more like a silver dustcart with a hint of red here and there. This relic was like our previous machine that had reached the end of its days, but much older!

Distant bell, click, LOUD BELLS, lights come on.

We didn't get a chance for a practice run, the bells dropped and we were on our way to a fire, multiple calls on Southwark's ground. From the radio traffic it sounded like they had a goer.

Granny said, 'We could drop this lump of shite off at the museum while we are there.' Frankie crunched his way through the gearbox.

'Can't you find one you like Frankie,' I yelled over the grating acoustics. This was all to the accompaniment of the Guvnors hand, sticking out of the roof and ringing the bell; he had quite a tempo. 'He's done that before,' I uttered to the rest of the crew.

'Well, he's old enough,' said Granny. The Guv looked over his shoulder, *he can't have heard that* I thought, Granny and I exchanged glances. The machine was full of strange noises, I'm sure it was some sort of old-fashioned mechanical language. The engine gave a grinding apology to the rest of the lorry, whose answer was tired and detached. I hoped it could see its way clear to keeping it all together, at least for the next few minutes.

Frankie seemed to get into the rhythm and we started to motor along nicely. 'She's certainly not slow for an old bird,' I said as we swerved around some traffic.

'Don't be rude to her Tommy, she's only just letting me play,' shouted Frankie from the front.

'Let's hope the Escape's still attached when we get there,' said Granny. The Escape is a fifty-foot wooden ladder housed on large cartwheels. For such a cumbersome thing we could move it around pretty fast, although it was just out of my reach when on the machine, good job I could jump. They hang precariously on the back of the appliance, released by just one lever.

'We'll be lucky if anything is still attached by the time we get there, we'll have to do a Hansel and Gretel to find the way home,' I said.

The Guvnor shouted back to us, 'Four, Persons, Brixton's Pump.' We hadn't heard the radio due to the racket of this old machine. He was cleverly managing to take off his white shirt, put on his tunic, talk on the radio and ring the bell at the same time, and my wife says only women can multi-task. What our Guv meant was that Southwark had asked for one more machine to help fight the fire, people were involved and Brixton had been ordered additionally to increase the normal three-appliance attendance.

It was time to rig in BA. 'This takes me back Gran,' I said, sounding like some old hand instead of one with just over three years in the job. The BA sets were not conveniently placed in easy-to-use brackets behind the seats like our newer machine. They were hanging on a wooden frame, between us and the front cab. We really should have waited until we arrived to put them on, but that would waste precious time and we loved a shortcut. I decided to show Noddy how it was done.

'Take the set off the peg and turn it upside down and back to front on your lap,' I demonstrated as I spoke, fortunately Noddy just watched, 'put your arms through the shoulder straps,' I waited as Frankie threw a left, 'then lift the whole thing straight over your head.' It should have been easy from there, just a matter of tightening the straps and retrieving the mask; it wasn't.

I had the BA set at the pinnacle of a perfect arc, all forty-eight pounds. The left turn was followed by a hard right. My cab door swung open and I was on my way out of the machine towards the tarmac of St. Georges Circus. I looked back in sheer disbelief, floating unnaturally, like a spaceman miles from home. My mind raced ahead and saw, and heard, every detail of my imminent demise reflected in Granny and Nod's tonsils. My facemask was happy to continue on its centrifugal journey but the cylinder was teetering on conversion to gravity. The BA set slid down my back and joined the road's attempted abduction. My hands reached for the evasive doorframe finding only air. Split second rescue hung like a breath, only a hearts vague suggestion. My skin was threatening a flayed trail along the junction, sharing itself between a double decker bus and our own rear wheels. The escape ladder loomed, I thought *well it's still there, I wonder if it will also grab a bit of me.*

A vice like grip brought time back into line, Noddy had seized hold of one wrist, arresting my continued momentum and swinging me back towards the appliance side. This tricked my other, near-orphaned hand, into another failed purchase. I was s*o close, so close*, Nod's cheap ploy was floundering, my mind was a fusion of disaster and triumph. I was going…then a giant, magic-like arm sprung from inside the appliance, a reflex, an automation, faster than any speeding Fire Engine. Granny wedged Nod on the seat and grabbed my tunic, excruciatingly clutching flesh at the same time.

And then I was back on the floor of the machine, the BA set still lazily attached. The engine swerved a little as it spun around another corner and the door slammed shut. I sat back on the bench seat, tightened the straps of my set and leant over and kissed Noddy on the forehead, I couldn't reach Granny but it was understood. I took a gasped breath and said, '…and that's how you put your set on.'

Granny added, 'Anyone going to the pub tonight?'

'Only if you stop all that pinching,' I said, rubbing my breast. I would have a bruise for days. My wife might think it was passion, she'd be right.

The Guvnor hollered, 'What's going on back there?' We all just howled in an attempt to get the blood flowing back in our veins; my heart was still pounding.

I wondered if it was health and safety that got the sets moved or just so the Guvnor could keep a check on the crew. Noddy got his set on with a little less drama than I, opting just to place it on the seat behind him. We were ready by the time we got to the job. No time for reflection.

Southwark were fighting a fire in a derelict warehouse, and it was steaming. Everyone had been accounted for by the time we got there, and now it was just a matter of extinguishing the blaze. There had been a report of an old tramp using it as a doss, but while searching he'd been spotted in the park opposite. There were holes everywhere, missing windows and loopholes. These allowed the smoke to dissipate and consequently visibility was reasonable. When there is someone involved, the urgency can be felt, a controlled haste exudes from everyone on the fireground, no matter what their task. It is calmer now, not relaxed but the tension has gone. Their Guv seemed to believe they had knocked out the seat of the fire and carried out a sweep to confirm there was no one involved. It should be relatively safe now; so he said.

We were detailed to take a branch up to the first floor and knock out the hot spots. This is playtime, I love putting on a set and crawling around a burning building, it's what we live for. I felt a great relief pour over me, the kind only escape from the clutches of a London Bus can allow. The fact that this place was alight, and perhaps dangerous, did not occur to me. I assumed Noddy would be gagging to get in, after all those months of staying outside. Our Guvnor's last words were to Nod, 'Listen to Tom; he'll show you how it's done.' This was going to be his first job bigger than the flats we regularly visited. My first fire seemed a long time ago, but I could remember the excitement, and my racing heart; I could see it now beaming from Noddy's face.

'You got that Nod, just listen to me,' I said, although by then Nod was too focused on the job to catch the irony; too new, too keen. He had obviously forgotten my recent lesson in rigging *en route*.

The place was cooking, the whole warehouse had felt the fire and was on the verge of becoming reacquainted. Crews were also still fighting the main seat on the ground floor, so much for *killed the blaze*. I also wondered how they had really carried out a search, it was huge and far too warm. We had only just cleared entry control when I spotted our first problem. I pulled Noddy down to a crouch and pointed to the stair that was meant to be our route to the next floor; it was glowing. I could see the reddened timber treads pretending to be secured to the stringer.

'That's not safe, we'll have to go and get a short extension to bridge it.' I was hoping Noddy had understood my rasping speech, he was nodding but that was normal. I could see his head study the stair, following the charcoaled brilliance of the radiant steps. It was a dogleg, the first flight stretching directly away from our position, the underneath of the second flight looked sound, hiding an even greater trap. Then as if to prove my point a firefighter, without BA, came from nowhere, leapt in front of us and ran up the stair. I couldn't work out what was more bizarre, that he had no breathing apparatus or that he thought he could climb the stair, but by sheer momentum he climbed.

Each temptress tread collapsed as he lifted his boot, only to destroy the next. He got to the half-landing and miraculously managed a one-hundred-and-eighty-degree turn. This was good of him as it allowed us a better view of his demise. He came crashing back down, together with most of the stair and a shower of brilliant embers. As the firework display subsided, Noddy and I looked at each other, and as one moved forward to help.

'He'll be in bits,' rasped Nod.

'He'll be fucking hot as well,' I said, 'get ready to hose him down.' He rose from the ashes, brushed himself momentarily, probably burning his hands, and ran off calling in his wake, 'I'll get you a ladder.' I grinned so much I could feel air leaking from my mask.

When he returned with a short extension ladder Nod and I were still in the process of extinguishing and destroying the timbers that he had missed. He'd actually done us a favour, we now had a definite pitch to the first, enabled by his fated climb. I doubted whether my first estimate of a bridge would have worked anyway. He dropped the ladder and stood back for a minute, hands on hips, 'You be careful up there,' he said with much authority, then turned and disappeared.

Nod looked at me, 'He's having a laugh, right.'

'He'll be a senior officer one day,' I said, 'state the bloody obvious and then vanish.' We tied off the ladder and pulled our hose up to the first floor. It might have been well ventilated but it was still stifling. I could feel the heat creeping over my raised flesh, searing the absurd goose bumps.

'How you doing Nod, warm enough?' He nodded but he didn't need to, his animation was intoxicating and he was already using the branch effectively. After a quick air check, we started to move across the first storey. There were pockets of fire everywhere, including holes in the floor that were obviously pre-fire and had probably promoted its spread. They were now emitting a smoky steam that was increasing the humidity and our discomfort. Sunlight streamed in an absurd saintly illumination through the vacant windows, and although it was still hazy, we could see.

We moved about in a combination of crawl, sit and squirt. All the time looking out for areas that may not take our weight. I sat and stamped my heels in front of us while Noddy used the jet over my shoulder. This is a well-known firefighting manoeuvre called, *making it up as you go along*. It was like creeping over burning coals, my whole body was tingling and I felt like my firegear was becoming detached, heating up from the inside. The fire, that was meant to be extinguished below, was still managing to keep us pretty warm. We were soaking everything, 'Put a bit of spray on Nod, I'm getting fucking warm in here,' I said. It didn't really help; we were already overheated. I tapped Nods hand to attract his attention again.

'What's up Tom?' I passed my flattened hand from side to side in front of my neck, the sign to knock off.

'Come on Nod, time to go. Leave the jet there, we've done our bit.' He went to stand and turn around at the same time, and almost stumbled. He looked me in the eye. 'Still hot up there?' I asked.

'Yeah,' was all he managed, with a couple of nods for good measure. I had been taking most of the heat from the forward position, we normally would have swapped round but I'd had enough. It's amazing how much protection a body can give you from the heat, another lesson for Noddy.

'Let's crawl back out then Nod.' We followed the hose back to the ladder.

By the time we got out we were roasted, my insides were starting to boil up into my head which had become hotter than the rest of me; we staggered away to rehydrate. The BA control officer chased us to return our tallies and maintain his count; we had forgotten to check out. We found a pump, cracked a delivery and used our helmets as oversize drinking vessels and then wore the final refill. We sat, propped against a wall, I shrugged off my set and pushed it aside.

'Undo your tunic Nod, let the heat out,' I looked up, it was Granny, 'You trying to break our new boy Tom?' he said, 'Stay there.' He picked up both our sets, one in each hand and took them back to our machine.

'Nod?' I asked.

'Yep.'

'Okay?'

'That was fucking top banana Tom, how are you?' I was shagged, I didn't know if I was wet from my own dowsing or still sweating. I certainly needed a while longer to regroup. I watched Gran walk away with what looked like two toy Breathing Apparatus sets.

'Yeah, everyone should have a Granny, init.'

'I think my leggings are well supple now, that was a scorcher, they're gonna be right comfy,' said Nod. Soft leggings are like a Badge of Office to a Junior Buck, evidence of confrontation with the beast.

'I'm afraid not.'

'Don't tell me they get warmer than that Tom.'

'Not much Nod, but the Guvnor likes us to have leggings that don't flap about like a pair of seventies flares.' He followed my gaze to the tear in his left leg.

'Aww bollocks.'

'Easy Nod, at least you won't have to clean them.'

We were first away, but not before we checked my door. The others were already investigating. 'It seems okay Tom. You sure you closed it properly?'

'I thought so Guv.'

'Okay let's check it again when we get back.'

'I think it could be this old machine Guv.'

'And I think it could be this old Tomato,' he said. He was probably right, we tested and tested it when we got back and it closed every time. 'I'm not happy, take it off,' he gave the order. The old beast came off the run and we looked forward to one of our favourite jobs, a re-stow. It's not until you transfer every bit of kit from one machine to another that you appreciate how much stuff we actually carry.

'Where's Ted?' I said to Nod, the re-stow was over and I realised something was missing. Nod jumped back into the old machine just to check but we all had a lump in our throats.

'Who's got him?' Nod was convinced we were having a joke, until he looked at our faces.

'Shit guys, you should have let me go and saved Ted,' I said, 'he must be half-way to Southwark, and probably very thin.' I was convinced Ted had taken a dive for me and disappeared when I nearly, unceremoniously dismounted. 'It would have been quick, those Routemasters don't muck around.'

'We'll have to go and have a look,' said Granny.

'God, that was ages ago, there's no chance,' said Nod, 'if he's not dead he'll have been stolen.'

'Still got to try,' I said, 'how will we break it to Toby when he comes back.' Although Nod was Fm Ted's designated carer, Toby had a soft spot for small furry creatures, he had one of his own in the unspeakable depths of his footlocker.

'I'm on my way,' said Bones. He took Rodney and the Turntable Ladder for a gallant but futile trip to the busy junction that was the scene of my extra vehicular activity.

They came back empty handed. I couldn't believe that Fm Ted had also taken a leap out of that old machine. I had an image of his knitted jacket under the wheels of the bus, it was better than the image I had earlier, of me under the bus. It felt like Ted had taken one for the team, one for me, saved by a bloody cuddly toy.

It was nearly change of watch and I'd found Granny sitting on his footlocker. The shoe and boot section of our lockers juts out to make a convenient, if not very comfortable, seat. I sat down nearby. Our Bear was already history and we needed another distraction; at this time of night, it would be the pub. I'm sure what I often imagined was his sixth sense was just a highly attuned awareness of everyone and everything. Certainly, on the fireground, whenever you needed something, Granny would be there with that bit of gear or his large helping hands. I wondered whether some things affected him more than the rest of us. He wouldn't take any thanks for saving my life earlier, that wasn't unusual, but it was the distant look in his eyes, a sort of refusal to believe what had happened. It was the look he always had when we found another stiff.

However good his intuition was he'd had a blind spot when it came to his latest acquisition. He was messing about with what looked like some type of multi-tool. He was turning it upside down and every way. Looking very confused.

'What's up Gran,' I said, he was a bit perplexed.

'Didn't you get one of these Tom?' he said.

'No, what is it?'

'Rubbish probably Tom. I don't know why I always fall for Rodney's junk; you must be a better judge.' He held out his massive hand with what looked like a toy in his palm. It was because of all these *special offers* that Rodney had got his nickname, he wanted to be called Delboy from *Only Fools and Horses* but the watch decided he wasn't clever enough and settled for his younger brother!

'I didn't get the offer; you know me and Rodney keep it on a strictly carbohydrate level.'

'Eh?'

'You know, food, what goes with what mince dish, so I can join in.'

65

'And there's me thinking Tomatoes went with anything.'

'Oy, I'm a married man you know,' I said. My thoughts immediately went to the phone number on the scrunched-up bit of paper, now smoothed and pinned to the back of my locker door.

'Look at this Tom, it's broken already. I'm sure half his bargains are hooky.'

'It's those Mitts, perhaps you need one in extra-large.'

'Yeah, I'll throw it on the pile with the rest. It's nearly six, are you having a beer?'

'What sort of question is that? See you there.' I left my cycle gear in my locker and went to the pub in some civilian clothes I keep for just these occasions. I had decided to stay at the station instead of cycling home, some of the floaties were going to join us for a pint or two; it had been that sort of day. I needed a beer. For some reason flying alongside the fire engine instead of sitting inside had given me a terrible thirst. I don't think I really ever fully processed that day. It certainly never occurred to me that those sort of things don't happen to most people.

I'd started storing the trauma somewhere without even realising. I didn't think about it much, I certainly didn't share any fear, if there was any, even though there should have been. It was acceptable however to have a few more beers than normal. A few pints with my brothers, they would understand; they probably had their own inner hiding places and they certainly wouldn't ask any difficult, probing questions. I didn't take it home either, there was nothing to gain, so I thought. The big bruise on my chest became the result of yet another skylark. I mentioned the door flying open but not my near fatal exit; it was Fm Ted who brought the farm, not me.

Granny and Jules, one of the fireboat crew, were already in the pub. Julie as we called him, loved the story about our old machine with the dodgy door, although he insisted they were the best fire engines in the fleet and easy to drive. Old hands love old stuff, especially sitting in the pub and reminiscing. It wasn't long before I was subjected to the standard squashed tomato jokes; it was my turn to take the flak.

After too many beers and the compulsory Indian meal, Granny and I made our way back to the station. We swore that we would one day have a curry before we got drunk, just to see whether it was tasty or not. We cut through the estates in an effort to save time and get out of the biting wind, it didn't work.

Granny was thirty-two, married and had no kids of his own; it would interfere with his social life, which seemed to consist of his rugby club and a long list of exotic holidays. He was always going on another *holiday of a lifetime*. I guess I was jealous to some degree, I was lucky if my wife and I got a weekend together. He was talking about rugby as usual, which was fine unless he lost, we would know because he'd have a face like a bulldog licking piss off a thistle. We had a way to break this mood.

'What do you reckon?' One of us would ask.

'Definitely, he lost, no doubt.'

'Whose turn is it then?'

'Yours, I did it last time.'

'Alright, I'll do it,' we went off to find Granny. 'Hey Gran, how did the game go today?'

He would mumble, 'We lost.'

'Aww, never mind, it's only a game.' You could see the temperature rising like steam erupting from an old warehouse floor; then we would run away. That's about when he would realise, we were taking the piss and would feign a chase.

Anyway, it was time to change the subject, something had been on my mind all night.

'This way,' said Gran.

'Okay', I was going through this block but it's much of a muchness,' I said, it all seemed a little different on foot but we sort of knew our way, we thought. Neither of us were ready to admit that we were a bit disorientated, not lost, we knew our ground but it was taking a little longer to get home than it should have. 'Did you ever call that woman from the Lion, Gran?' I asked.

'Blimey that was a while ago, what makes you think of that Tom?' He was on to me; I should have known better.

'Just wondering that's all.'

'I guess you might be thinking that I'm married but I took her number.'

'This way Gran. I'm not judging.'

'So, what's her name then?' he asked.

'Who?' He was definitely on to me.

'The nurse with the red hair.'

'Aww, you know.'

'We all know Tommy; you should realise that.' It's true, it's not that we're gossips, we just have to know about each other, with as much detail as possible, and then some embellishments for good measure.

'So, what are they saying Gran?'

'They're wondering when you're going to eventually give her a call, that's what they're saying Tom.'

'Well, I was thinking, there's no harm in having a chat; is there?'

'Don't ever think of being an officer, Tom?'

'What's that got to do with it?'

'You have to make decisions.'

I could see the bloody phone number every time I opened up my locker, see it and touch it, just to check it was real. I was in danger of wearing it out. I was going to call, I guess I knew that on some level, I just kept thinking about my marriage. I was fighting a sense of loss, and I couldn't decide whether it was of my wife or of not talking to Red; I'd already given her a pet name. If I didn't call soon, she wouldn't remember who I was, if she hadn't forgotten already.

'You still with me Tom?' We were almost at the rear gate.

'Yes, I'm here. So, you never said whether you called her Gran?'

'I'm happily married Tom.' He was, of course, I'd used it as a ruse to try and get some advice. Truthfully, I was really looking for support, I should have asked him directly; he would have helped. That was all about to become lost in misadventure.

'Have you got your key?' It was only when we arrived at the back of the station, we realised that neither of us had the key to the rear gate.

'We'll have to go round the front,' said Gran. All was quiet at this time of night and the back of the station isn't overlooked, we thought. I had a better idea, somewhere in the depths of my swollen beer belly came a plan to get out of the cold night much quicker. 'No we won't, look this new automatic gate will be easy to climb, just give me a leg up.' The bold red, metal was flirting, *climb me, climb me* it purred.

'What about me, who's going to give me a leg up?'

'I'll pull you up once I'm astride.' I was excited now, even Granny wasn't going to change my mind.

'You'll pull me bloody arm out of its socket before you lift me, Tommy.'

'Naw I won't, come on.' Everything seems easier than it really is when viewed through the blurriness of pub goggles. What happened next should have got us locked up, we had no idea, but we were being watched. Along with the new gate had come Closed Circuit Television.

It didn't go well from the start; every time I got above ground level my co-ordination took a dive and so did I. After several attempts and with more of a two-handed shove than a manmade step, I managed to get to the top of the gate. Although I'm sure Granny must have just dumped me there out of frustration. I remained horizontal, cuddling the uncomfortable metalwork and threw down a casual arm to pull up Granny. 'Sling us one up, Gran,' I said.

Once again, the giant arm stretched out, but now it was my turn to pull. He suddenly became a lot heavier than I'd imagined in my pre-climb assessment, I thought he'd stuck his feet to the ground. About this time several things happened at once.

Firstly, the bells dropped and our White Watch had a call out. 'Aww we could have gone around the front Gran; they've got a shout. We could have walked right in.' I sat upright having abandoned my weightlifting career before it really started.

'Better come down,' said Granny, but I couldn't hear because what I thought were Fire Engine sirens were too loud. I thought he would be on his way to the front of the station and a much more relaxing entrance. Contemplating my lonely descent to the station yard, I was having flashbacks to my earlier tarmac torment and still unaware of the impending calamity.

Secondly the gate I was sitting on started to move. 'Whoa, Gran, how'd you do that,' I screamed and turned back in his direction. I nearly fell and started to sway about, I grabbed at the steel with one hand and threw out the other arm, in a vain attempt at balance.

The third, fourth, fifth, etc. things had been the arrival of several police cars, with lights pulsing and two-tones bawling, adding a cacophony to the noise of our departing PL. My directional hearing had gone way up the spout, the extra noise that I had imagined were weird and loud echoes, were actually the boys in blue, and they were right behind me. Their cars were parked in a fan arrangement, pointing full beam towards our mistaken trespass. Granny was standing there as if he had just got caught going over the Berlin Wall. He had both his hands in the air; I couldn't, I was in danger of falling off of the moving gate.

The gate stopped moving and a fire brigade officer came into view. He had his hands in the air too, but not as high as us; I had joined Granny in his reach for the stars. For my life I had no idea who he was but he knew us. 'You bloody two, I might have guessed.' His hands were flapping, like he was patting two invisible balls. It was a brave attempt to calm things down. He raised his voice and spoke to the police, 'It's alright they're with us.'

'I can cancel the other cars then?'

'Yes, yes, call it all off.'

'Other cars, call it all off? What's happened?' I asked, still not realising that we were their focal point and could become headline news.

'We bloody happened; shut up Tom,' Granny whispered loudly.

'I must admit they don't look much like terrorists, especially Wild Bill Hitchcock up there,' said the sergeant, 'we'll cross this one off.'

'Thanks, thanks,' said our senior officer, 'simple mistake.' I think he was hoping his superior rank could smooth things over; it was working. Granny helped me down from the gate whilst the police cars drove off. The officer closed the gate and we waited for our bollocking. 'Fucking idiots,' he was shaking his head, 'go on, get lost.'

'Cheers Guv, sorry,' I said.

'Yeah, thanks,' added Granny, as we scuttled away, I nearly fell over my own feet, trying to look at Granny and our way into the station at the same time.

'He was alright, do you know him?' I asked Granny.

'Covering his own back I'd say, he'd look pretty silly himself, starting a terrorist alert on Fire Brigade HQ for you and me Tom.'

'Still nice about it though.'

'I suppose. Now go and find your Tomato patch before the White's get back.'

Granny had turned into Mother. I turned into my pit, but not before wondering if my wife would find out about this, she was in antiterrorism, she could have even been there!

6

Early March 1984
Rat Stations

Toby was his normal jolly self this evening, exuding energy that you couldn't help but absorb. I jokingly asked him how many marathons he'd run this week, he didn't even blink, thinking it was an everyday question. He replied that he'd only done two, ten-mile training runs and was going to have to run around the bridges before we went on duty. After a fair bit of badgering, I agreed to do a couple, Westminster and Lambeth was all I could manage after my twelve-mile cycle.

I guess we all had different reasons for joining the fire service. I knew Toby's, he'd told me: *I just want to save lives*. Given our heavy stiff to low rescue ratio, I thought he must be having a tough time. That wasn't the case, he loved it all, just like the rest of us. It's a filthy job most of the time, cleaning up when there's no one else to call, but for Toby every job was a mission, every call was a rescue, you could feed off of his positive energy. Every watch should have a Toby.

We had time for a quick pint before we started work, more important than the run around the bridges.

'You cycle in Tobe, then have a run, why don't you go the whole hog and do a triathlon,' I said.

'I can't bloody swim!' he answered, 'I get frightened in the bath!'

'You've got to be kidding, you be careful the next time the lions have a drink.'

'The floaties will save me, but won't the Thames Barrier stop that now?'

'What lions?' Noddy had become inquisitive. My mind was racing, trying to think up a wheeze, but Toby wasn't on the same wavelength, the truth won.

71

'They're on the river wall, lion's heads with rings in their mouths, have a look next time you're down there. We've seen the river so high the water was coming through the cracks in the pavement,' said Toby.

'And that's when they take a drink,' I finished his sentence for him. Noddy looked at us both, disbelief plastered all over him, he'd learnt to be careful when listening to our stories; every tale has the potential to become a practical joke.

As I was looking back at him, I couldn't take my eyes from his nose and chin. It was only after he'd told us that he was a Punch and Judy man that I noticed how pointy they were. The more I looked the more pointed they got; I bet Punch had a nodding head as well.

'Any new fiddles Nod,' I asked.

'Yeah, I've been shelling showers.'

'That's easy for you to say!' Toby laughed, 'How many have you sold?'

'None yet, but it's early days.' Noddy was an optimist, fortunately.

'Why don't you just get promoted,' although I really thought that was the toughest way to make money. Nod looked introspective, maybe the Lions had been replaced by dreams of leadership.

'Come on, or we will be late,' I said, we rushed back to the station, just in time for roll call.

We'd lost more than Fm Ted recently, we were down at least a hydrant bar, a ceiling hook, and according to our Blue Watch, a length of hard suction hose. These bits of equipment can just walk away when you're not looking, but hard suction is huge, not easy to mislay, and we certainly hadn't used it recently. Most gear is marked up with a station number, but that doesn't seem to stop it vanishing, especially when you're busy and firefighters from other stations are around.

Apparently, it's easier to get a replacement for broken equipment than have to do the paperwork for a missing item. Especially when you back on to Brigade Workshops and can purloin anything to be substituted at a later date.

'Tom and Toby, take a radio and nip down Doulton's Drive,' said Bones. Doulton Pottery began its existence in the area in the late nineteenth century and a Doulton Building can still be found on the corner of Lambeth High St and Black Prince Rd. Doulton's Drive now leads into Brigade Workshops.

'What do we need?' Toby asked. Bones produced a list. 'You're having a laugh, Bones, what are we doing another re-stow?'

'Just see what's around, but don't talk about it on the radio, you never know who's listening,' said Bones. I ignored this remark, it was like telling a burglar not to wear bright clothes.

'Let's take Nod and show him around,' I said to Toby as we made our way out.

'No, send him to me,' Bones almost shouted, 'I don't want him getting into bad habits.'

'Alright for us though,' I said.

'There's no hope for you two,' answered Bones.

A weekend night was an ideal time to climb over the gate and have a rummage, it was deserted. We knew where the cameras were now and they didn't point at these gates. They were much higher than our back gate but somehow easier to climb when you've not had a skinful of ale. Inside there were loads of ladders laying on the floor, we didn't need any of them. We were probably only going to find stuff that was to be thrown out, still serviceable but not good enough to issue, ideal for our purposes. Toby and I had a reputation for breaking and entering, it was part of the job. Of course, if you had a Granny around there tended to be a lot more breaking, with a lot more noise; tonight, we were going to have to be more subtle. We found a stock of old hydrant gear easy, a skip full, all battered and bruised.

'There,' Toby had spotted a good hydrant key with a telescopic hidden bar in amongst the trash, we were in luck.

'That's a good start Tobe,' I said, 'we'll leave it here and pick it up on the way back. We went further along, under the railway arch, trying doors on the way without much luck. I turned on my torch to make up for the loss of borrowed streetlight. We were right at the back of workshops now; the main block wasn't easy to enter but the old stores at the back were sometimes left open. It was eerily quiet so we tiptoed along, trying unsuccessfully to keep in character. I could hear the slight breeze funnelling through the arch, a backdrop to our not so soft footsteps.'

'Maybe we can find a window,' I whispered. A train ran above and suddenly the silence wasn't the only thing destroyed. I nearly wet myself and Toby's hand grabbed his heart. We became part of the wall, neither of us able to move until we bravely turned our heads to check the other hadn't been spirited away by the hush invading Ghost Train. The whole place had to stop vibrating before we could return to our disappointing investigation.

73

'Jesus, that frightened the shit out of me,' Toby got even closer to the wall, cleverly hiding his long shadow. I felt a shiver, which was from more than just the evening shade, accentuated under the ancient, damp arch. It was still only March and I was thinking that I should have put on an extra layer of clothing.

'What about that old skip,' I pointed to what I thought was only a pile of old hose. The more I looked the more concerned I became.

'There's someone laying there!' Toby's eyes widened to reflect the dimness and reveal a deeper worry. We couldn't be sure, so we crept forward. There was just enough light to turn our adventure into a disaster. Any remote warmth in the evening air was completely replaced with a cold fear and I began to tremble.

'No, just rubbish,' I muttered, I hoped, but there was someone there. Whoever he was he didn't look comfortable.

I'm sure I heard him moan but it was Toby, 'Oooo…shit Tom, what are we going to do?' He grabbed my arm and we were now locked in symbiotic nervousness.

'Yo-you alr-right m-mate?' I stuttered but he didn't move. My mind was racing now, trying to think up excuses for being here whilst at the same time imagining performing cardiac massage on top of a pile of hose. It wasn't far, just a few steps but what should have been a rush took an age. I had a cold, goosy feeling that went from Toby's hand to right up the back of my neck. There was definitely a figure amongst the reels of yesterday's fire hose. Toby was already climbing in, but we both shone our Bardic Torches from the rim of the skip, as if a bit of hesitation would remove the suspected horror.

'It's a fucking dummy,' screamed Toby. It was an old drill dummy, its guts were ripped apart, spilling a pink intestine of non-percolating 70mm hose into the skip.

'Who sends a drill dummy to Workshops?' I was trying to revert to the, *I wasn't scared* mode.

'Someone who wants to frighten the shit out of us Tom, that's who.'

'Have we had enough?'

'Naw, come on.' Had I been on my own that would definitely have been the end of this excursion. Toby was relying on some phantom joint bravado; I don't know where it came from but he found some.

'Yeah, okay,' I said. We delved deeper into the recesses of the dimly lit workshop buildings. 'Better test the radio Tobe, we're a long way from home.'

'Shall I tell them you've been chatting up a right dummy?'

'No but ask them for the First Aid kit for my new arm injury, you pinch harder than Granny.'

'Bravo two-two-one, report my signals, over,' Toby tried the reception without the hushed tones of a little earlier.

'Loud and clear,' answered Noddy.

'They're working well tonight,' said Toby, but I didn't really hear, I'd just found an unlocked door. My seesaw adrenalin had gone up a notch, again. 'Wow, should we?' Toby was hesitant. We both stood on the brink, staring into the blackness beyond and reasserted in our former plundering role. The skip event almost scratched from our minds.

'Of course,' I said as I slowly pushed the door wide open. I was expecting it to creak like some deserted crypt.

'What do you reckon's in there Tom?'

'Only one way to find out.' I could see nothing, I took a sideways glance and tentatively put my foot over the threshold.

As if in answer to my step there came a shout, 'OY YOU! WHAT YOU DOING?'

It was loud and it echoed, it could have come from anywhere, but it was distant enough to invite escape. Toby and I stared at each other for a nano-second and intuitively decided that *run away* was the best response. We flew like buggery through the dimly lit warren. I must have been legging it as I nearly tripped over Toby's heels; I don't normally move that fast. But something was wrong, there was no follow up shout, no *come back 'ere, you're for it*, no *wait till I tell your Mum*, we sped on anyway. Toby passed the hydrant key and bar and turned to see where I was, he must have heard me slow down. I stopped to pick up our previous booty.

'Come on Tom,' he hissed, impatiently.

'Listen,' I said. We both cocked an ear towards the sky because it's well known that that is the best way to hear a would-be assailant. There was only silence. Luckily, we hadn't turned into the main stretch of Doulton's Drive, the bit that could be seen from the road. 'Have we been had Tom?' asked Toby.

'Almost Tobe, almost,' I said, 'fancy a stroll?' We rounded the corner just in time to see our machine pull up at the gate, I wished I could whistle. I had a sneaking feeling they had recently been parked behind the back of workshops.

'You didn't need to come and meet us guys,' I said. They weren't sure, they exchanged little glances, and I ignored them.

'We got a new key and bar but no luck on anything else,' said Toby.

Nod couldn't help himself, 'What's it like in there guys, no one around?'

'No, it's deserted this time of night Nod,' I said, straining to keep a straight face, 'just me and Toby.' They looked confused but we all knew the shouting didn't come from a man made of hose.

Having returned from our excursion and now patiently waiting for supper, Toby had a suggestion, 'That bit of mischief has inspired me Tom, fancy a bit of *Rat Stations* tonight?' Rodrick was the oldest hand on the station. He lived with Toby, who was more like a custodian than a Carer. Rodrick was a rat. No one knew how old he was, but his last steward had been retired five years, which could put his birthday around the late fifties, early sixties, he was certainly showing signs of his longevity. He was a dirty brown colour and much of it was dirt. He was more Coney than rat, he had no legs, was blind and his tail was short and flat. However, in the dim gutters of Albert Embankment he was the biggest, filthiest rat you've ever seen.

'There'll be lots of people walking home past the station tonight,' said Toby, 'there's a Do at the Hospital.'

'Yeah, Doctors' Mess, Vanessa said she might put a shout in, if it gets boring.'

'What, the nurse with the gorgeous red hair? So you did give her a call.'

'Yeah, well no.'

'Who's Rodrick?' asked Noddy, looking up from his eternal polishing but interrupting at just the right moment. I'd let slip about my phone call and now it would be hard to keep it quiet.

'Come here,' Toby beckoned us over and started rummaging in his footlocker. He pulled out a tatty old, rolled up plastic bag, the type that had started to degrade even though they live for a thousand years. He bravely delved inside, 'Ta da,' he announced.

Nod was unimpressed, 'It's an old bit of fur on a fishing line.'

'Easy Nod, you'll hurt his feelings,' I said. As Toby began to stroke his pet's matted thatch, Nod looked from him to Rodrick and back to him. I could see he was wondering whose feelings Toby's or Rodrick's. '*Rat Stations* after supper then?'

'Sounds like a plan to me,' said Toby, 'So what's she like?' I knew I wouldn't get away with it.

'We haven't been out, I just thought it would be polite to call her, being as she gave me her number.'

'So, when are you seeing her?' said Toby.

'I don't know, I didn't speak to her,' I said.

'What are you talking about?' said Noddy, I didn't know whether he was confused about my phone call, *Rat Stations*, or the prospect that we might get a spurious shout to a party. He was still the new boy, even after all these months.

'She wasn't in, I spoke to her flatmate.'

'So, who might call us Tom?' said Toby.

'Well, I was trying to act like it didn't matter that Red wasn't in and we sort of got talking.'

'So, who are you going to ask out Tom?' Noddy said.

'Who said I was going to ask anyone out, I...'

'SCOFF IT AND HOP IT,' Rodney's voiced echoed around the station. Supper was ready and that got me out of any further explanation. Truth was that I was disappointed, I'd finally decided to give Red a call and she wasn't there; that wasn't the name she'd written on my now faded note, but I'd already given Jenny a new name. I'd fooled myself that I only wanted to chat but now I was convinced I had to see her, and we hadn't even spoken.

'Don't be last,' I shouted as I sprinted away to the mess. We had been waiting, supper was late, as usual.

'Are we doing the booze cruise again then Tom,' asked Frankie between mouthfuls. We were slowly finishing supper; it was always a Le Mons type start just in case we got a shout but then we relaxed into a more digestible pace. Some would make a one-slice sandwich of whatever we were eating and leave it to one side; if we got a shout it would go with them. I didn't bother, I think it was the idea of a *veg. curry butty* somehow only making it to the pole. I'd never get over the disaster of seeing my supper all over broken comrades as they fell down the newly greased fire pole. I don't know where their *butties* went between Mess and machine, but these fast food foldings would end up on the back shelf with the BA face masks, both requiring the same level of protection.

Another empty plate clattered as Bones finished and his fork hit the Delph. 'That was shit Rodney,' he said. Rod was trying not to smile but you could tell he was enjoying the kudos.

'If you mean, am I going to organise another European adventure to indulge in fine cuisine and, per chance, return with some local wares, I don't see why not,' I said, trying to add an air of elegance not normally present in the firefighters Mess.

'I remember it more as Muscles and Chips, missing the ferry and losing me duty free,' said Toby.

'Where did you get to?' asked Gran.

'I wish I knew but I'm afraid of going back to Boulogne in case I get recognised.'

'You're lucky you didn't get kidnapped by the French Resistance and taken back to Rene's café,' said Granny.

'That was a big disappointment for me, the waiter didn't look anything like Michelle or Mimi,' said Frankie.

'He had his eye on you though Frank,' I said.

'That's 'cause I'm nearly fluent in the lingo, init.'

'Yeah, he was definitely impressed with your Benidorm French. How did it go? *Mucho vino por favour*,' said Rodney.

'I still think you could have been on, Frank, the way he kept looking at you from across the bar!'

'I think he was more Cockney than you Frank,' said Granny. 'Maybe we should do something for Anglo-French relations and go somewhere completely different.'

'What was you thinking,' I asked.

'Well how about a weekend away somewhere.'

'Now you're talking,' said Toby.

'What about Butlin's, they do mini breaks,' Frankie seemed keen.

'I was thinking of something more sophisticated,' Granny just managed to say. Suddenly everyone was a travel agent and we were talking about themed weekends, sixties nights and group discounts.

'Do you take your wives?' Noddy asked. That caused a brief silence, we'd only ever taken them out at Christmas.

'It's the only way it would work for me, Julie would never give me a pass for the whole weekend,' Bones managed one of his hard done by looks.

'Why not?' said Toby, the only single man on the watch and the only one still eating.

'You got to remember Tobe, we want to get away for the weekend, you just want a chance to get up to your nuts with the latest girlfriend,' this was ironic coming from Frankie who was just as likely to bring his most recent conquest than his wife.

'My wife would love it, count me in.' That statement from Gran sealed it and Toby still hadn't finished Noddy's leftovers.

'Over to you Tom?' Frankie said it as a question, what he really meant was, can you sort it out. I was the watch excursion organiser.

'Leave it with me,' I said but they had already moved on to a bet whether the phone would ring for Frankie as we were about to do the washing up.

The first time I tried to organise anything it nearly didn't happen. I made the mistake of giving everyone options on what, when and where, and World War Three broke out. Now I don't ask, I just tell. There's still a choice but a small one and most of the watch like to be in rather than out.

The pay phone was ringing. We had our own call box for private calls, except it wasn't that private, just a recess in the corridor. I didn't normally answer it, it was never for me, and I might end up lying to someone.

Frankie was in the habit of having the night off without telling his wife; he would leave a note stuck to the phone saying he was out on a big fire if anyone called. I had dropped him in it once, when he forgot to leave a note. I answered the phone to a lady who asked for Frankie, without thinking I quickly replied that he was on leave, only to be met with floods of tears and a sobbing voice, *He must be there.* Fortunately for me Bones was walking past and I threw him the phone before he knew what was happening, mouthing the words, *Frankie's wife.* Bones spent the next half an hour convincing her that I was a stand-by who didn't know anything; partially right I suppose.

'A and B,' shouted Gran, even though we'd all heard. It wasn't that old a system but for some reason that's what it was still called.

'Told you, that will be Frankie's get out of the washing-up call,' said Rodney.

'Now how would anyone know what time we finish supper, Rodders?' said Frankie as he went to get up, but I was nearest the door. I stood.

'I'll go,' I said.

'Expecting someone Tomato,' said Granny.

'Frankie, A and B,' Bones voice came from the distance, he'd beaten us all to the phone.

'See, told ya,' said Rodney.

'Well, we've got to get a rat out of his cage,' I said, trying to cover up my disappointment that the call wasn't for me.

'Not until you've done the washing-up, you're not,' I don't know what was wrong with Rodney, he always gave me a dirty look on top of one of his digs, but no one else seemed to notice. I wondered, not for the first time, if it was just my imagination.

'Of course, Rodders. Pass your plates down everyone.' We all help with the washing up, always, I don't know why Rodney gets so excited. But Frankie does seem to have an uncanny knack of timing his incoming phone calls.

Toby loved *Rat Stations*, we all did, there is a waist high balcony all the way around our floor, except it's more aesthetic than of any use. There is just enough room to walk around and of course, to hide. We went to the Chummery to make our plan.

If the watch had a soul, it was the Chummery. On nights it was a place to sit and chat to your chums. But it was also a place to listen, I'm sure I learnt more about the job from the little details in the grand stories that were told again and again. Even if each time was with greater exuberance and less authenticity than the last. The snippets were there all the same, little procedures veiled behind the animation. We also relived some of our unheroic and mischievous exploits. The telling becoming more fantastic and even funnier than they had ever been at birth.

There was a time when most stations would have had an actual bar, these had disappeared by the time I joined, the permissible ones anyway. There was an acceptance however that we would have a drink at work. This was supplied through the 'Nutty Cupboard', a spare locker full of chocolate bars, bags of crisps, soft cans of drink and cheap tins of ale and lager. If the Chummery was the soul of the watch then the Nutty was its heart, or more accurately, its stomach.

Like the Mess, this was a place where the watch really got together, it was where we got to know each other. The jokers revelled, the politicians aired their controversy, and those with real brains eventually got found out. We played Trivial Pursuit once; never again, I hardly ever got a go!

Most of all it was where attachments were corroborated, lasting friendships forged from everything we have to share; born in the fire. The benefits this created for the watch cannot be understated. We needed to be a team and this kind of socialising brought us together more than training ever could.

Typically, sometime after supper we would gather and the Nutty would be unlocked and left open. We would take up our pews, footlockers normally although there was always a bit of mattress and a table and chairs. This was our time to unwind before we eventually went to our respective pits. Officially we weren't meant to put our beds down until midnight but there were always those who would drift off early. However it was only the floaties that could really get away with an early night, they had a much quieter life on the river.

I was a night bird; afraid I'd miss any of the fun and mischief or even worse become a target. I worked on the principle that if I was at the heart of the revelry, I wouldn't be the one that got nabbed. It didn't always work. Generally though, we didn't mess with bedding, that and grub were sacrosanct.

This was where we learnt about each other, our other lives, what we got up to in our other homes. It was where we found out if anyone needed a hand or if there was some paid work available. It was where we relaxed and larked, it was also where we schemed. It was the best part of night duties. Tonight, we were going to play with Rodrick but there were always other matters to deal with.

'You should be called Dylan,' said Toby to Rodney, who was dozing on his bed, 'you know, the hippy rabbit from the Magic Roundabout.'

'And you would have to be Dougal, Toby, you've got the hair,' added Gran.

'It's a good job the Guvnor isn't here, he'd get you both to the barbers,' I was risking it, I normally lose any discussions about hair, being follicly challenged myself.

'That's a good idea Tom, I wish I had thought of that,' the Guvnor made a rare appearance.

'Hello Guv, are you going to join us for a beer?' Frankie asked. The Guvnor made a pretence of not knowing exactly where the Nutty locker was situated. He stood with his back to us studying the wares.

'Just a coke, ooh, and maybe a KitKat. Cheers boys, carry on.' He must have been aware of the unnecessary silence, but that probably helped him maintain his authority. I would have welcomed him to sit down and have a chat, I'm sure we all would, but he was very old school and preferred to leave us to our mischief.

'Do you think the Guvnor is Zebedee?' I said.

'He was having an affair with Florence you know,' said Gran with knowledge.

'You must be whatsisname Tommy, you need to get on your bike, dropping us in it with our hair,' said Rodney.

I ignored the obvious dig, 'Oh yeah, the guy on the little tricycle who used to wiz around. Did he have a name?'

'Of course, he did, it was Mr Something?' said Toby. We were all blank.

'You've done it now, Rodders, none of us will get any sleep,' said Gran.

'I'll sort it,' said Frankie as he picked up the phone, 'Control will know or they'll find out.' Mobilising Control were in contact with the whole brigade, for the next ten minutes, every time a machine booked back, they were also asked, *who was the guy on the trike.*

Frankie snatched up the phone before the first ring had finished, if anyone was going to chat to the girls in Control it would be him. We soon thought it was someone else as he nattered away, so we continued our new discussion. We had moved on to the Woodentops, but I couldn't remember any of their names except Spot the Dog. When he eventually put the phone down, he interrupted the current dialogue.

'Mr McHenry,' he announced.

'That was quick, they're getting better,' I said.

'Yeah, we'll have to ask them something more difficult next time,' said Gran, 'Cor who dropped that?' He raised his fingers and squeezed his nose.

'It's Rodney's fault, mince A always has that effect,' said Toby.

'It was dou den,' Gran was now squeezing his hooter.

'I never said that,' Toby was in denial.

'We should light them,' suggested Nod. We all looked at him in confused disbelief.

'What you talking about, Nodders?' Frankie asked.

'It was in Spike Milligan's book, when he was a squaddie, they used to light their farts.'

'It might get rid of the smell,' I didn't believe it but felt a little encouragement at this point wouldn't go amiss. None was needed, Toby was up and doing the, I need a crap dance. Both hands on his arse, and legs like a spider.

'Quick, quick, I've got one brewing, matches, lighter or something.' Rodney produced a box of matches from somewhere and threw them at Toby. Toby now did an upturned crab impression, laying on his curved back, knees around his prominent ears, desperately trying to light a match. He was failing, he was striking and missing, he gravely needed help but there was no point asking, no one was going any closer. The Chummery already seemed to have shrunk as we all tried to find a corner to hide. Then he lit one, now it was a matter of keeping it alight and not burning his fingers. He gingerly moved it towards his target, let out an almighty flatulent gust of wind and simulated a Harley Davidson backfiring.

'Shit, shit, I've had a blowback,' he continued his spider dance all the way to the toilet. No one was in any state to help, we were now all rolling about like upturned crabs; no one else tried it either.

If you visited during the day, it was just a locker room. Tonight, it was the backdrop to a much more intricate operation.

'Anyone fancy another beer?' I asked, although with Rodrick in our sights we didn't really need any extra laughter lubrication. 'We're getting Rodrick out for a run.' Unbelievably there were a few groans but I knew they would all be involved when we got our first bite. Toby and I decided to give Nod a bit of instruction. Experience had taught us that the fishing line had to go around the lamppost outside the Watchroom first, then along the kerb to where we laid Rodrick, inconspicuous in the gutter. We set up our ambush and returned to our balcony hideout.

'Here's someone,' whispered Nod.

Toby quietly called, 'Rat Stations.' We all crouched below the parapet, peeping. Along came a gentleman, briefcase in one hand and umbrella in the other.

'He's not from the doctors' mess,' I said. Toby jerked the line just enough to move Rodrick, just a twitch. He didn't see him.

'He's as blind as Rodrick,' said Noddy. Toby tugged a little harder, Rodrick jumped, the man jumped, we had caught one. He tiptoed forward, holding his briefcase in his outstretched arm and his umbrella aloft, poised, ready for battle, his sword and shield, flimsy but deadly. Despite only city gent chainmail, he lent bravely forward, intrigued perhaps, then he suddenly changed his posture raising his cleaver for a strike.

'He's going to hit him, quick Tobe,' I panicked. Toby was already on the case as Rodrick sprinted along the gutter, chased by this pin striped Viking Warrior. His long *Cleese* like legs, swifter than they should have been, were gaining good ground. I swear he landed one but Rodrick flew up the lamppost and made the ten-foot leap to the safety of the balcony.

We couldn't speak, we had been holding our breath, then it all came out as we hid from view, we giggled and giggled like proper little kids. The unworthy attacker had disappeared by the time we managed to stand up. Granny and

Frankie were making a racket climbing through the windows, unable to resist joining the furore.

'Quick, *Rat Stations*,' Noddy had spotted someone else and was already crouched, trying to signal for everyone to join him.

'It's no good Nod,' I said, he looked disappointed.

'Because Rodrick's up here,' said Toby, 'it's your turn to set him up, and don't be seen.' It wasn't long before another couple of victims were sited.

'*Rat Stations*,' called Toby. What we hadn't noticed was that the approaching young couple also had weapons. The most deadly of all—beer cans.

There was a loud shriek as Rodrick made his first move. The pair were now locked in a frightened embrace, pussycats against the mighty rodent. They disentangled and quickly conjured up some courage. Toby jerked the line and Rodrick narrowly missed the first flying tinny. The final retreat of our rat didn't go according to plan. As Toby pulled the line something snapped, Rodrick's last leap failed and now he lay lifeless, in full lamplight. We looked down, unsure how this tragedy would unfurl. Was the anti-hero really dead, would the couple run off into the sunset; they certainly would, well Albert Embankment.

The girl, having realised the prank, was on Rodrick with lightning speed, 'It's a lump of rags,' she shouted. She held him aloft in triumph, a display for us, her anxious audience. The dramatic pause nearly over, she looked up directly into our vanquished faces, 'We've got your toy.' They turned and exited stage right, at breakneck speed away from the station, south along the Embankment.

I was down the pole and in pursuit before the rest could take a breath. I got to the Old Father Thames before I stopped, they were nowhere to be seen, gone and Rodrick was lost; all those years of service and now he'd vanished. I wondered how I was going to tell the rest of the watch, not only was tonight's game up, but we had also lost another pet. I couldn't believe it, I thought of running on in blind hope but I knew it was useless. They might have gone straight on but there were plenty of side turnings, I gave up my chase and turned back towards the station. I was wondering what the Guv would think of taking the machine out on a hunt, only to see our Pump Ladder pull out towards Lambeth Bridge, lights flashing and sirens blaring. 'Shit I should be on that,' I was talking to myself, 'that's me fucked.'

Then I saw him, lying in the gutter, I must have run straight past him. If he had had eyes, they would have been staring up at me. 'Rodney,' I cried, then laughed, 'oops, sorry Rodrick, I didn't mean to be so rude.' Luckily no one was around. Those kids obviously gave up the idea of keeping a dirty old bit of fur, they can't have known how much we loved Rodrick. He was wet and traumatised but, apart from a missing line, he was unscathed. I thought I could present him as evidence for my defence, I could hear the Guvnor, *oh in that case Tomato, well done, take the rest of the night off.*

The boys were back soon so I made my way to the office to get my bollocking. Toby grabbed me before I got there and bundled me into the TV room. 'He doesn't know Tom.'

'What about Rodrick,' I said, confused.

'No, we got turned back, we never got off the machine. I don't think he realised you weren't there.' I was sure he was sharper than that.

'You sure Tobe?'

'Well, he never said anything. Wait until he calls for you; I bet he doesn't.' I walked out of the TV room and came face to face with the Guv.

'Tom,' he said, in a greeting kind of way and walked straight past me. I was still holding my breath as Toby and I got back to the dormitory.

'Cheers Tobe, I could have dropped myself in it there.'

'You were a bit of a wanker running off like that.'

'I know, I got caught up in the euphoria of it all.'

'Any luck getting Rodrick back?'

'Well, I did but I'm afraid he almost bought the farm,' I said, as he came into view draped over Noddy's lap, 'he's never been on such a run.'

'I think I'll take him around the bridges next time I go, just so he'll know his way home,' said Toby.

'I could take him and clean him up,' said Noddy.

'I don't think he would survive your washing machine, anyway he's a gutter rat, he can't be shiny,' said Toby.

Granny turned up, 'Did you catch them, Tom?' I thought about making up a story to save Rodrick's feelings but he deserved the real story.

'No, they just threw him away,' I said.

'I bet he escaped,' said Toby, wanting his pet to maintain the Senior Hand respect, 'just a few minor repairs to his leash and he'll be back on the run. There's plenty of life left in the old bugger.'

7

Late March 1984
An Errand

'I'm afraid I've got some bad news,' Bones read us out a note at roll call that we had received through the internal mail; it came with Fm Teds little knitted jacket.

DON'T CALL THE POLICE OR HE GETS IT
IT'S GONNA COST YA
YOU'LL BE HEARING FROM US
WE'VE GOT A CHOPPER AND
WE'RE NOT AFRAID TO USE IT

We sat around the Mess table, mugs of steaming tea acting like Cowboy covered wagons, protecting all we had of Ted. Bones had laid out his tunic together with the note, in the centre of table.

'Bastards,' he said as he retreated to his own mug of tea. Mesmerised, we looked on as Frankie snatched up the note and read it again.

'This is great news,' I said, snapping out of the team discomfort, 'it means he's alive. He didn't buy the farm under a London Routemaster.'

'They might just know we've lost him and be having us on,' said Noddy.

'And where do you think they got his jacket from Nodders?' asked Frankie. Toby got up, screamed and ran around the mess table, he stopped and turned to us, pretending to bite all of his fingers at once.

'I can't stand it,' he hollered, 'next it will be an ear or even a paw.' I had to join in, I got up threw my hands in the air and chased him around the table.

'Quick, who's going to go and secretly not tell the police,' Frankie bent his long frame over the table and gave everyone a stare, note still in hand.

'I'll do it, I'll go alone,' I said.

'No, you won't,' said Toby, 'we'll both go alone.'

'You better get baking Rod; I reckon this will be more than a one cake demand!' said Granny.

But we never heard from the kidnappers again.

Once we'd calmed down, it was time for me to make an announcement. 'Listen up. We are going on a three-day mini cruise to Guernsey,' I hadn't even told them how much and they were all signing up. 'Whoa, deposits on nights will do.'

Distant bell, click, LOUD BELLS, lights come on.

'I don't bloody know where it is,' said Rodney, 'sort it out boys.' We'd raced all the way onto Brixton's ground and now we were dawdling around, trying to locate an errant lift.

'Look, over there, it's an estate map,' I pointed across the road. 'Hold on here, I'll have a look.' I'd become the flats expert; well, everyone's got to be good at something. We weren't far away; I got back on board and gave directions. The Guv gave the two-tones a blast and off we went again. Hoping to find the person stuck in the lift before their bladder gave way.

We found the broken elevator and reassured the occupants that they would be out shortly. We now had to split the crew; the Guv and Toby stayed at floor level whilst Noddy and I went to the roof or top floor, Rodney stayed on the machine. We had to climb seven more flights of stairs to get to the lift motor room. Once there it was a matter of hand winding the lift car to the floor level where Toby and the Guv were waiting. This was all co-ordinated by the Guv via handheld radios, if we could hear them; we often found ourselves yelling up and down the lift shaft. Today the radios were working, they must have new batteries or been blessed when we crossed the station border. I could not only hear our Guv I could hear the local station; they must be nearby and working hard by the sound of the radio traffic.

Nod knew the lift room procedure; we get enough of them so he'd had plenty of practice. As we were locking up, I could still hear the masses of thank you being bandied about below, the sound being carried up the lift shaft.

I spoke loudly to Noddy as we were reunited with the rest of the team, '…and then having done all the graft you get back down and find all the lavish praise being given to the floor landing crew.'

'It can be a tough job Nod, but someone's got to do it,' declared Toby.

The Guv was still talking on his radio, 'Okay, be right there.'

'What's up Guv?' I asked.

'We've got an errand,' was all he said.

'I knew I could smell something,' said Rodney, as we rounded the corner. I thought it was me, we all smelled of fire, it gets into your firegear, and we don't always have a change of tunic to put on the run. There was no doubt now, in amongst the tower blocks a street of houses had become a dense smoky haze. I could hear the sound of the fire pump, the dropping of equipment and some occasional shouts. There was obviously a crew here but I couldn't see them.

As we pulled up our Guv jumped out, 'Wait here boys,' he said.

'Any idea what's going on Rod, did you hear anything?' said Toby. A slight breeze cleared the fog and the job came into full view.

'I'm not sure but it looks like that's where we're going.' Just ahead of us we could now see a half boarded up terraced block. Signs of disuse in the form of overgrown gardens and broken upstairs windows gave a sad look to this burning building. Smoke was percolating from the whole roof; it looked like the whole terrace was alight.

'Fucking hell,' I said, 'why hasn't he made them up?'

'I think he sent the stop,' said Rodney, who had been sitting on the machine since the lift job and had heard the main radio traffic. It was starting to make some kind of sense.

'There's only one machine here, isn't there?' I said.

'This is going to be fun,' said Toby. Nod was looking from side to side, trying to make sense of what was going on.

'Looks like we're going to help them put their fire out Nod,' I said.

'I don't really understand why he doesn't call Control for help.'

'Think about it Nod,' Toby took on schoolteacher mode, 'He's told them he's put it out, now he'll have to tell them he was wrong.'

'They haven't got a book big enough to throw at him,' added Rodney.

'You're going to be wearing that set again,' I said. His head started nodding; we had got through.

The two Guvnors came back, straight to the rear cab, opened the door and their Boss said, 'Really appreciate this lads, now four in sets, quick as you like.' I looked over at our Guv who just nodded his head. I jumped off so Rodney could get to his BA set. The two chiefs wandered off probably discussing the weather for all I knew, I guess we'd get to know what our part was going to be soon enough.

When our Guv, came back from his chat he got us to gather around. 'Right guys, I have to ask you this, they need help but can't ask Control without a lot of trouble.'

'You don't have to ask Guv,' said Rodney, before he'd finished.

'Are you all okay with that?'

'Of course,' Toby and I answered at the same time, Nod just nodded. We didn't care about how or why, we were about to get another fire to play with, why would we worry about that.

His next speech was longer than I'd ever heard before, 'Good lads. Listen up: this house closest is house one of an unoccupied terrace of six. They have put out a small fire on the first floor of house three. There was another fire in that attic which they missed. That has spread to houses two and four and maybe further, via a common roof void. Got it so far?'

We all said, 'Yep.' I didn't see Nod's head move once. I was starting to get confused but couldn't bring myself to say.

'They are doing houses three and four; Rodney and Tom, you have house two, Toby and Nod you've got house one. We'll use their Pump if we can, in case we need to get away, we're still at the lift as far as anyone knows.' He paused, I don't know if it was for dramatic effect or he was weighing up the possibility of Control wondering what was taking us so long; then he continued, 'Now, remember to be aware of other crews working, as far as we know all the attics are linked. And Toby, look after Noddy!'

I thought, *who's going to look after me, not bloody Rodney?* I couldn't remember going into a fire with Rod, the drivers normally got stuck at the machine, operating the pump. I knew it shouldn't matter but I didn't feel as close to him as I did the rest of the guys. It was more the little things that I picked up on, like he always seemed to leave a room just as I got there and when I spoke directly to him, he answered me in one-word sentences. I'd asked Granny what he thought, if anyone would have noticed it would be him. He just said it's probably nothing to do with any of us on the station. I didn't really know what Granny meant and now I just accept that Rodney is a little bit grumpy. Anyway, we were about to become closer, there's nothing like fighting a fire together to test a relationship.

I assumed I had all the information I needed: loft, house two, Rodney. It didn't start well, I grabbed the Large Applicator, our *go to* branch for cars and attics. It's long so you can poke it places that are difficult to reach.

'You can leave that behind,' said Rodney, 'you don't know where anyone else will be.' He was right of course; I had been too lost in my vague thoughts and this roof void wasn't empty. We could hardly thrust its Rose Nozzle into the loft without checking first, it can turn hot fire products into masses of superheated steam. There was only one way we would be of any use in this job and that would be climbing right into the loft. 'Get a branch and a ceiling hook.'

'What about hose?' I asked, accepting his lead. He raised his voice again so we could all hear.

'Take all our 45s, we'll use their 70s.' That made sense as well, they would have already used all their lighter, smaller, 45mm hose. He'd morphed from our flower power driver to the respected senior hand and team leader. We also needed pieces of the short extension for access. 'And don't forget the dividing breaching so we can split one hose line.' Rod was thinking on his feet, it made me appreciate why senior hands should have respect.

'How are we going to carry this lot,' I said, 'we'll have to make two trips.' It wasn't that far but now we were here we were keen to get to work.

'Use the ladder as a stretcher,' said Noddy.

'Aww, I'm going back to school,' I laughed, 'you got anything to add Toby?'

'You could put your set on Tom, if you fancy it, that is.' I made an inane grasp at my shoulders as if to grab the set that I now realised wasn't there.

'I'm going to shut up now,' I said. I'm sure I heard Rodney mumble *that I'll be a change*, but I was diving back in the machine to slip on my B.A. set.

We laid out as much hose as we could before charging it with water. This was easier than dragging full, heavy hose into the houses. There was no trouble getting into the terrace, it had been well visited by the local kids who'd left the front door open. An old pram stood limp and lonely in the tatty front yard; it gave the place a bit of personality, not much but enough to make it seem abandoned rather than derelict.

There was a lot of running backwards and forwards before we could actually start-up and get to work; my last trip was to BA entry control. Fortunately, the council had only boarded up the ground floor which gave us a bit of light at the top of the stairs. Rod was surprisingly fit for his age, which I had as a sedate fifty, I was much more used to hearing him bitch about having more *time-in* than us *Bucks* than actually seeing him out of the driver's seat. We finally started our sets up just before entering the loft, a while after handing in our tallies.

Any discrepancy would be in our favour, but we never considered that we would get in a position to need the extra time. I was momentarily distracted noticing how Rod's facial hair actually missed the facemask seal; I wondered if he had a stencil in his shaving kit. You can get a seal over a beard, not that I've ever tried, but it's not guaranteed, especially when your air supply is low.

I opened the loft hatch again and clouds of sooty dust rolled down our ladder. I'd already opened it once but Rodney made me close it until we were ready. Rod led from the front, holding the top of the ladder while I followed him up into darkness; I couldn't see a thing. A thick obscurity fell across my mask, a transition to immediate blindness, my sight was sucked away. I was exhausted already from setting up our gear and we now started the task of lifting fully charged hose into the pitch night of the communal loft.

A task only achieved by putting the long pole of the ceiling hook down and afterwards desperately trying find it again; on more than one occasion I thought it was lost. It was difficult to move around, there were only a few floorboards and balancing on the joists was like walking on a tightrope. I held onto Rod as he followed the sloping line of the roof, I certainly couldn't see him, we bounced off of old bits of furniture and junk. The murkiness had a despairing effect and seemed thicker than ever. I was breaking tiles with the hook as much as I could in an attempt to clear some of the smoke; it wasn't working.

Only tiny points of light pin pricked the roof and made no difference to our vision. Rodney made some huffing noises, but this was no time for training, although I could have done with some. We were trying to make our way towards house three and the seat of fire.

Moving around blindly you tend to build up a mental awareness of your environment, not really a picture, more of an outline drawing. It's distances that I always struggle with, I find it hard to judge how far across a room we have come. The hose became our lifeline, an umbilical cord between firefighters who are desperate not to be separated.

We made sluggish progress, fighting the hose's insistence on wanting to return to the floor below no matter how big a bight we pulled up. It wasn't until I'd returned to the hatch a few times that it finally gave up its struggle and decided it would stay. I still had to keep going back to haul more of it through the hatch, we could have done with someone feeding it up from below. I thought *at least I know the way out*, but in reality, if I'd have lost the hose, I'd have been lost myself.

The loft hatch was located somewhere in the middle of the attic and could easily be missed. Light from the broken tiles was disorienting as well as feint, especially with the unregimented clutter strewn all over the place; of course, there was always Rodney to help! '…hos…Tm…ook,' I could only guess what Rodney was saying as I crawled back towards him, dragging as much hose as possible. Then he was beside me and together we hoisted a large bight, probably all we had.

'Ta Rod,' I rasped, as I stumbled on some broken floorboards, we both fell back, 'Mind we don't break anything, it's probably all treasure.' Odd bits of flooring were making themselves known through different parts of my fire gear but my sarcasm got a strange response.

'Fuck! Fuck! Fuck!' Rodney was coming through loud and clear now. Our heads laying side by side like some star struck lovers staring into the inky sky.

'What?' I must have sounded impatient.

'My fucking foot!' if there was ever a time to turn on the lights, to take the blindfolds off, it was now. I even rubbed my facemask, as if I was cleaning my eyes. I ran my hands down Rods tunic, feeling buttons and BA straps, down the wrinkled plastic leggings to his boots. His right foot was trapped. Wedged between the ceiling below and a few boards. I shuffled around and his foot came free, free from my weight on a loose board.

'Got it,' I said. I didn't mean it to come out as a lie but Rodney wasn't aware of the whole manoeuvre; we were still working in the dark. I promised myself I'd tell him when the job was over. He got up and I could hear stomping, I guessed his ankle had survived.

Eventually we found a party wall with a window like opening, glowing fierce orange. I was sure the property had been stretched while we were inside, it seemed like we had travelled miles. The window was actually a small doorway but the lower half had been blocked by more old furniture. The fire was on the other side and we could hear another crew working, attacking the blaze.

'Let's leave them to it and ventilate,' said Rodney. The flames hadn't spread to our house, just all the filthy hot gasses. Rod grabbed the ceiling hook and took over breaking holes in the roof, he made it look easy; I could hear the tiles smashing on the ground outside.

I was still finding it hard to see my air gauge as we were covered with a layer of soot, so thick it had left a coating on everything. I wiped my mask and discovered visibility, the loft was clearer than I thought. I was in an attic much smaller than I'd imagined; much smaller. My earlier mental image had been way off scale. The hatch to the party wall was now only a few paces but I could see where Rod and I had shared a few horizontal moments. Fortunately, the evidence of false entrapment was lost among the more prominent struggle left by our tunics.

We even found Toby and Nod who had come right through the door in the other party wall. We came out of those houses, filthy and knackered. We were black with soot, ash smeared and totally shagged. We gathered up our stained equipment and returned to our machine.

'Cheers Rod, that was a tough one,' I said.

'Yeah, thanks Tom,' he said. I must have looked shocked. 'You okay Tom?' he added.

'Err, yeah fine.' I wondered if we'd gone through some weird space portal and I'd come out with a different hippy. I didn't say another word, nor did Rodney. We never overdo thanks, we expect help, the odd pull or push, it's like helping ourselves. There is no room for the maverick, we rely on each other too much. I decided it wouldn't hurt if maybe Rod didn't know it was me on his foot, I might even get a bigger portion of rice on nights.

The attics in each house were connected through the party walls by doors. This had been the reason why the fire had spread; most of the doors were missing. They never should have been there in the first place, perhaps that's why the terrace was vacant.

We helped them make up their hose and returned to our Station. 'Are we still on the lift job Guv?' I asked.

'Yes, get one set done quickly, you take that Tom. Toby, take my set. Then we can go back on the run.'

'Right Guv,' Toby said. After a big job like that we normally took a few minutes off the run to service our B.A. sets and get cleaned up ourselves. Not today though, we'd only been to a person stuck in lift. We were manky, the lower floors of the houses obviously weren't that clear of smoke and we had been working hard before we even started up. It was hard to clean the BA sets without re-contaminating them, smut was dribbling from our noses and out of our sweaty skin. We showered one by one to reduce the risk of a slow turn out if we got a shout, or at least to make sure there was only one naked firefighter on the back of the machine. We were lucky, all was quiet. I knew I was going to need a complete change of rags, even my under-crackers were smoke stained.

We had the statutory couple of pints before cycling home, it had been that sort of day, but then they all were really.

'What about the beer kitty?' Granny said, getting straight down to the most important business, our weekend away.

'I hope those floaties weren't spoiling you today, Gran, while we've been smoke eating and everything,' said Toby. Gran ignored him, when the fireboat needed a spare bod, he liked to volunteer.

'What do you mean Gran,' I asked, 'do you want another pint?' He often finished before the rest of us but his glass was still full. Our proposed excursion had been the subject of discussion all day but this was a new angle.

'No, a weekend beer kitty, might as well start saving now.'

'We do football cards at my club,' said Noddy, 'you know, guess the team and win the prize; the rest goes to the club.'

'Can you get some Nod?' I'd been trying to co-ordinate the nod of his head as he took a mouthful of beer for ages, but without success. I would have to get Toby on board, we must be able to get him to dribble at least.

He moved his pint away from another mouthful, as he nodded and said, 'Yep, next week probably.'

'What about a raffle? We could get some prizes donated,' if anyone could do this Frankie could.

'What are you going to tell them it's for Frankie?' Nod asked.

'Well, the Red Watch Welfare of course.'

'We could all donate a prize,' said Toby.

'As long as it's not a pair of your old socks,' I said.

'Naw, but I've got some new ones,' he downed his pint, 'See ya tomorrow.' That was the cue and we were soon all on our way.

The evening was balmy and I was in no rush to get home. I always find my pushbike to be the fastest form of transport in town. I get exhilarated as I push those pedals and etch a few more global miles. Sitting on a locker somewhere in the station one tour, Toby and I had worked out that we would be halfway to New Zealand if we had just kept going when we left work; I reckon I would need a new bike for the way home. Some of the other guys used to cycle now and again but we were the stalwarts, all through the year, even Christmas day, we were on our bicycles.

London traffic really is the pits but I often sped past all the jams. I've also found quite a lot of short cuts over the years. They actually make the journey longer but I love nipping through parks and alleyways, just me, the bike and some *Prog Rock* over the Walkman. I always leave really early for work, I hate rushing around and prefer to arrive refreshed and ready for anything. I'd sneak out with the dawn, the first one hundred yards was a minor slope so I'd just kick once and then glide to freedom. It is a great unwind after work as well, although if we stay too long in the pub it has to include a few piss stops, which is easier in the park than Peckham High Street. There's always someone who'll complain if you have a leak in the bus lane.

My wife was always late home so I was surprised to see her car parked outside. I dumped my bike in our side alley and quickly went through the front door.

'Hi ya,' I shouted, 'just having a leak.' I ran upstairs, breaking my neck for the loo. I had an uneasy feeling of guilt which I thought was because I was disappointed that she was home early. There was a lovely smell of food, I started thinking that I'd forgotten something. I wondered what we had arranged, it would be so unusual that I'm sure I would have remembered. The front door slammed, I thought *I can't have closed it properly*. That was the first real clue that I managed to miss.

Downstairs the table was set for two and my wife was looking very slinky, especially compared to my sweaty cycle kit. I started to apologise for being late and that's when I really noticed the table. It was set for two but they had started without me. There were two half-eaten plates of something that definitely wasn't Mince A or B. I never said a word, my wife was saying plenty but it didn't sound like apologies, more like *you're meant to be on nights*. I could see her mouth moving but I was no longer paying any real attention to what she was saying. I think she was telling me off because she had got my shifts wrong. Strangely all I could think was, *it wasn't even vegetarian*. I just turned and left. That was the last time I set foot in that house.

I got back on my bike and went to see Toby. I thought *I wonder if he fancies another beer;* I was feeling quite euphoric.

8

April 1984
Canisters

There were occasions when we actually got around to drills at Lambeth. Drills were the Guvnors affectionate term for basic training: pitching ladders, getting hoses working, etc.

He would threaten us by shouting something like, 'Right you lot, Boots and Leggings, in the yard, now!', and we would all groan. This is one of those strange fire service terms which actually meant, 'Gentlemen, if you wouldn't mind, could you please assemble in the drill yard, dressed in your firegear and at your earliest convenience.' We had to groan, it was expected; we had to pretend that the Guvnor was being really cruel, it gave him more of a sense of purpose. He was a pretty good Guvnor, he had those expected qualities; firm, fair and friendly, not many Guvs could achieve that. He avoided socialising with us though, I think he liked to maintain a little bit of aloofness. He was confident, especially on the fire ground and that's where it really counts in the end.

In reality we couldn't wait to get out to the drill yard, it was a chance to play with our favourite toys. Although I should clarify this, I think some of the senior hands were really groaning. Toby and I had four and three years' service respectively, little enough to still be keen and long enough to think we knew it all. We are also the youngest on the watch, in our mid-twenties. I had recently moved into Toby's back room after a couple of nights on his sofa. It had been a storeroom until I turned up; it still was. We just piled the boxes a little higher and wedged both bikes between them, balanced on their back wheels. I spent my nights on a put-you-up bed expecting to wake up wearing pedals and cardboard boxes.

The Guvnor had a routine, firstly he would ask for a simple ladder pitch, normally to the third floor of the tower and just for good measure, take a hose up there and squirt some water. He would then introduce different levels of complication, depending on his creative mood. Today didn't seem any different; well not yet.

We were parked in the yard in our normal position for drills. The back of the machine pointing towards the tower and the front towards the appliance room and the front doors, just in case we got a shout. That was still our quickest route out, everything was designed around a possible shout. Midweek it was virtually impossible to drill due to all the Staff Cars using the yard as a carpark. Today was a Saturday and the Guv had been doing a bit of forward planning.

The Guvnor said, 'The appliance has just pulled up at a building fire, the tower is the building, deal with it as you find it. Carry on.' I thought *he's lost it today.* The sun was streaming into the yard, even though it was still only spring, we considered it a heat wave. I wasn't really in the mood and I wasn't really listening. The Guv was mixing it up a bit today, he liked to add a bit of variety. I just wish he'd give us a warning when he was feeling inventive; we didn't adapt well to change. We'd pitched the ladder up against the tower so many times we could do it in our sleep.

'Stand-by to slip,' I shouted, someone had to give the order. Everyone followed my lead and slipped the huge, wheeled escape ladder off of the machine. We dutifully went through the normal procedure and pitched it to the third floor, as we always do. The great red cartwheels spun around in our hands as soon as they hit the yard floor. I also hit the floor at about the same time, at the end of my controlled leap for the trunnion bar; I am too short to reach this without a jump. The escape ladder crashed elegantly around and into the tower, it was already being wound aloft as we stopped its horizontal journey. The Guv had the courtesy to wait until we were finished.

'Knock-off and make-up,' he shouted. 'Who asked you to pitch the ladder?' he demanded once we had put it away.

'The third floor's always alight Guv,' I said, my cheek as normal, running ahead of my brain. *He ignored me,* I thought.

'Start again, this time investigate properly. Nod you're in charge. Get to work.' I had no idea what was going on but it definitely didn't involve the Escape Ladder.

We looked at each other, looked at the Guvnor, who was just about to speak when Noddy said, 'Right, let's go and have a gander.' We moved in a huddle, following Nod right into the base of the tower via the side door. There was a group feeling of malaise brought about by the unusual April sunshine and the angry disappointment on our Guvnor's face. I had to take some responsibility, everyone remembered who had given the order to pitch the ladder.

'Hey guys, I'm sorry I was on automatic. You didn't have to follow,' I said.

'No worries Tom, but we could hardly start arguing about it, could we?' Granny was giving a reasonable interpretation, as usual.

Then we saw it, a twenty-five-litre plastic foam canister with PROPANE written on the side in black marker pen.

'Oh! It's a cylinder drill,' whispered Rodney, 'that's meant to be a propane cylinder involved in a fire.'

'So what, we don't do anything just get it wet, and run away?' I said. Cylinders and fires don't mix, they tend to behave like bombs, and at quite low temperatures.

'Yeah, maybe the Guv didn't want us running around, pitching ladders and stuff in this hot weather,' Rodney joined in with the gripe and he hadn't even been part of the ladder crew.

'Get a hose-reel off and lash it in place, spraying the foam canist—I mean cylinder.' Nod had gone into officer mode, but at least the Guvnor looked pleased. Nod ran over to the boss, came to attention, and started telling him in a raised voice, what he could already see. I wondered *is he taking the piss or is this some sort of promotion stuff*. Nod was still the Junior Buck but he was going places.

'Okay,' barked the Guvnor, 'the cylinder is now cool to the touch. Carry on.'

Noddy turned and shouted to no one in particular, 'Build a dam.' He didn't seem bothered by throwing orders around but we were only playing. We normally do cylinder drills in the summer months, a pool of water is just too inviting to resist when the sun is beating down. However, this early in the year I made a mental note not to get too close to the dam. It didn't take long to sling a salvage sheet into the triangle made by breaking up a triple extension ladder and then fill her with water. I'd woken up a bit now and was thinking, *it's not just the cylinder that's going to end up in that dam.*

I said aside to Toby, 'Shall we get Nod?' he just grinned. I also said to Gran, 'We are going to get Toby.' I then stood well back from the edge of the dam. As they started to wrestle, I joined in, it should have been an easy push by then. I probably should have realised that they were acting but I was too pleased with how clever I thought I had been.

'Now,' shouted the Guvnor. Suddenly I was very damp, oozing betrayal and looking up at the sky. The Guv's smirking head came into focus, 'Wring yourself out on the third Tomato, it must be warm up there, it's always alight.' The rest of the drill session became a wetter affair with many stray branches providing a cooling respite, but everyone else avoided the dam.

After drills I went straight to my locker to change into dry clothes, this turned out to be a grave error. I was wondering what all the noise was about, all the warning signs were there, I just hadn't processed them. I got far enough into the Mess to nearly have my legs taken away by Frankie, slithering out of the same door. He was being pursued by about half a gallon of flying water; I managed to protect him from most of it. My second set of clothes were now also soaked; I didn't have another clean change. I squelched my way into the mess to grab my own water-carrying weapon, there were few left, certainly all the best ones were gone. I couldn't find anything with that required mix of lightness for moving around and ample capacity to ensure a worthy hit. And then I saw just the thing, written all over it was, *I'll be perfect.*

We spent the best part of the next hour sneaking around the station with pots and pans full of water until everyone and everywhere was drenched. Well nearly everyone, we never bucketed the Guv and a couple of the older floaties just didn't play. I wondered what age it was that you lost your need for fun.

There comes a point where we somehow agree a truce and we spend another hour mopping up the old wooden floors. That time was getting close; it should have come sooner.

I quelled my schoolboy excitement, hiding behind the locker room door with my new sleek weapon, a ceramic jug. I don't know why I hadn't thought of it before, it was easy to carry and easy to conceal, a stealth launcher extraordinaire. If I hadn't had been so wet, I'm sure I'd have been sweating. The anticipation was too much, I was sure my heart and my breath could be heard; I tried to stop both. Toby crept noisily along the main corridor, he was rubbish at keeping quiet and the old floorboards weren't helping. He was right in the open, a prime target, I needed just a few more steps. He stopped for a moment, I was sure I'd been rumbled, then the creaking recommenced. I thought *I'd better go for it.* I'd convinced myself that he would turn around at any minute and retrace his steps; I wanted this to be an ambush not a chase. With an excited yell I swung my jug blindly around the corner, hoping for a direct hit; I got one. The sound was more shattering than dousing, more smash than splash.

'Ow, fuck,' gasped Toby, rather non-dramatically, considering. I looked down at my jug, it wasn't there, just the handle in my clenched fist; it had fired its last shot. Nervously, I peeped around the corner. Toby was holding his head, blood running through his fingers and dripping onto a pile of broken crockery, my former pitcher.

'Shit, sorry, shit, oh fuck,' I was whimpering more than him and thinking how good he'd been to me. This was no way to treat my new landlord, it could turn out to be a more temporary arrangement than I'd first imagined.

'No worries, Tom, it's not that bad, I caught the rebound off the wall.' I was hoping the water had mixed with the blood and it really wasn't *that bad*, it looked pretty serious.

I don't know what they said to him at A&E; we got a shout as we dropped him off.

'Bravo, two, two, one, PRIORITY, over.'

He looked up at me sadly as we sped off to a fire on Peckham's ground. Control had given us the address first so we could be on our way, this meant that the Guv had to take the rest of the details as Frankie performed his usual dance through the traffic. In the back we took our time rigging and then sat back to enjoy the nice long ride.

We pulled up to a three storey, mid-terrace home that had black smoke pouring out and fire-fighters pouring in. It looked Victorian, there were a few steps up to the entrance which hid an additional lower level.

'Wait there,' said the Guv, as he disappeared to find their boss.

'Can't we just get on with it?' Nod said.

'He's gone to find out where we're wanted,' said Gran, 'he prefers us to still be here when he gets back.' We didn't have to wait long.

'They're still searching up top, he wants us to tackle the fire which he thinks is in the basement.' *He* was obviously Peckham's Guvnor, the officer in charge of this little conflagration, and *us* meant me and Noddy.

'Do we know what's down there Guv?' I asked.

'No idea Tom, so be careful. There's a basement window but we don't want to break it in case it feeds the fire, there are lots of crews searching the upper floors.' There was a chance that the fire wasn't getting enough oxygen and breaking that window might cause a backdraft. An explosion. It could rip right through the house. It had to be tackled from the inside while there was a possibility of anyone still being at home, including the fire crews.

'Come on Nod, it won't put itself out,' I said. I wasn't sure if he understood the full gravity of what we had been asked to do, but I figured the quicker we got in the better. When they get going, fires are prone to keep doubling in size and they don't hang around for slow firefighters.

The entrance hallway was once, not so very long ago, well decorated in an old-fashioned type of style. It now wore an ashen fug, with hose disappearing straight through to some unknown destination towards the back. Even now I could see the smear of sweaty firefighters' handprints on the staircase and glass from a broken picture on the floor. The smoke seemed to be coming from behind these stairs, that was our target, the dungeon entrance.

The hose already laid in the hallway made movement difficult as we attempted to drag our own line through the dim, gloomy corridor. This task became just too much; our charged hose and Nod parted company and he crashed to the floor. He was fine but I was finding it so hard to stop grinning that my facemask seal kept letting by, wasting my precious air. I dusted him down, we had a quick air check and together pulled the hose into a large bight at the top of the stairs. Nod was moaning about his ankle but not enough to call off our attack.

A swarthy darkness surged from the crypt, increasingly black and filling the hallway. The door was already open, allowing plenty of air for the fire, there was no pulsing breath, no throbbing quest for oxygen, just plenty of smoke. *No chance of a backdraft* I told myself, not that I'd ever experienced one; I was working on theory. I was also finding it hard to contain a growing dread, a sudden jitteriness was reminding me of a claustrophobia I thought I'd long since extinguished; I hoped Nod wouldn't notice.

I figured one of the other crews must have opened the door and then been redirected to search upstairs, it would have been nice to know what the conditions were like then. It would have been nice to know what the conditions were like now! You can over-think these things, it was time to just get on and go and fight the fire.

This was our portal, our artery into the intimidating abyss. I sat at this pinnacle and took an audible gasp of air, stamped in front of me and I was off, my descent committed. I squeezed myself against the wall, wishing for its protection, but at a jaunty angle forced by the bottom of my Breathing Apparatus which had scant regard for the stair strength. I had no idea what we might find, Noddy was crouched, waiting to sit behind me and help feed down the hose.

We bumped down a few steps at a time. I could only see pitch, but I stared hopingly into the depths, seeking a change, a clue. There were none. Sounds of the other firefighters started to fade, replaced by the rhythm of my exhalation valve and Noddy's own uncoordinated scuffling, comfortingly following and providing my back-up. Whilst going down I waved the back of my hand blindly into the void, hoping to find anything before it found me. It was warming up, I could feel a tingling sensation on my exposed wrists and ears, there was no doubt we were entering the fire zone.

My insides were turning into a hot soup. Slowly submerging into the baking cavern, I wondered what sort of hellish creature might have burrowed into this shrouded inferno. It certainly wouldn't expect a visit from the likes of us, arriving unnaturally through its stifling mantle, waving our clumsy, yellow legs to herald our arrival.

Out of nowhere, as if to waken my musing, I was hit by an immense, searing heat. The previous tingling turned to pain as my plastic over-trousers started to melt into me and the staircase. My whole body was enveloped by a sudden invisible oven, I couldn't remember ever having been so hot. I thought I was about to spontaneously combust. I tried to tell Nod to get low, this was a reflex action as it didn't mean much on the incline that I was fusing into, even if Nod could have seen me. I was hit by two instincts at once, get out or hit the deck; unfortunately, they were two different directions. A quick grope behind found Nod's boot bearing my way.

It was a snap decision of self-preservation; the quickest way out of the furnace was down. Up would have meant clambering right over Nod, that would have been a problem, it wasn't politeness but the realisation that we would have ended up wrestling in the cauldron. Any stair safety procedure evaporated, it was that or me. I plunged to the ground, only fractions of a second before Nod. I'm not sure if I consciously pulled the hose with me or it had just come along for the ride, but it was there. Thank fuck.

It was cooler at the foot of the stair, my reflexes had opted to get out of the impossible scorching layer the fastest possible way. My subconscious hadn't bothered to remember that low was also a cellar with no other way out as far as we knew. I was wishing for another dump in the improvised dam we had built earlier and half expecting to be running back up and out to the cool, safe Saturday afternoon. However, the thought of going through the stifling layer again destroyed all traces of eagerness for such a proposal. I was sure my hands were burnt from my excursion through the blistering forge.

I held my hands up to my face but there was nothing there, it was like they had been removed even though I could still feel them, I expected them to be glowing. My torch wasn't powerful enough to penetrate the enveloping darkness but comforting enough to confirm this wasn't the bottom of a suburban chasm.

We were entwined at the foot of the stair, trapped by an impenetrable burning exclusion, inches above our heads. I put my arm out and fumbled Nod until we were embracing like alien lovers, masked and simmering. I'm sure he said, 'What the fuck!' I said it as well, again.

'You okay?' I asked.

'Yep, you?'

'Yep.' These peculiar husky sounds were all we had to help achieve an element of unwarranted calm. Our torches probed, unseeing into the vault and came to rest on our air gauges; I had to press mine against my mask. I felt my legs and then head, not for injury but just to be sure I still had them. There was no way to tell the size of this room, just a memory of the upstairs, we could have been sitting in the corner of the whole street, there was no echo, just hell. Our world had shrunk to a couple of feet around the bottom step. I kicked about and found nothing.

'What now?' Noddy said.

I mumbled into the darkness, to where I thought his ear should be, 'Well we are down here, the fire is obviously down here, we better get on with it.'

Nod nodded, I was that close I could feel his head moving. I thought *we had better get on with it fast*. We had plunged into the heart of a demon, and his passion was growing. As we crept away from the stair we encountered junk, bags, furniture, boxes, fuel for the beast. There was some shelter behind a stack of something, I added a bit of spray to the jet, just to protect ourselves, and gave the darkness a drink, a bloody good drink. We were lucky the fire was there somewhere and we found it, I gave it another drink. There was a crack of light from what must have been the far wall, we may have broken the window with the jet.

Conditions improved, slightly, I felt like I had stopped cooking. I sprayed the jet around again and again, so much that I was in danger of filling up this abyss.

I looked at Nod and decided we'd had enough. I pointed to the stair and he didn't argue. We left the hose where it was and crawled back up. The roasting crust had now vanished but everything was still blistering to the touch. I wondered if that might just have been my tender hands.

We sat on the pavement outside, away from the action. 'What was that then Tom?' Nod asked.

'Not sure Nod, I think we fell through a hot ceiling layer, it was probably thinking of flashing over.' We should really have gone up rather than down, but that's easy to say in retrospect, I didn't think we had much of a choice at the time, the heat took over, and of course there was a fire to put out. Flashover can start at a temperature of about 600°C, I was starting to feel like I was back in the fire.

'Shit Tom that sounds dodgy.'

'Yeah, it was, good job you was with someone who knew what they were doing!' Nod looked perplexed. He was steaming, we both were, I could feel pools of sweat soaking the calves inside of my boots but I was too weak to take them off. The adrenaline that had kept us alive was giving way to an overheated, brain led, exhaustion. My limbs had taken on a heavy slump as we waited for the fatigue to piss-off. Nod recovered faster than me.

'That was so scary, I felt like it was happening to someone else Tom, it was just too unreal.'

'It was definitely you Nod.'

'Didn't it frighten you?'

'Did I look scared to you?' Actually, I was close to shitting myself but there was no point losing a rare bit of kudos.

'Well, I couldn't see you, could I?'

'That's why fires are dark Nod, so we can all look big and brave. Come on, you never know what you're going to find, let's get rid of these sets and go and have a look downstairs.'

That was about as close as we ever got to confessing fear. Most of all we didn't want to admit it to ourselves, it might stop us doing it again. We seldom get time to do more than react to a situation, any thoughts are focused on putting out the fire, remembering the way out, and, of course, looking after your buddy. Even that isn't altruistic; they are there for you as well as you for them. Far from being scared of fire, we lap it up. The chance to get to work is exhilarating. We have a different view to the public, for us fire is a desire, exciting and adrenaline inducing. Having no fear is not a sign of bravery. How can it be brave, doing what you love? We can't let it become scary, it would spoil the fun. *Today was different.*

'You ever been in a backdraft Tom?'

'Naw, they're as rare as chicken shit. Fires flash all the time but conditions have to be just right for a backdraft.'

'Tom?'

'Go on Nod, what's the matter?'

'Chicken shit's not rare.'

'Well, it is in Lambeth Nod, and it's normally behind closed doors.'

Downstairs was a mess, if it ever had any order, it had now been replaced; it looked like it someone had set light to a Jumble Sale. The front window was completely broken and was the only source of light. There was a back room which housed even more junk but this was all untouched by the fire, protected by a closed door we hadn't found. It was now propped open. We hadn't bothered to search on our first visit but another crew had been looking round. The back room opened out onto a small courtyard.

'We got a cylinder here Tom,' Noddy shouted.

'Keep it down Nod,' I replied, as if whispering would make it safer. Noddy had been rooting around in the debris.

'Shouldn't we do cylinder procedure Tom?'

'Yes, of course, I didn't mean keep it secret. Put your hand on it Nod, it must be cold, there's been no fire in here.'

'Yep, cold.'

'Looks like the only one, can you see any others?' Noddy looked around but it was alone. 'It looks like a foam canister to me Nod, what do yer reckon?'

'I reckon you're right.' It was a propane cylinder. 'Not another dam Tommy,' Nod was grinning.

'No, but let's put it in that garden just to be on the safe side.' I had come out in a cold sweat. 'Good job it wasn't in that first room!' Nod's smile vanished.

Toby was already home when we got back to the station. Five stitches, and the rest of the tour off but he was more upset at having missed the job. He did have some consolation, a nurse's phone number, I hoped she didn't have red hair.

9

Late April 1984
The Dance

The White Watch seem pretty excited. 'You're lively this morning,' I said to the few jostling around the locker room, 'you must have had a quite night?'

'No Tommy, the usual, but it's tonight we're going to be extra busy,' replied Patty.

I sat down on a spare footlocker, intrigued, 'Go on then, spill the beans.' I was still in my cycle gear but the shower could wait a few more minutes.

'Well, that would be telling, wouldn't it,' Patty was talking for them all. I just waited, it was obvious it wasn't really a secret. 'We had a visit from three of St Thomas's finest and they are just gagging for us to go to their party tonight. Ain't that true boys.' There were some murmurs of agreement and I'm sure H was about to clarify when Patty butted in again, 'They were devastated when they found out we was working, but I told them not to worry, we would be there.'

'Yeah, anything for a Nurse,' H finally got a word in.

'And what are you going to do about that little matter of being on duty?' I said sarcastically.

Rodney joined us. 'Just listen to yourselves, will you be sharing out your sweets with them?' I exchanged a glance with Patty that was mutual confusion as to where the sweets had come from.

'We all know you're past it Rodders, guess you'll be at home with your funny fags?' bellowed H.

'I probably will, Joss Sticks and me pipe too.' This was sharp for Rodney, and as if he had exhausted his repartee, he left.

'So what are you planning Pat?' I said.

'Wait and see,' they all replied. Well this was the White Watch, anything could happen. I got in early once, only to come face to face with a fine young lady taking advantage of our showering facilities. I don't know who was more surprised?

'We'll see you there then,' I left and went to investigate the showers, this morning there was no female company, sadly.

I bumped into Bones in the corridor, 'Morning Bonesy, how's it hanging?' He hadn't been to the Mess this morning for a cuppa.

'I'm good Tom thanks, you okay? Is Nod around he's out to Brixton for the watch?'

'He's still in the Mess, shall I go and tell him?'

'Please Tom, and tell the rest of the troops, Boots and Leggings in the yard.' It looked like the Guvnor had some training planed. It wasn't going to happen. As I started to walk away Bones had something more to say, 'You okay with your wife stuff?'

It was a funny way of putting it, but all the guys had checked up on me in their own way. The Guvnor even asked if I wanted some time off, he knew though, that I'd rather be with my brothers. I was relieved about the whole issue, the way you are when something's bothering you but you didn't realise. Whoever he was, eating a meal at my table, he had done me a favour. That didn't stop all the aggravation of dividing up our meagre assets and working out the divorce. My soon to be ex-wife was keen to get everything settled, a suspicious man might have thought she'd been planning it for some time.

'Yeah, should have happened ages ago. I've known for a long time but just let things carry on, you know.' I got the feeling he wanted to talk more but we were due on the drill ground; then the bells dropped.

Distant bell, click, LOUD BELLS, lights come on.

Toby had the sledgehammer over his shoulder, it was our opening gambit for a person locked out. The Lambeth community had worked out that we were good at opening doors, especially when they had forgotten their key. We had become their personal doormen.

'What's that for mate?' The punter was glaring at Tobe's shoulder.

'You're locked out, aren't you?' said Toby.

'Yes, but...'

'This is our universal key,' Toby continued. The punter was now showing definite signs of uncertainty and confusion.

'We need proof of occupation and a signature,' said the Guv, he hated these calls as much as we did.

'You know who I am, you've been here before,' he said. He was getting a bit shirty and had just admitted to serial, expected conciergeing.

'Not us, it must have been someone else,' I said.

'I ain't signing nufin.'

'Then we can't let you in,' said the Guvnor, he was getting impatient. I thought *that's handy we're going home.*

'Alright gis it,' he scribbled something, it could have been Micky Mouse. The Guvnor looked at it with contempt.

'Just proof you live here now,' said the Guvnor. Toby was getting itchy, I mentioned that he should put the sledgehammer down. We were about to try slipping the lock but the Guvnor held us back and looked disdainfully at the prospective occupier.

'Just open the fucking door, I pay your fucking wages,' he said, unfortunately for him.

That was it, the last words had hardly been drunkenly spat out, when our Guv turned his back and spoke to us, 'Mount up guys, we're on our way.' He never said another word, nor did the punter.

As we pulled into the yard the Guv told Frankie to park up and for us to stay rigged. We were going straight into drills.

'Stand-by to slip,' he shouted and we dutifully threw the Escape up the tower.

Distant bell, click, LOUD BELLS, lights come on.

We had the ladder pitched and hose out when the bells dropped, this wasn't unusual but it was always inconvenient. We returned the ladder to the appliance, along with most of the gear we couldn't do without and we were out of the doors with only a couple of minutes delay. The call was to a fire in a tower block, Prince Point, one of the tallest in our part of Lambeth. Unfortunately, this estate, like much of our ground, suffered from acute vandalism. The lifts were often out of order and the long staircases were darkened by broken lights. They both got used as urinals, a smell that was occasionally topped up with a bucket of bleach, a temporary but not successful solution.

Apart from making it unpleasant for the residents, this thoughtlessness often included the fire protection measures put in place for our use and their safety. We always found difficulties, today was no exception.

We were on our way, according to the tele-printer call slip, to a flat alight on the twenty-second floor. This was never going to be easy, fires that high up require amended tactics, amended even more with only one appliance. On the way Control informed us that they had had multiple calls to this address. It wasn't far from the station, the end of Black Prince Rd., but we were already rigged having been playing in the yard so I sat back and enjoyed the short ride.

'Can you see it Bones?' I asked, I was trying to look out of the front window but on the wrong side of the machine to get a good view. Frankie pulled into the estate and stopped.

'That's not the twenty-second,' said Bones. I could see it myself now.

'That's about the sixteenth,' I said, doing a quick count. Sometimes the transfer of information between caller, Control and ourselves is a bit of a guessing game, especially when Control have to deal with many different reports. Of course, as far as the public are concerned it's always our fault.

We were once called to a person shut in lift at Foggit House; none of us knew Foggit House. It certainly wasn't in my new flats book, I immediately thought what a waste of time that had been. However, even after a search of the estate we were still perplexed, so we asked Mobilising Control to re-contact the caller. He met us on the corner of Army House and took us to a lift, in Army House. He didn't speak much English but I had to ask why he called us to Foggit House. He said, 'No, no, this House, I foggit house, I no remember name of house, I tell lady on phone, foggit house.' He was polite enough not to blame us.

Today it seemed we had the right place but the wrong floor. Toby counted, 'That looks like the sixteenth to me, you're right Tom.' It didn't matter because at that moment we weren't going anywhere, a car was parked in our way.

Frankie sighed in frustration, 'It's no good guys, I can't get through, you're going to have to bump it.' We have a technique for this, we man handle the car with a combination of bumping up and down and pushing to one side when the weight is off. This is one of those jobs that definitely shouldn't be tried at home. It obviously has to happen fast but we also have to be sure not to take any of us out at the same time. We worked like a machine, five of us in unison, all watching and taking subtle clues in movement and looks from the other four.

Some grunts of commands from the Guv and a thumbs up from Frankie and off we went again. Not fast though, the parking was horrendous, and all the time we could see the smoke pumping out of the tower block, it looked like a huge chimney with a breach in the side. Eventually we got to the foot of the tower, well near enough, we still had to work around a couple of cars that had strayed from the roadway.

The Guvnor had already made it up, just by the sight of so much smoke pumping out of a flat so high up. This was now a four-pump fire, if the other appliances could get anywhere near. Toby and Bones were in BA, both grabbed a length of hose and went to call the firefighting lift, I grabbed the still wet branch, the BA board, sledgehammer and followed.

We have a special key that can summon the lift, bringing it straight to ground floor for our sole use and allowing fast access to remote floors.

It didn't work.

This fire-fighting lift was out of order, there was no sign but no lights either and no hint of movement. I could already feel the strain of the sixteen-floor climb ahead, although we were all hoping for either of the lifts to miraculously arrive. An exchange of glances confirmed a joint realisation; we couldn't wait forever. We were already late for our appointment with fire. I started to feel a terrible apprehension, we had already had too many delays and it was catching up with me. I looked at Bones and Toby, I think we were all suffering from this pause.

It was unusual for Bones to be with us but the TL was defective and we'd been told that there were no spares. Being our Leading Hand, he was in charge of our small troupe; we waited briefly, then Bones said, 'Let's do it.'

I thought he had all the makings of a great Guvnor; I snapped out of my despair and got ready for the climb. At that moment he had the same limited vocabulary as the Boss, he just needed to knock a few words off here and there. He was also the one most badly designed for a multi-floor climb.

We entered the bland concrete shaft that housed a stair running the entire height of the building. It was bland on purpose, there shouldn't be anything in here that could burn. This was the firefighting shaft, designed for our use with a two-hour protection from the flats. The sixteenth floor seemed an awful long way away. 'Come on boys,' Toby said, 'this is just like doing drills at Training School.'

'I don't know what School you went to but we never had a tower this big where I came from,' wheezed Bones.

'That's floor six, only ten to go,' I added, it didn't help. Toby thought things like this were training runs. When he wasn't keeping amazingly fit, he was the station Union Rep, that meant we were well informed about any March or Demonstration; they were always good for a beer or two.

Bones looked directly at Toby, 'There should be a Demo about the state of this building,' he said. No one, even Toby, seemed ready for a political discussion. While the others were counting the floors, I was counting the amount of stair doors broken or even completely missing. These buildings, supposedly the more modern on our ground were the most abused. It wasn't unusual for both the lifts to be out of order, confining many of the older residents to their flats, sometimes for days.

As we approached the not so shiny eighth floor, we heard screams, muffled but definitely shouting, 'Fire, fire. In here.' We looked at each other in disbelief.

Toby said, 'What the fuck?' We all knew we had much further to climb, or at least thought we knew. I started to doubt my first assessment of the fire floor from outside, *did I count sixteen?* If I could have poked my head out of the sealed window I would have, just to check.

We went to the flat where the panicked cries were coming from, knocked, and called out. A woman's voice hollered, 'Quick, help, fire, fire, I'm in here.' This verbal evidence overruled our hesitation and we asked her to open the door. 'It's locked,' she was sobbing. We told her to stand back and kicked down the door, another break-in courtesy of Toby & Bro. It didn't look on fire, there was no smoke.

'Where's the fire then love?' Bones asked.

'Somewhere, some flat somewhere' she cried, 'I don't know.'

'Is your flat on fire?' Bones asked a little sharply, wanting a straight answer.

'No, not me, somewhere, I don't know.' She didn't bloody know! We were flummoxed, and angry.

'Why was you locked in?' Toby asked just as brusquely.

'My husband locks the door when he goes out,' she was crying now.

'We've got to go on,' I pointed out.

'We've got to go love,' Bones said, he'd quickly calmed down, probably due to the tears. We all returned to the staircase. The discussion of why she had been locked in took up a few flights, but all it really amounted to was more vital lost minutes.

By the time we got to the sixteenth floor we were being hotly pursued by another crew. While we always appreciate the help, I couldn't stop thinking that the fire should have been extinguished by now. To top it all I'd connected to the Dry Rising Main and the pressure was crap, water seemed to only be thinking of forming a jet, this was going to be a difficult fire to put out.

'We're going to have to give it a go, you okay with that Tobe?' said Bones.

'We can't stand around here, moaning won't put it out,' he answered. They started up.

'See what you can get done about this water Tom, or we'll be out before we've even got in.' Bones put his arm around my shoulder and smiled, it sort of made me think I could achieve the impossible, but not for long. I'm sure it was on everyone's mind, but I was more worried about how long the little water we had, would last.

Clapham's crew reached the fire floor as Bones and Toby entered the flat. 'The mains is fucked,' they said.

'What do you mean?' I was worried now, the dry rising main was our only source of water. We could never haul up the hose, it wouldn't take its own weight at this height and it would take forever to lay hose up the staircase. I was wondering how many extinguishers we had, if you was lucky, you could knock out a room with one, but not a whole flat that had had time to cook. When my imagination got to a lift full of buckets, stacked on top of each other, I realised that I was losing it, and the lift was out of order anyway.

'Well, the drain valves gone at the base and some floors are leaking to fuck. The outlets are open but all the hand-wheels are missing, we couldn't close them.' They brought me back to the real world, this main had been wrecked good and proper.

'Look, take this,' I said. Fortunately, I could give them our own hand-wheel to go back and close the floor outlets. The on/off valves were controlled by a brass hand wheel secured by a thin leather strap. They were far too valuable and far too easy to be stolen, so we had stolen one of our own. Clapham were impressed at this little bit of ingenuity. The drain valve was another matter, hopefully Frankie would be able to pump more water in than must have been flooding out.

I could hear the sliding of my boys' boots disappearing into the flat, they weren't keeping quiet which was a comfort. I could also hear them talking to each other but it was too distant to understand. I took the brief time available to finish their time-out calculations and enter them on the BA board. They had thirty-five and forty minutes of air supply, although if they were taking a punishment at the fire face they would be out much sooner. Heat and hard work can do marvels to your air consumption rate. I could feel some improvement in the hose, it was getting heavier, I pushed some more through the door. I knew I wouldn't be alone for long, I could hear Clapham's crew getting closer but the smoke was getting thicker so I decided it was time to move down a floor to where the Bridge Head should have been in the first place. I met Clapham on the stairs and we all manoeuvred some more limp hose up to the fire floor; it was much better than it had been, it might even be enough to put out the fire.

'They should have found it by now,' I said. 'Are you going in?'

'Suppose we should,' they feigned disinterest. I took their tallies, added them to my board and off they went, up to the fire. The hose had stopped moving so I assumed they may have been tackling the blaze. Clapham's Sub Officer arrived to take charge of the Bridge Head. He wheezed, held on to the handrail and held out his hand in a stop sign. He wasn't a young man and the sixteen floors had taken it out of him. He unbuttoned the top of his tunic and took off his helmet, revealing a mass of soggy grey curls, I thought it could be Toby in twenty years' time.

When he eventually spoke, he panted, 'Bloody song and dance, this. What you got Tom?' I thought *no, Toby would never be out of breath.*

'Flat alight, next floor up, two crews of two inside, shit water,' I said. He called my Guv on his hand-held radio and relayed the information. His conversation with me was over.

The first stages of a job often look like chaos: hose is being thrown all over the place, firefighters are running to and fro trying to find a hydrant, the door is being battered to pieces and the Guvnor is looking everywhere and pointing a lot. This goes on until water meets fire, we might have been at that point but it had been an effort and too long getting there today.

I had some moments to reflect, we'd overcome a nightmare of problems and now I was just standing outside, lonely, and a floor below the action. Breathing Apparatus Control Officer may be the most important job on the fireground, but it's also the most frustrating. I moved back to the fire-floor, still waiting for the others to return, all the while keeping an eye on their estimated remaining air. After what seemed like days, the boys came back out, removing helmets and lifting facemasks. Their reddened faces framed by the mark of the pneumatic rubber seal. They looked dishevelled and exhausted.

'That was like pissing on it,' said Bones.

'You got it though?' asked the Sub O.

'Yeah, we stamped most of it out,' said Toby. Clapham's crew followed them out, I returned all their tallies, and they trotted off down the stairs to get rid of the sets. I entered the flat to have a look around and maybe squirt a bit more water about. It was empty except for the room that had been alight where there were scattered burnt remains. The Sub had already asked for more guys to finish off and clear up.

When I eventually got back to ground floor level the place was like a lake. The drain valve of the riser had been smashed and water was pouring all over the place. 'Could have done with that lot up there,' Bones said to Frankie, pointing at the water, it sounded a bit critical. We were all feeling it, the fire was out but we knew it wasn't our best day. That's where the tension came from, it might not have been our fault but we were all angry that we were prevented from doing our job well.

Frankie bit, 'Do it yourself next time, I've been running my fucking arse off down here.' It was unlike both of them, I guess all the problems had got to them and unknown to us, they both had a couple of their own to top it up. We would find out their secrets soon enough but for now there was an unusual tension. They glared at each other for a moment and then both burst into laughter, I'd fallen on my arse and was now soaked through.

'Look there's a tomato going for a swim,' Granny howled, he'd stayed downstairs to help Frankie and was now ensuring brotherly love returned, albeit at my expense. Everyone was pretty wet, there was so much water around, but I'd just managed to win first prize. I seemed to be doing well at full immersion lately and wondered if the drill would have involved another dam.

There weren't many days with so many problems; we get over one or two, nothing is ever textbook straight forward. It's the potential added risk that nags, I know in my heart that not many people survive a fire, and often premises are empty, especially in the middle of the day, but there is always the fear that we could have done better and didn't. We aren't the sort of people to dwell on *if only* scenarios, the job would be too hard if we did. Today I think we all felt a little frustrated. The flat was vacant though, so no one was hurt this time, just the decor. The Guvnor was often on the phone to the local council complaining about the sorry condition of these homes, but nothing ever changed. I had another thought of how bad it could have been and then remembered how wet I was. And Clapham's boys, well they only went and nicked our hand-wheel; you just can't trust anyone.

When we got back the Guvnor had given up on the idea of drills, which gave me time to do a little bit of investigating. It just so happened that we were planning a few beers after work, and of course we couldn't let the nurses down if it was their Easter Ball, it just wouldn't be gentlemanly. So, at great sacrifice to ourselves we decided we should include their party in our night's entertainment. We needed a bit more detail than we could trust the Whites to give us so I had a great excuse to give Red another call. She still wasn't home, but I was getting to know Vanessa pretty well, apparently, they were both on nights all week. I exaggerated my disappointment, 'Awe that's a shame we were planning on whisking you off your feet.'

'You should be careful with an offer like that, you could give me unnecessary dreams.' It dawned on me that I had probably woken her up.

'Oh sorry, were you in bed?'

'Now Tommy, we haven't even met.' She was a great tease and probably great company too. 'The Dance is at Guy's Hospital, do you know the tower block?'

'Yes, that's a terrific venue, but now you won't be there I don't know that we'll bother.'

'It might be wise, I think all the tickets were sold.' I let Vanessa go back to her sleep, I wondered what it must be like doing a whole week of nights instead of our two. I had to think of something to take my mind off of Vanessa in her bed and whatever she might or might not be wearing.

The idea of a ticket sellout and the White Watch story didn't really add up, but we decided to give it a go, the concept being refused entry wasn't in our vocabulary; we always got in, anywhere. We aimed to pub-crawl over to Guy's and get there for about ten o/clock, just right to make an entrance. As usual the plan went astray, we stayed in a few pubs too long and visited more of them than we should have. It was gone eleven o'clock by the time we got to the hospital but we just walked straight in, unnoticed.

This turned out to be due to the bar closing at eleven even though the dance went on until midnight. Big mistake on our part but the party was raving. This whole upper floor was open plan and also seemed to be full of firefighters, I even recognised a few of the local constabulary; the girls must have done a good recruiting job. True to their word, there were members of our White Watch, resplendent in their uniform light blue t-shirts and trousers. H was carrying a Brigade Radio but I'm sure he wouldn't hear it; the music was deafening.

Patty came over and asked in his normal cocky way, 'Where have you lot been? Never mind you're just in time to help, we've got a surprise for the nurses, come on.' He turned and I looked around, everyone had dispersed, only Frankie and me were there, we joined Patty, the other White Watch crew and some firefighters from Westminster Station. We filed through the kitchen area where a couple of the Whites picked up piles of dinner plates.

'What are they for?' I shouted but there didn't seem to be enough time to get a decent answer. I found myself led backstage. The music changed and the curtains opened to *Sexual Healing* by Marvin Gaye. Everyone seemed to know what was happening but me. I just joined in as the drapes pulled back and we all started gyrating on the stage.

As I looked out into the darkness, I slowly became aware of a growth of faces and arms appearing before me. Heads sprouted above other heads, slowly at first. Then some shouting and screaming above the music and I was witnessing a stage crush. An unnatural vertical wall of expectant, insatiable, mass female desire, was growing before my very eyes. The stage seemed to be surrounded, leaving no escape as we were carried along on the enveloping intoxication. I glanced to my left and right, I was at the end of the front row of sensual performers. I recognised Frankie and two of the Westminster boys on my right. I was in a frightened trance.

What on earth had happened, how did I get here? My heart was scolding me, telling me not to be there but my brain couldn't find a way to stop showing off. As we all threw off our shirts a million arms surged forward, grabbing and making us step back. The timing couldn't have been more perfect, at this time of night our voyeur audience were primed with inhibition, and they wanted satisfaction.

They pulsated like a single entity with never ending tentacles, creating energy like only the Beatles could have known. I was now waving my jeans around my head when the shout went up for plates, I turned back to see where they were coming from and realised, we were the only four on the stage. Frankie

116

was grinning from ear to ear as he thrust a plate into my hands, he was on top of the world. I wasn't.

Finally dread took over. My alcohol-induced haze showed some signs of clarity, turning hot perspiration into cold sweat. My fellow exhibitionists were now turning back and forth, passing the plates in front of their crutches and arses as they mimed pulling off their pants. They, at least, seemed to be loving it. A chant had arisen,

'OFF...OFF...OFF!' I nearly pissed myself.

I stumbled backwards in my cowardliness, grabbing my clothes and finally made out the redhead at the side of the stage. She was out of sync with the general melee that had replaced the Nurses Easter Ball and she was pointing behind me. As soon as she had gotten my attention she disappeared, displaced by the throng. There was no trap so I just fled, cowering to the back of the stage to find Jenny beckoning me.

She was unsuccessfully trying not to giggle, 'You look as frightened as some of my patients when I bring out a needle, you're a better mover though, I'll give you that.' I was putting my clothes back on and starting to come to what little sense I had left. Red was still tittering and I couldn't help joining her infectious laugh. Her hair was hypnotic, I doubted if I would ever be able to call her Jenny.

I whined, 'I've lost my bloody shirt.'

'Why don't you go back and get it,' she said teasingly, her gorgeousness clearing any worry about my current exposure. She was wearing a little black dress, comfortably covering her creamy, voluptuous curves. The light from the distant kitchen set her head ablaze and she gave me another sexy look, 'I've got a shirt at home that will fit you.'

We crept to the back of the hall beyond the climatic performance. The White Watch were there, I saw them but not before they had seen me. 'Captured,' they cried, 'Got you. Sucker.'

Red grabbed my arm, put her hand on my bare chest and pulled me into a long passionate kiss. I thought to myself, *what a great wheeze.* But Red had given me the out.

I looked up from the embrace and said to them all. 'Yes, captured.' I could feel their eyes on my back as we walked away. *I could love this girl,* I thought.

'They'll be talking about that for a while,' she said.

'What, my dance or that kiss?'

'You quite like getting your kit off, don't you?'

'I don't know what you mean?'

'Well, you seemed to be having fun.'

'I just got caught up in the euphoria of it all. I thought you were meant to be working, anyway?' I said changing the subject.

'What gave you that idea?'

'I called and spoke to your flatmate, she told…'

'Aww, she doesn't know whether she's coming or going,' Red interrupted, 'Are you cold?' I was but I wasn't going to admit to that. Her flat was only a short walk away and we were soon inspecting her fridge for a bottle of wine. 'Take that white one, it's Vanessa's, she's the one on nights and I think she owes us a drink. Pour us a couple and I'll go and get you that shirt.'

I was still looking for the glasses when I heard her come back. 'Do you think this will fit?' she said. I turned to find that she was modelling the shirt and it didn't look like she was wearing much else. I felt goose bumps all over, she was stunning.

'Oh! I think that will do just fine.'

Captured I thought.

10

May 1984
Jumpers

Toby answered the internal phone, 'That was Frankie, he says there's a geezer downstairs who's our mate.'

'Why doesn't he send him up then?' I said.

'You know Frankie, it sounded a bit suspicious. Shall we go and see?'

We slid down to the appliance bay to find Frankie talking to an old boy in a wheelchair, it was Del the local vehicular vagabond. We would often see him about, wheeling his bag laden home around Lambeth. He was always so happy, I wondered if there was something more attractive than I could imagine about his vagrant lifestyle. He should have been frozen; it was May but there was a distinct breeze coming through the still open bay door. He had no socks or coat, although I couldn't count the amount of jumpers he wore, they were held together by grime and disguised like a multitude of woolly string vests.

'Here they are. Have you got your puncture outfits? Del needs a mend,' said Frankie. I stopped before I got too close as he needed a shower more than anything else; he stank.

'Hello Del,' said Toby, 'what's the problem?'

'Whatcha son...' he started to ramble.

'I'll go and get my kit,' I said, 'Do you want a cup of tea Del?' I left without waiting for an answer, I could see the rims of his wheels meeting the appliance room floor where there should have been tyres and I knew he wouldn't say no to a cuppa.

By the time I got back Rod had turned up and they were manhandling Del out of his chair. Toby and I nipped into the BA room where there was a sink, and we set about mending the many punctures in both his larger tyres.

'I'm sure he's chucking up more than usual,' I said to Toby.

'Yeah, but are you going to give him a bath?'

'No, I guess not. I think I might get some new cycle togs though, he looks smarter than I did this morning.'

'There you go mate,' said Toby, wheeling out his chair, 'that'll keep you going for a while.'

'What did you give him?' Rod said to Frankie as we waved him goodbye.

'I just slipped him a Pearl Diver,' said Frank, he had that grin on his face again.

'He did alright then, so did I,' said Rodney.

'You deserve medals just for lifting him up by his armpits,' I said.

'I know the stinking bastard, I'm going for a shower,' Frankie was sniffing and pulling his shirt, hoping his elongated face would somehow remove the smell.

Distant bell, click, LOUD BELLS, lights come on.

'We've got a Jumper,' shouted Frankie, as he handed the slip to the Guvnor and started up the machine. We broke into song before we were even out of the station.

Peter Cook and Dudley Moore had written a song just for us about someone threatening to jump into a blanket. It had become our idea of a silent approach. The two-tones weren't being as uncompassionate as us and were switched off. It's not a nice song but we just can't help ourselves. Perhaps if we got more involved with the people threatening to jump, we wouldn't be so callous. We normally spent most of the time at these incidents in the background, we are strictly tidy up detail.

It's not that being called to a person threatening to jump is a regular occurrence, but we do get a few. For some reason the bridges over the Thames seem to be an attraction for those poor souls wanting to take their own lives. I don't think they realise that these leaps are often quite successful, perhaps believing the watery landing won't be too final. Apart from the impact, which I'm told can be a bit like hitting concrete, these free divers often don't resurface immediately.

The Thames in London is no ordinary river, it is subject to the influence of the lunar cycle. Twice a day there is a battle, where for some time there will be a split-tide, water will be flowing in different directions in the centre than at the edges of the channel. Additionally, obstructions such as jetties, moorings and bridge supports cause under-tows which add to the mix. After about a week the build-up of gases wins and their bloated bodies resurface for retrieval, hopefully by the River Police and not our floaties. They hate that job, and only ever tow them to the Police River Station.

I suppose we should have more understanding for those attempting suicide, it's quite common in our own profession. I used to play footy with a great winger. He killed himself and I never even knew anything was wrong. I hate to think what drives people to such despair, and what stopped him getting help. Our biggest problem is that we spend our time trying to save people, we find it quite disturbing that someone would want to destroy what we consider to be our ultimate purpose. Our success rate isn't that high though; most fire victims are gone before we turn out of the station doors.

Today we are called to a person threatening to jump from Castle Point, a tower block not far from the station. We arrived after two verses of our inappropriate song; it didn't occur to me that this person might actually jump, not mid-harmony. We often don't have time to worry about our casualties, we either leave them because they are obviously dead, or we pull them out and send them off in an ambulance. This black humour is a defence mechanism, we just have to be careful not to let it overspill in front of the public. In truth we take a little of every tragedy on board; this is our subliminal way to pretend we are unaffected. I often think that counselling might help, just the chance to talk, but I'm not sure whether it would be accepted in our profession.

The idea of a silent approach is an attempt not to scare the jumper into committing their act. However, from the roof of this thirteen-storey tower he couldn't really have missed our arrival. From his vantage he would see the busy life at the junction, the muted traffic waiting at the crossroads for their turn, the park dwellers, dog walkers and those inaudibly chatting. He wouldn't hear the pedestrians who only now, with our arrival, will have noticed something was amiss.

'I can't see bugger all,' said Toby, looking skywards.

Then he appeared, 'There, there,' I pointed. A silhouetted head and shoulders looked back down at us from a roof top structure, a small tower on top of a tower. It was a confirming glance, he gazed straight at me, into my soul. He must have recognised a link between *purpose* and *interference*, then he disappeared again.

An old lady had stopped and was also staring, I wondered if he could feel her compassion, see her long life.

At this point most people threatening to jump become introverted and self-reflecting; it is now that their rescue can take place, verbally. I imagined him sitting up there alone for just a little longer. Meanwhile we began our wait for his return to the safety of the ground floor. Life at the junction continued its normality, only slightly intrigued by our presence.

'Tom, go and tell the police where he is,' ordered the Guv. I turned to see a squad car just pulling up behind our machine. Although we are quite willing to try, the police normally take over in this type of incident, they have trained suicide negotiators.

'You got anything mate,' said one of the coppers, getting out of the car and reaching for his cap. These two would be the first to make the long internal journey to try and *talk him down.*

'He's up there,' I turned, pointed up, and as if on cue he flew off the top of the tower. 'No, he isn't,' I mumbled.

There was a moment when all sound was swallowed up. I couldn't hear anything, the disbelief of my vision had shut off my other senses. He had disappeared to give himself a run up, and he was still running as he sailed out into his last breath, arms windmilling to increase his irretrievable progress. Gravity took over, not cartoonesque, there was no sudden realisation of a missing floor, this was more of an arc. About halfway down, the run turned into a scamper, as if he had changed his mind and was trying to climb back up, fighting an invisible scree.

It seemed to be working, his feet were making steps out of air and leaving his head and shoulders behind as his body became more horizontal. He had switched from perpendicular to laid-back and was now flying reclined.

Then…THUMP.

A dead sound, a loud, dull thud. Not unlike the sound one of our line bags makes when they hit the ground, but louder, much louder. A final, non-resonant thump. I was holding my breath, as if it wasn't really happening. He landed before I processed that he had actually jumped. I never saw him hit the deck, I had turned away, eyes closed and shoulders scrunched in reflex. It was the turn of my ears to have sensual priority to his slamming finale.

Our jumper was now recumbent on the pavement. If I hadn't seen his flight, I might have thought he'd just taken a lie down, he looked relaxed; asleep. My mind switched from astonished inaction to overdrive as I ran towards the supine form. I was recalling stories of people surviving great falls as I thrust my fingers to his carotid artery. I felt a pulse, no doubt. I put my ear to his mouth to check for breathing and looked along his body.

I couldn't believe he might need resuscitation. He definitely wasn't conscious, I thought *he must be dead, I bet he bloody hurts if he's alive!* I tried to imagine a pain worse than anything I'd ever felt but he didn't even have a grimace. There was no breath, no last thoughts, no soul. I was starting to wonder if his last moments had been of remorse or success as his being came into focus…

He was wearing a skirt. He had a beard and a skirt.

My mind screamed AIDS and simultaneously theorised that that was his reason for suicide. I hesitated, I didn't even think of my resuscitation pack and its safety shield; I hesitated. A fraction of a second later the ambulance crew took over.

'I felt a pulse, mate,' I said.

'Doubt it, last throws of life, is all,' said the paramedic, dismissively.

Is all, where does he come from, I thought. Thank the stars he's here though. I was conflicted, I had thought of myself first. I'd actually thought of kissing Red, or not being allowed to kiss Red. I couldn't believe that my relationship might be over before it had finally got going. I'd stopped doing my job, albeit momentarily, and even though the outcome would have been futile, I'd hesitated. It was so fleeting that it wasn't noticed.

We talked about it afterwards, just what happened, not how we felt. There's a level of detail we go into before someone cracks a joke. That's when it's time to move on, it's unsaid but there is a point we don't go beyond, a point where exposure is uncomfortable. This is a dangerous area where discussion that might have helped is suppressed. By the time we get a casualty update from the hospital, or morgue, we are already planning our next beer.

Compared to the amount of time on duty, the amount of fun and the great friendships, *stiffs* are just another occupational hazard. At least that's what I tell myself. I don't know how everyone else copes, or even if it bothers them; I haven't got the courage to ask. They might admit it hurts and I don't know if that would help me. I have a dark inner cupboard where I store all the memories I'd rather not have. I don't go in, I just shove them into the brimming recessed crypt. They stay there shut away, until I have to put another one in, then I sneak the door open again, like a frightened child. This is how I stop them messing up my day.

At a watch level *stiffs*, so called because of their habit of becoming, stiff, are met with a type of intrigue. We talk about them briefly over a cup of tea around the mess table. Often with a little bit of black humour, cringe worthy comments that shouldn't be repeated anywhere else. Then they are hardly ever mentioned again and we continue life: eating, training, cleaning the shit off of our gear…drinking. We are by-standers to tragedies that don't belong to us, brief visitors who try to keep their own lives undisturbed. This coping mechanism doesn't mix well with compassion but when we are in our second home, the station, it isn't our first consideration. Presenting a bold, unaffected exterior is the expected brotherly attitude. This isn't just a matter of face, it is a shared strength, a silent support. Personally, I would have liked to talk about these things more, but who could I tell. As far as I know, most of the guys don't take it home to their families, they say they don't want them to experience any of the suffering, there's no need. Maybe there is a need.

Macabrely, when people find out that I am a firefighter they say things like, *Ooo, I bet you've seen some sights,* and even ask, *what's the worst thing you've ever seen?* I change the subject, they are asking to open the door of my cupboard. In reality we probably all hold onto some adversity, a bit from those dark moments, a bit we'd rather not have.

I was asked at my interview how I might react upon discovering a corpse. I replied that I couldn't really say as I had never seen a dead person but I was sure I would cope. It didn't take long to find out. There was nothing, no reaction, I didn't register that they had ever been a person. She was just another part of the fire; I didn't see her as human. To me she seemed more like a Tailor's dummy than anything that had once breathed, walked and talked. There was still something vaguely human about her but she was very badly burnt.

It had been a slow burn and she had managed to become part of the fire and completely lose her lower right leg. I had no inkling that she was ever alive, all I really noticed was that I didn't freak. My first ever dead person and I had passed some self-imposed test, I coped. I can still see her now, lying on the floor over charred floorboards, staring unseeing at the ceiling. Sometimes my cupboard is a picture gallery.

The non-association with real people is a sub-conscious defence mechanism. I certainly never dreamed it up and it worked well, for a while. Ironically it is the least burnt that have the most effect, the ones that might be sleeping. Although their souls have gone, they just hold onto enough humanity to reach mine. When I had that interview, I never realised there would be so many, or that some would be children.

There are two very distinct scenarios, they are either alive or dead and the response is very different. In a fire it's not always easy to tell which is which. Sometimes conditions are just too unsustainable for life to survive, or like my first, the casualty was too badly burnt. We are not qualified to pronounce death, so the official term for a stiff is a person *apparently dead*. It is our call though, there is no one else to ask. We can't drag a doctor into the fire or bring out badly charred remains. So, erring on the side of safety we occasionally move someone who should have been left in place.

Once we make this decision we are committed and have to treat them as alive until we can hand them over to someone more qualified, normally the London Ambulance Service. There is no allowance for changing your mind.

This procedure had an unfortunate ending on one particular occasion. We had pulled a woman from a smoky ground floor flat to the street outside. Toby and Gran began an attempt at resuscitation, but it now seemed clear that she wasn't going to survive. In all the palaver I had managed to gouge my hand on a broken vase.

'You better come with us mate, she's not going to mind,' said one of the Ambulance crew.

'Go on Tom, we'll pick you up on our way home,' said the Guv.

She was pronounced dead on arrival at A&E, and I was whisked away to be cleaned up. My wound was more blood than gash so I was soon in the nurses' rest room being treated to a cup of tea. Thinking I'd ended up with a result, I had no idea of the blunder I was about to commit.

After a short while I was joined by two more nurses, 'God, that was horrible,' said the first.

'You're telling me, I've never seen anything so gross,' said the second.

'Why? What's happened?' I asked.

They took a real look at me, an intense study, then the first nurse said, 'Well, you brought her in!' She was referring to my ambulance companion; disgust beat her disappointment by just a margin. There was no coming back, I had miscalculated the difference between our two jobs. I hadn't appreciated the

125

condition of our casualty and had turned from compassionate hero to heartless bastard, in one beat.

Splat, we had already christened our flyer, was still lying on the pavement. We got the job of moving his body; it was like trying to pick up a giant sack of nuts and bolts. His skeleton must have been shattered by the impact, it was hard to get a grip. We gathered around and slipped him, as discretely as possible, onto a salvage sheet. It was still like trying to lift a pair of pyjamas, tied at the ends and filled with marbles. I think I had become a little attached to our deceased aviator, probably just compensating for the reluctance I first felt when we finally met face to face.

I had still felt a pulse, or something, and I was probably the last person he saw whilst alive, even if that was thirteen stories away. In the next few months, we would find many more people who needed our help, but only a couple of them would still be alive. Splat didn't make it, no surprise there. We talked about him wearing a skirt and wondered where he came from; he didn't look local. I never mentioned my initial apprehension that was still my battle. It wasn't much really, I would have started CPR if the ambulance crew hadn't turned up. I would have used my face shield. I'd just switched off autopilot and engaged rationality; it still nags at my subconscious.

'Tom,' shouted Toby, we were on our way home in the back cab, we all slipped straight back into Peter and Dudley's song.

11

June 1984.

Traps

'I dunno why we had to lose so many of our car parking places? Look at all those motors down there, they're not all essential users I bet,' said Frankie. We were standing on the first-floor balcony, overlooking what was left of our yard.

'You'll have to get your bike out Frankie,' I said. I'd come out for a bit of post lunch fresh air instead of the normal forty winks; Frankie had the same idea. It wasn't one of the best outlooks in London, the rear of the station was enclosed by other buildings; it was also about to be framed by one more. There was a much better view from the front of the station but only from the tiny veranda beyond our windows. The roof provided excellent London vistas, including the Houses of Parliament and St Stephens Tower, better known as Big Ben. You could have sold tickets for that view, but it was out of range to respond to our call bells, so we rarely got up there.

There were a few people moving around in the yard and beyond the rear gates, enough to add a bit of interest. We could just see our local, the Windmill, temptingly close on such a sunny afternoon. We both left that thought unsaid and Frank returned to his original moan.

'That's not the point Tom.' He was in an unusual mood, he hadn't really been with us all morning, there but distant at the same time.

'I know, I know, we firefighters get in the way a bit. The brigade would run a lot better without us hanging around.' We often got the feeling that we were surplus to requirements, we'd certainly been an afterthought when they allocated car parking. There just weren't enough spaces for the whole watch, this made change-over a nightmare and a bit of a car shuffle. I was glad I didn't have to join in, my pushbike was right behind me on the balcony. I glanced behind just to be sure.

'You're right Tom, let's put in a *Brigade Suggestion*, we could all become Staff Car drivers.' He was perking up but I decided to change the subject anyway.

'I reckon a barbeque would go down well on nights, it's pretty warm.' We were in the middle of one of those rare occasions when summer actually felt like summer.

'That's a funny thing for you to suggest Tom, do you fancy a bit of red meat?' He paused and when I didn't answer straight away, he carried on, 'How's the house hunting going, you found anywhere yet?'

'No, I'm still in Toby's back room. Has he said something?'

'Naw, you know Toby, he's so laid-back he'll fall over one day.'

'He's got no time to fall over, too much running to do.' Toby had been a star but it really was time for me to move on. 'Why, do you know of any flats going?'

'Maybe Tom, leave it with me.' It was encouraging, but it was also Frankie; it could be anything, anywhere. Meanwhile there was a barbeque to plan.

'Don't worry I'll leave the dead animals for you guys. It's the ambiance I was thinking of.'

'What this building site that was our old yard?'

'You've got to have somewhere to throw the empty cans and chicken bones, besides it's almost secluded at night.' It was true, we only had faint glimpses of the real world, but that worked two ways. No one could see us either.

'Let's see what Rodney thinks, he won't have done the shopping yet.' I was determined not to let Frankie start complaining again. It was bad enough; them taking our yard and parking, pretty soon he'd be on about the locker rooms as well. Things were changing, London was investing in a new centralised Mobilising Control and it was going to be attached to HQ, and that meant connected to us as well. It was our station and our yard that would be affected the most, and they never even asked our permission.

'I reckon we were about up to Mince D last week, he won't be able to do an E, on the Barbi.' A, B, C, and D were, Curry, Spaghetti, Shepherd's Pie and Chilli, I'd never thought of an E until now.

'I wouldn't put it past him Frank, haven't you heard of burgers?' I decided on a complete change of subject, one I knew would interest Frankie. 'This new Central Mobilising thingy, it will be good when it's finished, haven't you thought about all the control girls walking around?'

'Yeah,' Frankie went off in a dream, 'they all wear *suzzies*, you know Tom.' I thought I'd cracked it and Frankie was back to his old self but somehow, I managed to lose it again.

'Easy Frankie, it'll be ages before they move in, they've only just broken ground.'

'That's another point Tom, they nicked me lockers. I had a twin set in Rose Cottage.' Some of the locker rooms had nicknames too and Rose Cottage was about to be lost to modernisation. Above all I had failed to keep the conversation away from lockers! A few of the guys had recently been forced to move as part of our accommodation had also been claimed for the new building work. Our lockers are more than just a place to keep kit, they are our link to the building, our security, and our assurance that we are part of the team fabric.

We personalise them, keep our second lives in them, our phone numbers and our soft toilet rolls. Frank and a couple of floaties had been evicted; for them it was like being thrown out on the street. Frankie had already had a moan about having to move, I'd heard it a few times now, but he certainly wasn't his normal self, something else was bothering him. I really should have asked how he was, but as usual, I was too wrapped up in my own world.

'Go on Frankie, go and ask Rodney about a Barbi.' I thought he would have more luck than I would.

It had been a long time since the balconies at the rear of our floor had been used by Head Quarters. There was a time when they were the viewing galleries for parades and exhibitions; those days were long gone. However, they still didn't count as our accommodation, so we had a mobile Barbeque to avoid any complaints. Well only just mobile. It had melted into the raised seating platform the first time it was used; if it wasn't for a crowbar and several strained firefighters, it would still be a fixture. It made it easy and stable tonight, the legs slotted right back into the holes we had left that no one had ever asked about.

We normally created more of an evening than just sitting around the mess table, a few cans of beer and a drop of wine made it a more sociable event; we could even pretend we weren't at work. However, tonight the rest of Lambeth was having a party and the chicken didn't know whether it was being cooked or not. The corn-on-the-cob that Rodney had brought, just for me, was getting mullered in the hot plate. I don't know what this special treatment was about, but relations between us had improved. Maybe I'd come up to a greater standard in our recent loft job than I realised. Generally, the evening was going well, at least that's what it looked like when we managed not to be on a shout. Even the TL was quiet and they were keeping the Floaties company.

Distant bell, click, LOUD BELLS, lights come on.

The bells dropped again and we were off to one of our regular destinations, a fire in a railway arch, Mepham St. Just a tramp's bonfire. I kept thinking that I must congratulate Bones when we get back, he'd told us he was going to be a father again. Although that would be his sixth and he sure didn't seem that pleased himself.

We got back to the station to find the floaties bunched around the fading barbi. 'What's that remind you of Tom, lots of old men, drinking out of tin cans, crowded around a dying blaze?' said Granny.

'I thought I recognised some of the dossers under that arch!' I said, pondering the similarity to our last shout. We finally got a chance to sit around and take in the atmosphere that was our corner of Lambeth. A chance to chin wag and slurp wine from our crystal flutes, well builders' tea mugs to anyone else.

'Have you joined the cycling troop then Nod,' I asked.

'I don't think I'll last long,' he replied. The barbeque area is also the bike park and we'd discovered an extra pair of wheels when we cleared them out of the way. 'I'm having a go at cycle courier work in the City.'

'Do you carry your tools in case you get an emergency plumbing job,' said Granny.

'I might go back to that, it'll be a lot safer.'

'It's good money though, ain't it?' said Frankie who'd spent most of the night on the phone.

'If you know where you're going,' added Bones.

'I don't think I earnt anything today, I got an unexpected overhead.' I thought he must have damaged his bike but it had looked okay.

'What did you do?' Granny asked.

'I got nicked running a red light. I was looking for an address and I crashed straight into a giant copper.'

'Didn't you try the, I'm a fireman, angle?' Rodney said.

'He wasn't having it, he was more worried about the tyre marks on his shiny shoes.'

'You didn't muck about then, you really ran into him,' I said.

'You didn't give him your real address though,' said Rodney.

'I had to, he was going to impound my bike, he said I'd get a summons.'

'Oh, he was probably bluffing, you'll be okay,' said Bones.

'No, I don't think so. I was pretty fed up already and I reckon I pushed him more than I needed to.' This didn't sound like Noddy, we waited for him to continue as Granny topped up our mugs. He looked at us all, almost sheepishly, 'Well he looked down at me and asked what I'd got to say for myself. I did a bit of a Tomato and spoke without thinking.'

'Oy, oy,' I shouted.

'Get on with it Nod, what did you say?' Granny asked.

'*Up the Miners!* He wasn't impressed.' As we fell about laughing, I thought we'd have to hear it all again when Toby was around, he was always on about doing more for the striking miners.

The call bells remained silent and we'd eventually finished our meal; we cleared up by throwing most of the debris into the footings of London's newest call centre. 'That's going to be an eyesore, used to be a bandstand you know,' said Jules, the old floaty had been at Lambeth since the late 50s.

'Yeah, we know, and a bar,' I said.

'More of a pub really, we used to have kegs delivered, right there by the old back gate,' he had started to reminisce; we'd heard it all before; the old boys did love to *swing the lamp*.

'Hey Tom let's go and see how they are doing with our old locker rooms,' said Granny. It was a great rescue; Frankie came along as well, we couldn't have kept him away. We left Nod to listen politely to his local history lesson.

A plastic sheet, hanging by a bit of masking tape, was the only barrier between us and our old accommodation, so in we went.

'What have they done then?' I said.

'Doesn't look like anything to me,' said Frankie. It was kind of eerie, we'd only been kicked out a few days previously but it already had an alien feel. It was deserted. Just empty lockers, some with the doors left open, but lonely and abandoned. The beds and chairs were gone and everywhere had a layer of builders' dust.

'I wonder what they're going to use this for,' I said. I was expecting Frankie to start imagining the control girls again but he had already been distracted.

'They've broken some of the lockers away from the walls, look, the whole things are just standing there,' said Frankie. What were once integral were now freestanding lockers.

'Why don't we take your pair home with us then Frank?' Granny said.

'I think I will, give us a hand,' he said to us all.

'You've got to be kidding, you'll never move them, they should be fixtures, they aren't meant to be mobile,' I said. Frankie had already started to shuffle a bank of two around.

'Come on, think of it as another Red Watch shifting job,' he said.

The watch had a part time number for a local removal company. It wasn't a big firm; old Murphy owned a couple of lorries and called us whenever he got a job. We even met other firefighters in the course of our *Murphing*. We were on a removal once where an old piano was sitting in the corner.

'Do you want us to move that, Mam?' Frankie said.

'Oh no, no, I've got a team of professional piano movers coming, don't touch my old girl,' she said affectionately. Half an hour later the Green watch turned up with a piano trolley.

'Hello boys,' I said, 'fancy meeting you here.' I didn't realise she was in earshot.

'Do you know each other then?' she asked. Their cover was nearly blown.

'We're always bumping into them Mam, got a good team there,' I said and quickly left them to negotiate the Joanna. As far as I know, the only thing that made them anywhere near *professional* piano movers was that one of them had got hold of a piano trolley.

The lockers were already on their way, unfortunately all the way. Frankie lost his grip and the pair fell crashing onto their side. 'See solid as a rock,' said Frankie. We could now lift them into the main dormitory where we plonked them against a spare bit of wall.

'They could do with a bit of company,' I said, 'they look lonely.'

The next dozen came out in various sections and started to transform the sleeping accommodation. The beds were getting partitioned off into semi-private sections. The vast dormitory was disappearing and becoming almost cosy. 'Do you think the builders would put me in an *en-suite*?' Granny said.

'We'll be lucky if they don't make us take these back,' I said.

'What's the matter Tom, you're not normally one to worry,' said Gran.

'I'm just concerned I won't get a whole terrace, I was thinking of sub-letting you know.'

Some of the lockers took a little more persuasion as the builders hadn't loosened them, but nothing that a bit of breaking-in gear and the help of the rest of the watch couldn't solve.

'I've got ten lockers now,' announced Frankie.

'You can hang a clean shirt in each one,' said Granny.

'How many have you got then Gran?' I said.

'Just one or two Tom, one or two here and one or two over there and...'

'We're the bloody Lambeth Locker Barons,' I said.

'We better save some for Toby, he wouldn't want to miss out,' said Frankie. Toby had taken the night off, apparently he had a hot date. I hoped it wasn't contrived around me, now I was his temporary lodger and out of the way for the night.

'All right, all right, listen though guys, if we give the other watches a few then no one will complain,' I said.

'You still don't think we'll get away with it do you Tommy?' Gran sounded like he was starting to have doubts himself.

'Just thinking of ways to beat the Man, I don't really want all these lockers, do you?' I'm sure Rodney kept more than he needed for his kit, but it's not all about firegear; apparently.

We had got a bit carried away and our rebuilding had reached over halfway down the once huge dormitory. This massive room was just what you'd expect for an army squad to billet, there were a few lockers but mainly just two rows of beds. Before our restructuring we could clear out all the bunks and end up with an indoor football pitch. The matches, however, would morph into murder ball and someone would always get hurt; after all, we couldn't even stay in one piece throwing water around. We were really making the dormitory a much safer place; not that the Brigade would see it that way.

It was easy to forget that there were three other watches on the station. It was our second home, but it was also second home to the Blues, the Whites and the Greens.

'Give a couple to each watch, pick the main boys. Good call Tom,' said Rodney as he wandered off to the Chummery.

'Who made him boss?' I said.

'He just agreed with you Tom,' said Frankie.

'Yeah, I suppose,' I still didn't believe we'd get away with it though.

We had been so busy mucking about with lockers we had forgotten our planned excursion the next day, it was now past eleven o'clock. 'Come on Granny, get the maps, let's sort out the route,' said Rodney. I thought *we better not let Rodney have too much of a hand, he was a terrible driver and even worse at map reading.*

'Five, three, three, in the Chummery,' I shouted from the door to anyone who wasn't already there. Out came the Ordinance Survey maps of Kent, our preferred destination and we began to look for spots with the prerequisite association of car park, footpaths and pubs. We'd been all over Kent, maybe it was time to spread our wings, but that would mean investment in another map.

'There,' pointed Noddy.

'Naw, only one pub, remember that time the pub was closed!' Rodney said. I thought *he's getting better*, and he doesn't even drink. Eventually a location was found. A perfect car park on a circular route, about five miles to lunch and three miles back.

'That will do,' said Gran, 'three village pubs. What could go wrong?'

The next morning it was larruping down. We would need some extra layers to go out walking today. But there were more important things to deal with first.

I thought I was first there. It wasn't a race but it didn't do to hang around after a fifteen hour wait. There were five traps in the firemen's washroom and just after change of watch was their busy period. If you had to go during a shift, you had to go, but if you could wait it was a much more relaxed affair, relaxed and social.

'Hi ya Tobe,' I said, 'you came in then, even with all this weather.' Toby hadn't announced himself but after years of living together on the station, we all recognised each other by subtler noises. The way you open the door, a slight shuffle to your walk, but mostly by those little snorts and wheezes that you make and don't realise.

'Yo Tommy, got an emergency on,' said Toby as the bog door slammed. I could hear the speed as different melodies ran into each other: the door latch, the seat, the zip and all the while Toby was feigning the strain.

'Nnnnnnnnn, I wouldn't miss a walk, too much fun, nnnnnnn. It wasn't raining when I got my bike out.'

'Easy Tobe, have you got an intruder in your under crackers?' came Frankie's voice.

'Safe now,' said Toby, 'anyone got waterproofs?'

'I didn't hear you come in Frank,' I said.

'I've been here all along, just miles away Tom,' said Frankie.

'You've been miles away all week,' the door banged again, louder than normal and Granny joined the party. 'Now where shall I go, I don't want a hot seat?'

'Ain't they made you a bigger one yet, Gran?' I said.

'And then I'd miss you boys, with your witty repartee. What's wrong then Frank, come on spill the beans,' Granny was in counsellor mode.

'We're gonna get fucking wet,' said Toby. Like me he thought Frankie was talking about the weather. He wasn't, and we certainly weren't expecting his next announcement.

'Me Julie's up the fucking spout,' came Frankie's confession. We were all confused because Bones had told us he was about to become a father again, just last night, during the barbeque and in between shouts.

'Yeah, Bones' misses, Julie, we all know, I think it's meant to be good news Frank,' I said, after a moment of unresolved puzzlement.

'What are you talking about Frankie?' Toby had a curious tone, he had missed Bones' announcement.

'Whacha Tobe,' said Gran, then in almost the same breath, 'you better tell us now Frank.' There was silence, we were alone in the washroom, the pause was to make sure; we listened from our individual throne rooms.

That's when Frankie broke the news to his audience, squatting with their kacks around their ankles, 'I'm going to be a father again, and it's my girlfriend Julie, not Bones' misses.' He had also missed Bones' news, having spent most of the evening on the A & B and he wasn't discussing happy families. It looked like there were two Julies in the family way.

'Aw bollocks,' screamed Toby.

'Hey, have a heart,' I said.

'No not that, sorry Frank, I forgot to bring my bog roll in,' said Toby, 'I dumped my kit and ran straight here.'

'Now that is a travesty,' I said.

'What are you going to do Frank?' Gran said.

'Black bin liner, we'll go and see Josie, she'll kit us out,' said Frankie, he'd snapped out of his surprise parental problem and solved our rainwear dilemma at the same time. Perhaps feeling better having told the rest of his second family, knowing we couldn't do much to help but were there to listen.

'I've finished, you can borrow mine Toby,' I could hear the rebound as I threw my soft toilet roll over the door for Toby. No one used the greaseproof paper provided by the Brigade, we wanted to remove traces of what we'd been doing not spread it around. Besides as it has Council Property written on every sheet, it feels like theft.

'About Julie, Frank, what are you going…?' Granny didn't finish, the door slammed and someone from the day watch came in, at least we didn't recognise their acoustic shuffle.

That put an end to conversation about Frankie's news, but I couldn't help myself, 'Julie, Julie, Julie, our Jules is going to feel a bit left out.' It suddenly seemed like there was a Julie everywhere.

It wasn't until we were alone again and washing our hands that Granny said, 'So who's going to tell Bones that it was Frankie who got Julie in the family way?'

'He won't think that, surely,' I said, but it had made me wonder, 'Do you think it will be a while before the truth catches up with the rumour then Gran.'

'Are you kidding, they probably already know at Division!' Toby added.

We all rushed to see Josie the cleaner/men's outfitter to collect our new Macintoshes. 'Anyone know where to find an adult with a pair of scissors?' Toby asked.

I guess it's a good job that not many people were out and about, as we descended on Kent in dubious outdoor fashion. We did have some real walking accoutrements, Granny had a plastic wallet for the map and Toby had a compass. Why I always ended up navigating though, I'll never know; I manage to take a wrong turn nearly every outing.

Our trips to the Kent countryside had become very popular. Many of the floaties would also come along; we didn't mind waiting for the old boys to catch up. Today there had been a couple of cancellations, nothing to do with the weather; so they said!

The rain hadn't let up and the ramble had become more of a swim for the boozer.

'Cut across shorty,' Jules sang out.

'Not so much of the shorty, anyway this is a carefully thought-out circuit, I can't just go chopping it about without consulting the committee,' I said.

'Well,' said Toby, 'I think we should cut it, and I'm nearly the Chair.' I looked at him, his bin liner wasn't really holding out and his hair was a mass of sodden ringlets dripping down his neck. There was an alternate route ahead that might work.

'Okay, do a right here,' I shouted. Everyone was looking around. I looked up, made a point of turning the map one hundred and eighty degrees, and said, 'Left, left.' The grumbles indicated that this was no time for a joke.

Off we slid, it wasn't much of a detour, but enough to exchange a wet outside for a wet inside and sooner than they all expected.

After an hour of liquid refreshment and a sandwich, the sky had cleared and we were all in higher spirits. Well almost all.

'Where's me fucking trainers?' said Toby. We had all left our muddy footwear in the porch and now there was one less pair. It was a bit of a stretch anyway, calling them trainers, they were his Brigade issue plimsolls.

'But there's been no one around,' I said, 'they must be here, and who'd want them though, really?'

'Aw, they were old anyway,' shouted Toby as he ran off up the lane in his socks and virtually leapt over the stile before disappearing into the wood.

'Woah,' screamed Frankie and he pulled a pair of muddy sneakers from nowhere.

'You're living dangerously picking them up Frank, they might disintegrate in your hands,' said Gran.

'Fucking idiot, running off, they'd got pushed right behind the flowerpot. He didn't look very hard.'

'Well, you know Toby, three pints of Guinness and he'll do another marathon, he's probably home already,' I said.

He wasn't, he didn't know the way, and his landing on the other side of the stile must have been spectacular. He was waiting for us in the woods. He was unnaturally outlined in brown, most noticeable in his hair, like a cutout model with a dark border. His clean front was only a disguise for a new attire. Closer inspection revealed the mud that had crept all the way up one side, over his head and back down to his other stocking, a sort of gungy warning to his excited smirk. He gave us a pirouette, nearly falling again, and showing us his back, he was wearing most of the sticky path. Frankie slung him his superfluous slippers.

'Bastard,' said Bones who had suddenly been woken from an unusual quietness. He made a run for Frankie, and I thought back to our conversation in the toilets this morning. He was cornered, surrounded by worried firefighters. Bones floored him with a tackle that would be worthy of Granny any day.

'Hey, what'd I do to you,' yelled Frankie.

'Only fucked his missus,' quipped Jules.

'I didn't, honest, I've got a Julie,' said Frankie. Bones looked at him, they were both sprawled on the oozy path which wasn't really that big. We all looked at each other briefly, unaware of what might happen next, the mutual gaze quickly returning to our prone brothers. We were also trying not to fall over and become part of the action.

'I know Frankie,' said Bones, 'but I didn't see why Toby should have all the fun.' You could have set off a land-mine, as a host of brave firemen sprinted off in an attempt not to be the next Mr Squelchy. Jules didn't make it. I thought, *you deserve that*, it was an unnecessary remark however it was taken.

'Boys, boys, think of the cars, we've got to get home with all that mud,' said Granny, just as Jules took a flying tackle at his knees and nearly broke his shoulder. Gran didn't move, he didn't notice, Julie slid horizontally into the swamp. That was enough to call a temporary truce.

'Come on let's walk and dry off before the ride home,' I said. I was one of the few vertical players left. 'Our path's just down here on the right.' I was trying to refocus the group and stay as dry as the afternoon had become. It was never going to happen.

The alcohol had loosened more than our balance and Bones and Frankie were having quite an open chat about their prospective fatherhood. Apparently neither had planned this event and both were worried about accommodation.

'Remind me to talk to you about your gaff, Tom,' said Bones, he just couldn't stop looking out for us.

Frankie wanted to know if he would be able to get any paternity leave, due to his unusual situation. We all wanted to know what Mrs. Frank had to say about the whole affair; he wouldn't let on.

I could see the car park below. I turned back, 'Just down there guys,' I said and with that announcement, promptly fell off of the path. I wasn't that muddy, my fall had been broken by a thicket of brambles and stinging nettles.

'Do you mind awfully, if we take the footpath ahead,' said Granny as he held out his hand to help me up. 'Ow, they're nettles Tom, be careful.'

'I sort of know, ta, and those brambles have put an end to my best new raincoat.'

12

July 1984
Water Trouble

Distant bell, click, LOUD BELLS, lights come on.

I was just disrobing after evening roll call when the bells dropped, 'Leave 'em on boys,' shouted Granny from the Watchroom. I hadn't quite got my braces down as the awful realisation went through my brain, *I should have had that piss.* We were a bit late getting back from a couple of swift pints before duty and now I was going to pay. I had a small hope that it would be a false alarm and we would be back before I actually wet myself. It's not that I've got a problem, but this evening I'd just kept putting it off and that last pint of beer had definitely left me close to an unanticipated bladder catastrophe.

I briefly managed to get it out of my mind as I started to test my BA set whilst we screamed out of the station. Surely I had some control left and could manage another half an hour; it was going to be touch and go. I had one of those sinking feelings as the Guvnor shouted, 'Railway arches alight, Southwark's ground.' *Off our ground that would take longer!* There was still a chance that they wouldn't need us and we'd be turned around before we even got there. Fat chance!

We arrived to discover smoke pouring from an arch and Southwark still trying to break open the door. 'Come on Tobe let's show them how real burglars get in,' I said, eager to take my mind off of the impending self-swamp, and ultimately get on our way quickly.

'Stay there,' the Guvnor jumped out and strolled over to have a chat.

'Shit, doesn't he know there's an emergency going on back here,' I said to no one in particular but now I had their full attention; it must have been the way I was sitting scrunched up with my hands in my groin.

'Got a problem Tommy,' said Toby, as they all started to laugh. Granny dug me in the side, 'Can I be of assistance?' It was almost all over, now that I had the sympathy of the crew to help it wouldn't be long. There were just too many people enjoying mid-summer outside and they had all come to see the smoky entertainment. There was no chance of slipping out and getting relief hidden by the fire engine. Somewhere or other I was going to be putting on a sideshow, and soon.

'No, no, bucket, bucket, quick,' I was desperate and threw off my tunic, the only way to get to my braces. The crew dived out of the cab in an attempt at escape and just as I was slipping down my leggings a bucket was chucked in, followed by a slamming door. Even Rodney got out and he was sitting in the front. The first drops were absorbed by my trousers via my hand but then it was just full-on ecstasy, gushing relief. I thought I was going to fill the bucket but finally shook off the last few drops.

By the time the Guv got back and announced our return to base I was sure I wanted to go again, but I managed to hold it this time.

We'd only been back at the station for five minutes and the bells dropped again. Not before Toby had got ordered on an out duty.

Distant bell, click, LOUD BELLS, lights come on.

The Ethelred Estate is almost right behind the station, it is one of our regular haunts. We were now on our way to a car alight in one of the many, mainly unused garages that formed a maze beneath the concrete blocks. I can imagine the architect's model, gleaming white rows and towers of homely fantasy, punctuated by patches of green recreation. In reality it was grey and every bit of pavement, walkway and grass was a muddy parking space. The underground garages, that are unseen in such a model, are also places where you might never see your car again; should you be foolhardy enough to leave it there.

'That's as far as I go,' said Rodney. He'd pulled up at the entrance that was on the call slip; we could see signs of wispy smoke. It had an unpleasant petroleum smell that was probably the tyres alight. Although there were so many fires in these crypts, it wasn't always easy to tell what was currently burning and what had been left from a previous visit.

'Shall we take the reel?' Nod asked.

'Naw, let's go and see where it is first,' I answered. We walked nonchalantly into the darkness, happily breathing in the faint fumes of all the poisonous plastics, rubbers and whatever else might be alight. The entrance smelt of urine, a definite sign that these places were of spurious use. It was like walking onto a dystopian film set, most of the garage doors were either broken or not there at all, displaying empty or rubbish strewn shells. We passed a skeleton of a scooter, a prior encounter. Strangely, one or two garages were in use, heavily armoured with padlocks thicker than Gran's forearms. Who knows what may lay hidden behind such fortification but none had escaped the endless graffiti.

'Don't we ever wear sets for these Tom?' He was taking the piss, we both knew we should.

'It won't be that bad Nod, you know how big these spaces are.' We just never wore our sets for car fires, we didn't consider them real jobs. 'You know how many cars we get, we'd be servicing them every five minutes.'

'I thought we were saving them for a proper job Tommy.'

'Well, of course, that's the real reason,' I stuttered the half lie.

'But it's getting quite thick.' Nod didn't really need to ask these sort of questions anymore, he had passed his probation, but it had become a habit; he was still the Junior Buck and he played the part. Not always worthy as far as I was concerned; I'd recently passed my four yearly assessment with outstandingly *average* scores. I was upset that I hadn't been *good* at anything, but at least I'd passed.

We were both stooping to keep below the fumes and we still hadn't found the car. The smoke had become thicker and was now forming a definite upper layer. Our only view was of the floor with all its spilt oil, occasional paint and debris contaminating the central run off.

'If it's any further we might as well find another way in,' I said. The garages were only dimly lit with the occasional, rare working lamp, which were framed now by the slowly drifting smoke. They had countless entrances all over the estate. I shouted to Nod who was vanishing, becoming absorbed into the murky poisons, 'We must be right on top of it.'

It was also becoming quite uncomfortable, the heated cloud of fire products was reaching under my tunic and into my lungs. I crouched even lower. What had started as a gentle stroll in a murky warren had transformed into a crawl in venomous smog; and still we carried on!

'It must be here somewhere I can feel the heat,' said Nod. It was getting pretty warm and suddenly, there it was, going nicely. At the car a flamed vision returned, revealing a glowing shell as the fire moved to the last flammable components. Someone's pride and joy, now abandoned in the middle of the thoroughfare.

'What do you reckon Nod, three lengths?'

'Easy, maybe more.'

'Come on then, let's get some water on her.'

Back at the entrance, Granny and Rodney had got out some 45mm hose and the Large Applicator; our favourite branch for car fires.

'We'll take all four 45s, give us five minutes and then turn her on,' I bowed to Nod's increased estimate of the distance. We raced back in with our line of hose, covering as much ground as we could before it was charged and became heavy. I knew Granny would turn it on pretty sharpish to try and catch us out. We got back to the car much quicker than earlier but I could hear the snapping of the water pressure, filling and attempting to straighten the hose line right behind us. It was fully charged by the time we arrived, Granny always managed to time it just right, if we could run fast enough.

'Just thrust the applicator into the car, turn her on and stand back Nod.'

'What, like last time Tom?'

'Sorry Nod, but remember, you never stop learning.' Almost as soon as the rose nozzle started to work the fire died down.

'It looks a bit suspect Tom, parked right in the middle like that.'

'It is Noddy,' said the Guvnor who'd now bothered to take a look. He walked away.

'What's he mean, Tom?' Nod asked.

'He reckons, if there's a number plate it's suspicious, if not it's a derelict. Something to do with the Fire report, you better find out for when you're in charge Noddy.'

'It's probably stolen then.'

'Of course it is, this is Lambeth, these underground garages are designed for torching cars, you wouldn't trust parking your motor down here, would you?' We didn't bother tidying up, there wasn't much left anyway, a burnt-out shell that would become a feature until it was eventually removed by the council. We dragged the hose to the entrance for a good wash off before we made it up, ready for next time.

'You boys look shitty, were you having fun?' said Granny as we emerged from the depths.

'Yeah, but we've made everything a bit grubby,' I said.

'Leave it, me and old Rodders will tidy up after you boys.'

'Oy, not so much of the old,' gabbled Rodney. Just then another Machine appeared, it was Brixton.

'I wonder what they've been up to,' said Nod. They stopped and their engine sound changed. They had put in their power take off, I twigged before anyone else.

'They've put the pump in, run,' I shouted but there really wasn't anywhere to go. We were in a dead end, the only escape was subterranean and the machine wouldn't fit.

Two of their crew jumped off, pulled off some hose reel and used us as target practice. 'Suckers,' they cried. What they hadn't realised was that we were still set in ourselves, it didn't take much to reconnect a length of hose and Granny and Rod caught them with our forty-five. It wasn't a bad retaliation but they had to get so close; the Large Applicator was more a weapon of mass destruction than a close combat firearm. I don't know who was getting most wet. Then another reel appeared from around the back of their machine and it became two against one.

'Come on Tom, let's get our reel,' Nod was already heading that way and besides, we needed a wash. There were screams, orders for more pressure, we were all getting drowned.

Then their driver hit the two-tones and hollered out the window, 'Shout,' they had to stop and make up their reels. We helped, of course, wherever they were going they were going to get there well washed.

Now the water fight had ended and Brixton were well on their way, our Guv appeared, 'Come on boy's, I've got an idea.' We mounted up and drove off our ground to Brixton fire station. It was deserted, as the Guv had presumed, both machines were out so we parked outside and walked straight through the open bay doors. Brixton fire station is smaller than Lambeth with only three bays. It's a lot older as well, at the back of the two bays that are used today is the station office, converted long ago from the stables. A relic of times when horses would thunder through the streets pulling the pumps. You can still see the brick arch outlines of the old stable doors in the office wall, now incorporated into today's renovation.

'They'll be out of the way for a while, have a look around,' said the boss.

'What are we looking for Guv,' I asked. He gave me the key to their general store. Their key safe was wide open, just like ours would be back at base, we didn't expect anyone to break-in to a fire station. In fact, everything looked as if they should still be around, sitting at the office desks, chatting in the appliance bay; except it was empty.

I'd never noticed the deserted feeling at our station, as soon as we return from a shout it's like we've never been away. But here it was, all the paraphernalia of life without the bodies. It was like invading a ghost station, the firefighters having been mysteriously transported away, leaving their souls behind. The remnant energy raised goose pimples along my spine.

'Try in there,' he pointed without answering my question.

'Am I as filthy as you. Nod?' I asked. Despite our impromptu wash we were still fire stained and leaving black smudges everywhere.

'If there's an investigation Tom, they'll find our prints easy.' Nod and I opened the door to a treasure trove of spare fire gear, blank forms, blankets, and there, smiling under some pillows was Ted. 'Ted!' Nod shrieked.

'Right let's go,' said the Guv.

'How did you know Guv,' I said.

'Don't worry about that Tom,'

'Shouldn't we leave them a message?' said Granny.

'No, lock up,' said the Guvnor.

'They'll never know we've been here,' I said, looking at my dirty handprints everywhere.

'You're catching on quick today, Tomato,' said the Guv.

'Bravo, two, two, one, PRIORITY, over.'

Rodney was turning the machine around when we got a shout over the radio.

'Looks like our trip towards home is going to be a quick one,' said Noddy. He thought it might be a false alarm closer to home; it wasn't. We picked up a job on our ground but near Brixton's border, I wondered who our back up might be with Brixton otherwise engaged. Nod and I donned our sets.

'See Noddy, if we'd worn these earlier, we'd be fucked now,' I said.

'Yeah, me and Rodney would be going in, you'd be well fucked,' said Granny. The BA set looked like a toy on Gran's back, he reckoned he only got one good mouthful of air from a cylinder. There's almost as much air in our sets as there is in a phone box, I always thought Gran should wear one of them, just to make it look realistic. I'd go into a job with Gran any day. I'd go in on my own I suppose, I loved it that much; thankfully that was never the case.

To be honest I was dead scared of tying knots or pump operating, I was safe from potential mistakes by getting a roasting. It's not that I couldn't tie up the hose, I just didn't find it natural. I occasionally watched the others: the line would drop, their hands would blur, and off back up the building would go the hose, all neatly tied to the line. And as for pump operating, well that should be easy: water in, water out. It isn't. There are tanks, gauges, valves, pressures; give me the safety of a fire any day.

There were isolated pockets of wealth throughout our ground, little areas that were posher than the rest, this was one of those places. Despite the extra security, which was an absolute requirement, Gran still managed to put in the ground floor door with ease, releasing clouds of thick black smoke.

'Ooh, that was getting bottled up,' I said. Nod grabbed the branch as he threw his tally on the ground, 'Whoa, don't rush, let it breathe a bit,' I said, 'you know what we say about haste Nod.' It's always best to give a fire a second or two just to see if it's going to do anything unexpected, a sudden inrush of air can create all sorts of havoc.

'There are old firemen and there are bold firemen, but there are no old, bold firemen, that one Tom?'

'That one will do,' I said. This little chat was all the time we needed to allay any apprehension and we were in, on our bellies straight away due to the blinding heat. Granny was virtually pushing us along as he fed in the hose, he must have seen the soles of my fire boots disappearing with each thrust. Just a short sliver along the corridor was the first room.

It was going like a bastard.

The whole room looked ready to melt, glowing like a brilliant sunset that had caught the rest of the scenery alight. Fire danced with the furnishings, shimmied around the cornice and flirted above our heads. Nod gave the ceiling a drink, loosened the baked plaster and provided a simmering steam bath.

In we went.

The jet died in his hands and we immediately began to roast. I leaned over his shoulder, 'What's up,' I said.

'It won't fucking work.' He was turning the branch off and on but the water had stopped and the hose was rapidly going flat.

'Drop it Nod, let's get out of here.' I had to shuffle backwards to negotiate the doorway, I knew it wasn't far but I was cooking. My tunic and leggings were getting rucked up because I was keeping so tight against the floor and trying to operate in reverse. As we crawled back down the hallway, I felt the hose re-charge under my belly. We skulked around and groped our way back, following the hardened hose. In the short time we had taken going backwards and forwards, the fire had found a second fiercer bout of energy and was now licking out of the top of the doorway and taking hold in the corridor. It had totally ignored our first foray, almost treating it as an accelerant.

'Fucking hell,' I mumbled, as we both pulled on the hose to regain the branch. It was hard enough handling the charged hose in our narrow confines but something else was stopping us. We had been disarmed and the fire wasn't going to give back our weapon easily. 'The branch must be snagged,' I tried to say to Nod as he pulled harder and harder.

'We'll have to go in,' I had finally got Nods attention. The room was flashing over, flames were now racing across the ceiling providing an immense downward radiation.

I could also smell smoke, real smoke, that shouldn't have been possible. I put my hands around my face seal but I couldn't feel a leak. Occasionally there is a smell of disinfected rubber left over from the last clean but there should never be a smell of smoke. Probably just the remains of our underground car fire, oozing from my face not from the outside my mask. I wondered why I was only noticing this now. I told myself that we were close enough to the front door should I need to get out fast. I'm not a suspicious person, but things weren't quite going according to plan and now I might have a leak. I gave the mask straps a vicious tighten.

It was fucking hot. A prickly, unbearable, energy sapping heat. I started to feel apart from my firegear, everything had become untucked and dishevelled in our recent clamber around the corridor, but this was more, my tunic was threatening to burn my body.

The flames lit up the smoky corridor, we'd have the fire behind us as well as in front and we still didn't know why our water had failed once already. There was no time to hang around, Nod had been too busy trying to retrieve our branch to notice me fumbling about with my mask. We bundled into the fire room and

Noddy scrambled for the branch, which had got snagged on a furniture leg. He hit the ceiling first, masses of burning embers rained down on us, some went down my tunic neck and I scrunched up against them in an attempt to put them out.

I made a mental note to put a new neckerchief on the run, having lost mine somewhere. Noddy gave the whole room a drink and we rushed back out, following the fire that we had now pushed well into the hallway. 'Drown it Nod, there's no downstairs.' There wasn't much point worrying about water damage. I don't think he heard me completely but he certainly didn't hold back. He wasn't going to let this one get away again. We went back into the original fire room and gave that a good spray.

'I think that will do Nod, leave the jet here and we'll have a look around.' Right at the end of the single storey flat was a tiny kitchen with a back door, we opened that and came back to search the third and last room, the bedroom. The smoke was hanging around. I thought the bedroom would be empty as it was still early evening; it hadn't occurred to me that I could be wrong.

It was still quite warm so we crawled and crouched our way around. I found the bed and swept my hand across the charcoaled covers and landed straight on a soft lump, a leg. This was one of those times when I really wished I had a decent pair of gloves. I couldn't see, so I tentatively felt along to the foot. There was no doubt, there was a person laying on this bed. A physical anxiety overtook my body, rising from somewhere deep inside, below my stomach.

I held her foot for a brief moment, my sensuality against her slightly detached, spongey flesh. My head was slowly accepting her trauma while my heart was refusing to permit my own. Subconsciously I was still trying to find a reason for this not to be another stiff. Like when you've lost your keys and you still keep looking in the same place, as if somehow, they were there all along; except I was wishing she wasn't here. My hand was transfixed, stuck to her foot but I could feel every inch of the inside of my firegear, from my helmet, strapped tight under my chin to the backs of my fire boots. This was different the earlier scorching sensation, this was a mental detachment, a retreat into my soul. I couldn't feel her life, it had left long ago; this flat was no place for the living. Time restarted, and from the burning lump that was in my chest, I called out, 'We got one.' Nod came over.

'What?' It was still hard to see so I took his hand and placed it on the foot. He pulled it back, so fast it was a reflex.

147

'You bastard, Tom,' he gasped, 'she's dead init.'

'Well, I don't reckon she's just a heavy sleeper,' I said. I had already felt the pappiness of her heated flesh, I certainly didn't want to touch her again. 'Sorry Nod, you okay?' I didn't mean to give Nod the same shock as I had just been through, but as usual I acted before I thought.

'Yeah, no worries.' I couldn't tell whether he was bothered or not; it's hard to get much of an impression through a dirty facemask.

As the smoke cleared some more, we could see an old lady in a soot laden dressing gown, her mouth in a last rigid gasp. I guess it was the smallness of the foot that had made me unconsciously determine that the victim was female. It was a neat and ordinary bedroom, the only mess created by us and the black ash. For the second time today, I had a feeling of intrusion, but stronger, I was invading her last rest. There was a pair of worn slippers poking out from under the bed, abandoned old friends, I was fixated by them.

She had probably been dead before we even found Fm Ted in Brixton's store, killed by the fire gasses long before we arrived. It's rare that we find a live one, most are dead by the time someone notices the smoke and puts in the call.

'Come on, we better go and tell the Guvnor.' It dawned on me that I must have seemed a bit callous. Once we got out and had removed our masks I turned to Nod, 'Don't think I was being disrespectful Nod. That was your first stiff, wasn't it?' Before he could answer Rodney came over, looking very sheepish.

'Tom, Tom, I forgot to make sure the tank was full after the water fight.' A couple of days ago I might have thought that Rod was being careless because it was me, although I know that would never really happen. No, this was Rod being nice to me again, well as nice as you can be when you've just tried to roast someone.

'Just a minute, Rod,' I called to the Guv, there was no public around, 'Female stiff back bedroom Guv.'

'Okay guys, well done, go and get rid of your sets, then come back and talk to me.'

Granny and Bones went off to investigate. Our TL had turned up and although it wasn't needed, Bones would be writing all the reports, he liked a first-hand view. There is also something about a stiff, something that drives human curiosity to experience the macabre. At least for everyone else, I could do without the thrill.

I turned back to Rodney, 'No worries, Rod, it made it more fun.' I looked from him to Nod, trying to remind him that there were two of us. He caught on.

'Hey Nod, sorry man.' Rodney sometimes was the oldest hippy in town.

'No worries, we were all there, Rod,' said Noddy, putting his arm around his shoulders. He knew that although water was the driver's responsibility, we had all forgotten to fill up.

'Oy, that's enough of that you two, he did just try to kill us Nod, remember.'

We went back in, Nod went straight for the bedroom. 'Don't you want to see what a mess we made of the lounge,' I called as I left Nod and went into the front room. There was the normal wet old burnt smell, but apart from the ceiling being mostly on the floor, it wasn't that disturbed. The furniture was pretty well laid out, just a few pieces out of place, which was surprising when I thought of Noddy's attack. But it was black, a covering of ash veiled the whole room with just glimpses of old stripy wallpaper peeking from behind the sofa.

The corner, where there once had been a television was still glowing; I picked up the jet and dowsed the embers. Saggy ornaments stared at me from a shelving unit, clinging unsuccessfully to their former shape. I picked up a paperback book from a coffee table and saw only the rich veneer outline beneath, protected from the thick, penetrating ash. A flash of light caught my eye, as somehow a beam of streetlight had made it through the blackened windowpanes and was reflected in a mirror above the fireplace. I wiped the darkness with my hand to see a frightened child.

'Who's looking beautiful then?' Granny had come back from the bedroom and caught me staring in the mirror.

'I bet even I look better than her,' I said, in an attempt to cover my distress.

Nod came in, 'She don't look too bad, Tom, are you going through for a gander?'

'I don't think I'll bother,' I said. I'd also seen the state of my nose, I looked like a snotty kid with black, runny nostrils. That could have been my smelly mask problem, I wondered momentarily what the state of my lungs might look like and immediately went into a self-induced coughing fit.

'You don't half pick 'em up Tom,' said Gran, 'she's started to cook.' He gave Noddy a strange look, the sort that said *I wonder why you think she doesn't look bad*. I try to kid myself that I'm not too bothered by fire stiffs, this one wasn't really burnt but she'd definitely felt the heat. The old lady had been killed by poisonous gasses, she could have been asleep apart from the frozen gasp of her over ripe mouth. She disturbed me, I wasn't going back.

'She's very stiff, is that *rigor mortis*?' Nod asked.

'Probably just the heat, it tightens the muscles,' answered Gran.

I wondered whether I should visit her chamber but catching this bit of Nod and Gran's conversation kicked that notion well into touch. I decided the memory of my hand on her cold pulpy foot was enough. I walked out.

'Where's the boys?' the Guvnor asked.

'In the front lounge Guv,' I said, 'will we be preserving the scene?' That's the other thing I don't like about fires with stiffs. We end up hanging around for ages. Rodney gave Frankie instructions about cooking the supper. It was going to be a while before we got back tonight. I hoped there would be enough time in between his usual phone calls not to burn the dinner.

Bones had decided that I needed a talking to; he was only a couple of years older than me but he was coming across all fatherly. That was bones though, always looking out for his boys.

'You wanted to have a chat?' I said. He came straight to the point.

'Don't move out Tommy, that house is just as much yours as hers, you know that don't you?' he said.

'I've already left I suppose, but it's just as much the bank's to be honest Bones, we're in negative equity. She's welcome to it.' I had no desire to start wrangling over something that was probably worthless.

'So where are you going to stay? Are you still with Toby?'

'Yeah, he's been really good.' I was starting to think there was a conspiracy going on, I'd had this conversation with Frankie.

'I've got a room if you want it.' I tried, unsuccessfully to hide the horror from my face, I imagined his tribe running riot and that would be on one of their good days.

'No, no, Bones I couldn't, how can you have room anyway, have you built an extension?'

'No, not at home, I've got another gaff.' Bones looked briefly into the distance, probably adding up the cost of the next member of his tribe. 'I'm doing up another place. The thing is, I'm a bit worried about squatters and stuff; it's not that secure.'

'I think I'm interested Bones, if you're talking about a house sitter?'

'It's got to help me if someone's living there, but it's a bit rough, so no rent.'

'So how much of it is a building site?'

'Well, it's not the Ritz Tommy, and you will have to room shuffle as we develop; I could even find you some work if you want?' I was so keen I gave him a big hug. Although somewhere, in the back of my brain, I registered that he had said develop and not decorate.

'Easy Tom, have a look first. Have you got much stuff?'

'No, I'm walking away with half a suitcase of clothes and my CD player, that's all my worldly goods.'

'What's a CD player when it's at home?'

'It's easy to see why you've got loads of kids, Bones; it's music, the latest thing.'

'You'll have to tell me about it, when I can't sleep sometime. Have a look tomorrow, there's some furniture there from the last owners.'

That was me sorted, to be honest I loved the idea of roughing it for a while.

13

August 1984
Corridors

I never knew whether some of our games were original or had been passed down over the years. Sometimes we seemed to be chatting away, especially on nights, and before you knew it, we were larking about again. The internal corridor that linked the whole of our floor was one unbroken stretch, a narrow, wooden-decked, stadium. As far as we are concerned it was built for playtime. Sometimes it was a bowling alley but the snooker players used to moan that we were damaging their balls. It is ideal for Mattress Racing; one of those events where everyone knows the rules but no one knows the rules. We made them up as we went along.

'Come on Nod, your go,' I egged him on but he didn't need that much encouragement.

'How far can I go?' he asked.

'Far as you want,' I said.

'Lambeth bridge, if you feel like it,' said Toby. He moved further back for his run up. The mattress waited patiently, inverted, shiny side down and expectant. It was centrally placed in line with the previously talcumed course and variable starting line. We slept on almost four inches of non-luxury cushion, laid on top of a two-foot-wide metal bed. Okay for a few hours rest and ideal as a chariot for riding in the latest tournament.

All was set as Noddy began his approach. 'Go Noddy!' we cried. He launched himself and landed flat on the spongy, sports kart. It moved, but only in that it changed shape and tried to become flatter and wider. Nod was winded and dejected.

'Too high Nod, you've got to get the trajectory much lower,' advised Frankie. He seemed to have declared himself the expert but hadn't even had a go yet.

'Go on then Frank, give it a go,' I suggested.

'What and get that talc all over me new Jekyll's.' Franks light blue uniform trousers had a crease down the front that you could have shaved with.

'Surely not Frank, if you get the right *trajectory*,' said Rod.

'Alright, get ready for a record.' He adjusted the *Luge*, for it had now become a vehicle of infinite speed. He took a step back with one eye closed and then pretended, once more, to realign his future carriage on its whitened fairway.

'I hope you're not trying to gain an extra couple of inches,' I said. He held his hands in the air for dramatic effect, turned and walked slowly back towards the Mess.

'Get on with it, Frank, we're off duty at nine,' howled Toby. With that he stopped, spun to face waiting spectators and took up his starting position, a sort of frozen mid-run pose. He concentrated on his target, the baying crowd (us) faded into the background as his eyebrows furrowed. He swayed back and forth, once, twice. We got into his rhythm and then suddenly, without warning, he was running. He raced along the corridor like he was doing an Olympic hurdles course without the jumps, his long legs high enough to stride any fence. He took off like a torpedo, sleek and low. Before we knew it, Frankie and mattress were skidding along the floor. A great cheer went up as he picked himself up at the end of his record attempt.

'Not enough talc,' he said. Toby and Nod were already applying another couple of layers along our Cresta Run as Frankie pulled the bobsleigh back to the starting block.

'What's all the bloody row? What are you lot up to now?' The Guv had come out of his room.

'Oh dear,' I muttered under my breath as we all seemed lost for words. He had our attention and without another word he sprinted; I can't remember seeing him run before. 'It's just been re-talced Guv,' I said too late, as he unceremoniously flung himself into the air without any regard for technique. I swear he virtually took off; he went further than any of us, straight into the radiator beyond the pole house and stopped faster than he started. I thought it was going to come off the wall.

'Shit, we've broken the Guv,' whispered Toby.

He got up, took a bow and said, 'Anyone beaten that?'

'No, that takes all the prizes Guv,' I said, as we all started to clap.

'Alright, enough for tonight, put it away,' he said.

'Did your rank markings protect your shoulder from that radiator Guv?' I asked.

'I had to use something as a brake Tom, and they work better than tomatoes.'

'Night Guv,' we all said. I thought, *I bet his shoulder's killing him.*

We all went back to the Chummery to wind down before hitting our own mattresses, hoping they wouldn't move until morning.

Distant bell, click, LOUD BELLS, lights come on.

It must have been well into the night, the bells dropped and it felt like I'd been asleep for hours. It was unusual for a night duty, even if we don't go out ourselves, we are at least disturbed when the TL gets a shout. I always sleep light and wake up easily, but Toby could become comatose. He would pull his pit into the middle of the dormitory so we could kick him awake on our way out. He was on the second semi-naked lap of his disturbed bedding as I passed him by.

'Toby, wake-up!' I shouted. He finally came round and started to fumble with his trousers.

Dawn was threatening an appearance through the back of the appliance bay as I slipped down the pole. It has been a quiet night, I mused, wondering what time it really was.

'Automatic Fire-alarm Actuating, The Grand Hotel, Westminster's ground,' shouted Noddy.

'Again?' the Guvnor sighed; we had been there a few times already this tour. Frankie threw a left onto Lambeth Bridge and we could see clouds of thick smoke deep in Westminster's ground.

'Typical,' said Noddy, 'they've got a real job and we've only got an AFA.' We all just looked at him, trying to string the words together at this hour of the morning.

Finally, Frank managed it, 'That's us dumb klutz.' He was more awake than the rest of us, which was just as well, being as he was driving. So often a call to an AFA is due to a fault, so much so that we expect them to be false alarms. It must have been Nod's first shout to a fire alarm that wasn't malfunctioning and had actually done its job.

'He's made them up,' shouted the Guv. None of us had heard the radio traffic, being more interested in Nod's attempts to pretend he knew it was our shout; all he was really doing was reminding us that he was still the Junior Buck.

As we approached the Hotel, we could see Westminster's two machines scattered about the main entrance, they looked like they had been dropped from the sky and had landed between a sea of knitted hose that wove around the appliances and some parked vehicles who wouldn't be joining this morning's rush hour.

The Grand stood menacing, threatening the morning's peace. Several plumes of smoke coursed into the dawn sky, trespassing over the Victorian façade. A nine-story imposing backdrop to firefighters' shouts, flashing beacons and revving fire pumps. We were about to add to the chaos.

The Guv leaned over before we stopped and spoke, 'Nod, give them a hand with water supply, you two BA.' Toby and I were already in sets, we jumped off and gingerly picked our way through the melee to BA control. The crews had obviously been working hard but it looked like they might need more than just Nod's help, there was lots of unconnected hose lines and unfinished mayhem. The AFA was still screaming its warning for everyone to get out and we were getting ready to go in.

'Nod's got his work cut out,' I said to Toby. I was wondering how many machines would be here by the time we got back out to the street.

'Where's the fire Guv?' Toby asked the Station Officer who was standing in pole position at the front of the wailing building.

'Dining room, ground floor, my guys are in there, they've *got it*, you're search and rescue.' I was wondering how the place had got so full of smoke. We don't get taught much about fire prevention, but enough to know that smoke shouldn't be percolating from so many upper windows if the fire was in a ground floor dining room. More machines were turning into the street, I'd heard a firefighter say they had made it six, I looked again at the smoke and *thought it's going to need more machines than that.*

Toby and I were told to search the fourth floor, there had been reports of guests missing from levels three and four.

'I can see the stair over there Tobe,' I said pointing through the murky foyer.

'Yep, let's do it then,' he answered, we started up our sets, handed in our tallies and found our way through the lobby to the main stair. I could hear jets working, but couldn't work out where from, somewhere past reception. There was a line of hose leading that way and another going up the stair which was our target. The doors were propped open with service trollies.

'Not quite *got it* then,' I said. I wondered if there was some jargon I had missed, I thought *got it* meant the fire was virtually out. It was with this in mind that we began our climb. The hose disappeared into the first floor, clearing the staircase and making it easier to negotiate. I was trying hard to conserve air by keeping a steady rhythm; Toby didn't even seem to notice we were going upwards. The smoke was just thick enough to make vision difficult and keep our minds focused on remembering the way that would eventually become our exit.

We had only gone a few flights when we almost crashed into another crew on their way down. They were struggling with a large body.

'Do you need a hand,' Toby rasped.

'No, we're okay, we've only just found her, she was here on the stair. Mind her suitcase.' They sat her down to get a better lift. I could only just make out what they were saying, but then I saw her bag, poised to send us back to the ground floor. It stood, murderously imitating the vast Victorian block and probably having already killed its owner.

'Where were you meant to be searching?' I asked, as they made more than one attempt to lift her body, she was beyond giving them any help with her rescue.

'We are three,' they said.

'We are going to carry on to four,' I said. I moved her deadly belongings out of everyone's way, and we continued our ascent.

The higher we went the less we could see. The fire effluent must have been finding lots of background routes into the rest of the hotel. Creeping into service ducts and badly finished floors, into cupboards and around pipework; polluting accommodation levels as it expanded through previously ignored cracks and cavities. We arrived at the fourth-floor landing, the place was now thick with smoke and we couldn't see a thing, including each other. The stair doors were wedged open to the accommodation level; Toby closed them.

'How you doing, Tom?' Toby said.

'Good. You?'

'Yep, which way?' The speech diaphragms were performing to their usual standard and I could only just make out what he had said.

'Go right, it's as good as any.' I put my hand on Toby's shoulder and from now on we became a single creature; more afraid of losing each other than of

156

getting lost. It was like crossing an invisible threshold, gone was the vague safety of the stair as we delved further into the unknown. My heartbeat increased as I realised how far into this vast building we had already come. I wondered if we would find anyone else who thought they had enough time to pack before they responded to the alarm. I also realised that it was a classic safety message, even before I'd joined up, I could remember the warning not to go back for your luggage.

We continued along the passage, practicing the BA Shuffle. This is nothing like the Harlem Shuffle, but if you could see through the smoke, you might think we were doing a strange dance. It's a slow dance, a sweep of an outstretched leg and a wave of a protective arm, testing we weren't about to walk into a trap. We knew it was a corridor but it was still a sightless exploration, a greyed-out tube, luring us with an expectation of finding a *live one*. I could feel both walls, one with my spare arm and the other with my boot. Without having to agree a plan we begun to search opposite walls; Toby was also testing the way ahead.

Although our job was to find the remaining guests, I was more worried about remembering the way out. Self-preservation had become my prime function, the search only a secondary exercise. All the time that we had some idea of where we were and our route out, we could allow the luxury of attempting a rescue. I asked Toby again if he was okay but I think I just wanted to hear his rasping reply for my own comfort.

At the first room I felt for heat with the back of my hand, the door and handle were cooler than I was. Although the fire was supposedly downstairs, we still go through this safety procedure at every door, you never know what could be on the other side. We held our air gauges up to our masks and decided that we both had loads of air. I gingerly opened the door and Toby followed me inside. A massive sheet strewn bed centred the equally huge room, both were empty, as was the en-suite.

I wondered if Red and I could afford a night here; I could have slept on the carpet, it looked that comfortable. I thought I could hear someone shouting. I leant close to Toby's ear, 'Did you hear that?' Toby said something I didn't understand and shrugged his shoulders. I wasn't sure if he had heard anything or not but we moved on. I tried to put a Chinagraph cross on the door to indicate it had been searched.

'I can't see it Tobe.' He already had his axe out and scratched out a cross. 'That's better,' I said, feeling the damaged door with my fingertips. No one could ever accuse us of subtlety.

We shuffled along, through the obscure racetrack towards the next chamber. I was becoming a little more relaxed, something I can only explain by the lack of thick smoke in the bedrooms. I thought I had an awareness of my surroundings, it was certainly hallway shape but with every sweep of my boot I kicked and tripped over small items, thudding and smashing as I went. I couldn't understand what was littering the floor. We didn't have time to investigate, they weren't person sized, just a distraction. We searched a room on the opposite side of the aisle; it was empty. The next was also unoccupied but this time Toby pointed to my ear and put a cupped hand around his own.

We were both on the same page, we could hear someone or something, howling like an animal. Toby pulled me over to an open window, the howl was louder. There was smoke swirling around, probably coming up from the fire floor at ground level. As some of the grey clouds cleared, we could see a pyjama clad man on the ledge below and opposite.

'Ayiee, ayiee,' he squeaked repeatedly, a high-pitched whine that we couldn't understand, although it was quite obvious what he needed.

'What the fuck's he saying?' I said but Toby just shrugged. Shouting in a BA set is a waste of time so I tried waving out of the window to attract his attention. I suppose I was trying to mime, that he should stay there and we would come and get him. I probably wouldn't have been successful if we were standing face to face, let alone across a void, above his head and through the clouds of burnt fire gasses.

'Best to just go and get him,' said Toby, shaking his head at my impression of Marcel Marceau. I agreed and we both looked out the window to try and assess where he was. We hadn't realised but the hotel was built around a central open core; Mr Squeaky was one floor down and not quite opposite. He wasn't going anywhere, he was balanced on a ledge and squeezing the life out of a drainpipe.

He continued with his spooky song, 'Ayiee, ayiee.'

The smoke in the ring-road that linked the bedrooms hadn't got any thinner. We retraced our steps blindly, but as quickly as possible, and then down a flight. This new focus created an apprehension all of its own, our once careful navigation was now rushed and had the potential for costly mistakes. I was unnecessarily worried, Toby had become a super-firefighter and was moving as if guided by an inner radar.

'It must be circular Tobe, this way might be quicker,' I pointed left. I was assuming the layout of the third would be the same as upstairs.

'It might not,' Toby pointed right, the same way we had come above, 'we can work it out better if we go the same way.' It was reasonable logic, and it wouldn't make that much difference. We hurried as much as we could, attached to each other by hand and shoulder. I was still playing football with more strange and minor floor occupants that Toby somehow avoided. Any remnants of virtual awareness had vanished, I even managed to kick over what must have been a small table and smash what could have been a vase. The path stretched away under my feet, I had no idea how far round we had come. Toby stayed focused and soon stopped.

'Do you reckon we're there?' I said. Toby went straight through the bedroom to the window; we were only two rooms out. Strangely, I was glad, if he'd been right first time I'd have freaked, probably handed in my notice at the next opportunity and joined the Foreign Legion.

'Shall we mark this room,' said Toby.

'It might be confusing for anyone finding an isolated cross.'

'Yeah, leave it.' We moved on quickly.

Having found the right room, we went straight to the open window. Our masked heads, appearing from the gloom must have looked both alien and frightening. Our potential rescue, attempted to squash the drainpipe as if it was made of Playdough, and then shuffled backwards into the gap between it and the wall. He didn't look happy to see us which was quite disconcerting. I tried to speak but the noises from our exaggerated breathing valves were now louder than our foreign voices muffled by the speech diaphragms. I hoped our yellow helmets would relay the relief we thought he should be feeling. I wondered who else he would be expecting. He wasn't having it; Mr Squeaky stopped his strange chant but he wasn't about to leave his ledge. He also didn't understand English, so my mumbled powers of persuasion were not getting anywhere.

I looked down at what was now a clearer view of the lower floors and sub-basements. There was no way we were going to get a ladder to him, even if it could be manoeuvred into the central core it wouldn't reach. I was thinking of making a bridge with a short extension ladder from opposite, but the smoke was just as thick over there. It would also have been too dangerous; my mind was wandering again and getting a bit over creative. Then something changed his mind. I guess he didn't want to come back into the smoky room but had finally decided that Toby and I were his best option. He gave us his hands and we led him off of the windowsill and back into the hotel bedroom.

There was a second staircase much closer to his room, it became our only option. He wouldn't let go of either of our hands so we had to lead him in a three-person chain, sideways along the narrow escape path; it could have been a nursery school outing. He coughed and coughed but still wouldn't let go of our hands. We couldn't move him fast enough, thinking he was going to collapse any minute, but we were soon in the relative safety of a smoke free stair. Toby and I slipped off our facemasks, ready to escort him down and out of the building.

'We should have used this stair earlier, it's almost clear,' I said, 'I wonder where it leads?'

'You alright mate,' Toby asked Mr Squeaky, he obviously wasn't. Streaming red eyes glared vacantly from his soot-streaked face. He couldn't answer, he kept looking at each of us in turn with wide-eyed wonder. I thought perhaps he didn't know until that point that we were human. The removal of our masks seemed only to add to his confusion. I expected him to start squeaking again.

'Hi guys,' I said, two firefighters were coming up the stair but not in BA, 'are you busy?' They didn't answer straight away, as if we'd caught them out, then they saw all three of us.

'We're just checking for casualties,' they said.

'You couldn't take this guy out, could you? We just pulled him off an internal ledge,' said Toby.

'Of course, where are you going then?' One of them answered. They acted like we'd given them a present.

'We're searching the fourth,' I said.

We went back to our original place on the fourth floor, but we only had enough air to search a couple more rooms.

'What you on Tobe?' I asked for an air check.

'Pretty low, is it time to leave?'

'One more room?'

'Yeah, that should do us,' Toby dropped his air gauge and tried to open the next door. The way in was blocked and took a bit of shoving.

Face down and now un-wedged from behind the door was a semi-dressed gentleman. I don't know why but I wasn't expecting to find anyone else, I knew it was time for us to exit and had considered our task complete. It hadn't occurred to me that one more room could mean another person, I was thinking of it as another cross on a door.

This guy wasn't making as much noise as matey on the ledge, he was unconscious and we weren't sure if he had a pulse or not. We couldn't tell whether he would ultimately make it, but that wasn't our call. Toby and I looked at each other, checked our gauges and shrugged our shoulders. We would easily have got him out within safety margins before we found our other friend. The extra work of carrying him was going to push us to the limit, especially me; I had less air than Toby.

I grabbed him under his armpits whilst Toby grabbed his feet and we unceremoniously humped him back through the scatterings we had left strewn around what was now a rescue route. We were closer to the main stair so without really thinking we rushed for that exit. It was still smoke logged, which turned out to be a major miscalculation on our part.

When we arrived there was no help, and we were both exhausted, *typical* I thought. I looked again wanting two firefighters to be patrolling this stair, ready to take Mr Quiet, but we were alone. Toby and I repositioned ourselves for the carry down and had only gone a few steps when tragedy happened, at least that's what it felt like to me. My air supply had got dangerously low and my warning whistle started to sound. I answered Toby's question before he asked, 'No worries, we've not got far to go, I'll be okay.'

We could hardly have dumped him on the stair, it wasn't an option and it was far too smoky to remove our masks. We bumped him down, only supporting his upper torso. It was the best ride we could manage in the circumstances, probably uncomfortable but he wasn't objecting.

When we got to the main entrance and fresh air, my whistle was really giving it some volume, we both should have left the hotel ages ago. The first person I saw was a Senior Officer, glaring at me, he hadn't seen the casualty we had now laid gently on the steps. He certainly wasn't deaf though, and he was heading my way. I ripped off my mask and gave him a direct order before he could speak, 'I need a medic now.' I pointed towards Toby and our second rescue. I remember back in training school, being told that *anyone* could give an order to *anyone* on the fire ground in order to achieve an urgent goal. I never knew it was going to be so satisfying.

We passed Mr Quiet to an ambulance crew and took our sets back to the machine. We took our time getting back to the job, no one would grudge us a bit of a breather, and of course the Canteen Wagon had arrived, we had to make the standard detour to sample its delights. By the time we got back to the front of the hotel things were winding down. The fire was out and most of the smoke had cleared. There was lots of talk about the unlikely coincidence of so many false alarms followed by a major fire. This would be dealt with by our Fire Investigators and the Police.

I found an Officer and asked, 'We were search and rescue on the fourth Guv, can we go and have a gander?' It's always nice to go and put all the pieces together and see what the place was like that you previously only vacantly groped your way around.

'Of course you can guys, and well done by the way.'

'Thanks Guv,' I realised that this was the Officer I'd given an order to about half an hour ago. There was no mention of my less than glorious exit with my whistle sounding. I guess, due to the rescue, I'd gotten away with that one.

Once again, we passed the abandoned suitcase on the stair. It had been moved again and was now holding open some doors. Our internal soot laden corridor was a revelation; for such a limited space it held many surprises. Toby and I looked at the floor and then at each other, our major confusion answered. It was littered with teapots, broken crockery and the odd shoe; no one had told us we should have been delivering breakfast and a shoeshine service on our first visit. What was more dramatic was the sweeping artwork, drawn on the smoky carpet and walls by our feet and arms, it would have impressed any BA instructor.

My mental picture, created by touch and a fair amount of boot, was not replaced by this damaged reality. There was no light switch moment, no chasing away of the darkness, for me there will always be two corridors. This one for all to see, and the shadowy veil that we navigated earlier. The revelation for my senses that clarified and explained our route was limited to the superficial. The first path, the one we blindly navigated, was a monochromatic, manufactured image that I created whilst deep among the tension, that is the one I remember.

There was also no picture of vandalised doors in either memory! Toby was euphoric, I could see it in his face, even in his hands, everything said, *wow, I loved that.* His whole body radiated excitement. I didn't need to ask but I did because I wasn't feeling the same.

'How was it for you then Toby?' I said.

'Fucking great Tom, fucking great.'

'I knew someone would say something about the doors though, you and your sign of the cross.'

'Awe, take no notice Tom, the wanker must think we're schoolteachers.'

'Yeah, carry a bit of chalk! Like it's still gonna be there when we get to search the next hotel!' I was feeling better, Toby's energy was infectious. I know we pulled two people out but the second was dead; I had no doubt. I was also starting to regret handing over Mr Squeaky to the other firefighters. No one seemed to have heard about our drainpipe extraction. It dawned on me that I was expecting a bit of kudos. I had always told myself that I didn't need an accolade. I'd imagined trying to retreat from any praise, humbly congratulating the rest of the crew.

We often show people the way out or guide them to safety but this felt like a real rescue. I was shocked to discover that I wanted, or maybe needed, recognition. I thought again about our second rescue, wondering whether he would be alive if we had found him before Mr Squeaky.

'Mexican dogs,' yelled Toby, he brought me back from my thoughts to the now late morning; I would have to thank him one day.

'What's that?' Nod asked, he had found us and was having a look at our handy work. I think he thought we were talking about the damage to the corridor.

'Chihuahuas, Nod, two-hours, Mexican dogs,' I tried to explain, 'it's gone ten Nod, we've got two hours overtime. He sort of grinned, I'm sure he hadn't worked it out.

'What's the matter Nod, not been on any good AFAs lately?' Toby gave him a brotherly hug.

14

September 1984
Bunnies and Dogs

There was a big discussion in the mess. It was the tour before our weekend away and the boys were nervous.

'I'm not coming,' said Frankie.

'Really!' I said. I'd spent all summer organising, collecting money, getting tickets, changing tickets (Red), and most importantly overseeing the growing beer fund. I'd thought, briefly, that I would be going on my own when my wife left. That had thankfully changed when Red came on the scene. We'd been seeing each other for a few months and she was eager to meet the rest of the family.

'I can't, someone's bound to mention the baby, I haven't really sorted it out at home yet,' Frankie was unusually tense.

'We won't say anything, you must know us better than that,' Gran was upset.

'No, it's the wives, you know what they're like when they get together, I can't put Barbara through that.'

'I'm not going either,' Bones had just joined us.

'What! I mean what's wrong with you Bones?' I was beginning to think I might be going on my own after all.

'I shouldn't have said anything either, apparently it's far too early. I don't know what I was thinking about.'

'Well, I haven't even told the misses,' said Rodney.

'Yeah, but you're not going Rodders,' I said.

'Eileen knows but she won't say a word if that's the case,' said Granny. Nod said that his Linda wouldn't say a word and Toby insisted that Helen could be trusted.

'I dunno, it's too risky,' said Bones, 'you know what Julie's like.'

164

'Too risky for you! I'm talking major marital disaster,' Frank was worried, so was I. I could imagine it all going to rat shit instead of going to Guernsey. In the end the boys persuaded both Bones and Frank to come along. I think the biggest argument had been when Nod asked how they were going to tell their wives they weren't going. I didn't think it was that much of a problem, Frank was always mucking Barbara around, we all wondered how she put up with him, and as for Bones, well, he was always worried about Julie.

We met on the vast concourse of Waterloo Station, almost a full complement of landlubbers and one floaty, Jules and his misses, Kate. Only Rodney, the Guvnor and the rest of the floaties were missing. We'd decided to wear dark glasses and carry obscure newspapers to ensure we recognised each other. One or two of the many commuters turned their heads but that was all, we were still only a minor distraction. It was a toss-up between Toby's Morning Star and my Hastings Observer as to who had the best paper but Frankie won the Glasses outright. It wasn't that they were anything special really, but he insisted they were unbreakable.

'Yeah, easy to say,' I remarked.

'You'll have to prove it,' said Granny. He had an audience now, it was as if the whole station was waiting. He took them off, threw them on the floor and stood on them. The cavernous Dome of Waterloo Station waited.

The next few seconds lasted minutes, just enough for belief to creep in. Even Frankie's face turned from hesitation to assurance. He cracked a smug grin to welcome victory and it was as if that was all it needed.

CRR...UN...CHH!

It was long and drawn out and I was convinced it echoed. Then it was lost in the rapturous laughter that definitely got the rest of the station's attention. At this rate we wouldn't need much of the £300 beer kitty; we hadn't even had a drink. We changed its name from kitty to The Cat; for some reason we thought that would keep it safe.

A direct train took us to Portsmouth Harbour and that's where the games really began. I shouted, 'Dead Ants.' Eileen dived on her back and waved her arms and legs in the air. Everyone else looked on in amazement and wonder. Red thought she was having an epileptic fit and tried to get up the gangplank to help but couldn't get through. Granny's wife soon realised she was on her own and stood up, giggling.

'A bit premature,' said Granny.

'I was just trying it out for size, I didn't expect anyone to go, I haven't told them yet,' we were at the back of the queue.

'The missus has been on many a rugby tour, she knows the rules.' Eileen was totally unperturbed and was explaining the game to those around. Even some we'd never met before, innocent bystanders who, by the look on their faces, were thinking they should have got a different ferry. I caught up with Eileen as soon as I could to apologise.

'What?' she said, 'I thought it was a great call, imagine if we'd all gone for it on the gangplank.

'Yeah, we might not all be here,' Bones was pretending to be indignant but wasn't fooling anyone, least of all his wife. I wondered if she was thinking, *I thought I left the kids at home.* I also wondered if she'd be happy about the games and the drinking, but that was between her and Bones; we were sworn to silence. Julie was her normal resplendent self; she was never a skinny woman but she was hiding the pregnancy well.

By now the rumour had spread and everyone was on tender hooks, waiting for the next call. Mrs Granny could have fitted under his armpit, she was a very slim brunette with a cheeky grin. They still managed to look like they were made for each other, despite their difference in height. If you were pairing up strangers you would probably put them together, guided by some subconscious awareness.

'I think I'm due a free drink though Tommy, I might have been the only Dead Ant but that also makes me the last and now it's my call.'

'I think you deserve one Eileen, but it is meant to be a forfeit.'

'Anything that's wet Tom, anything.' I could see things getting out of hand; it was going to be a great crossing. We spent most of it in the bar, a rather unwelcoming room with an ambiguously sloped floor. We managed to make a base just off centre and began by playing Buzz, a drinking and counting game where you can't say any number with a three in it or that is divisible by three. When that became familiar, it never became easy, Granny added fives and we were playing Fizz, Buzz.

We had a go at Fizz, Fuzz, Buzz, not only replacing every three with a buzz, sevens with a fuzz and all fives with a fizz, but also changing direction around the circle after each fizz, fuzz and buzz. It really wasn't worth the effort, not only because of the sheer, drunken, memory impossibility, but also because someone was constantly at the bar buying another drink.

The wives and girlfriends were starting to relax and even join in, although there was still some reservation. Most of them had met before at our Christmas parties but that was about all; most of the boys just let them get on with it. Red was a natural mixer, although they all were gossiping like they'd known each other for years. I wondered if they were getting a little idea of the closeness we feel for each other; a brief glimpse into our world and our other family.

Granny told me how important these social gatherings were, he said our partners needed a support bubble of their own, just knowing there was someone else in the same position as them was a start. Someone else at home alone while we were on duty.

The weekend became a blur of pints, cocktails, drinking games and even some sightseeing. It had turned out that my decision to get a cheaper trip by going in September was a double success as a lot of the tourist trade had faded but left the sunshine behind, most of the time. Toby and I hired a couple of tandems for a day, with the excuse of seeing a bit more of the island, but they were really to blow out the accumulated hangovers. We were criss-crossing the cobbled old town streets to get used to them when it started to rain. We dived into the nearest pub just to get out of the drizzle; we had hardly begun cycling but there was no point getting wet. It turned out to be only a shower and we came out to a blazing afternoon. We also came out to just one tandem.

'Your bike's only been nicked Toby,' I said.

'What they moved yours and took ours from underneath,' he answered.

'Well, it was worth a try, we'll take a stroll back to the shop and face the music, see you guys back at the hotel if we don't bump into each other.' We could have arranged a meet, but I didn't know what sort of reception we would get at the bike shop.

'No, we'll go Tom, you carry on, it really could have been either bike, they all look the same.'

'Don't you dare Toby, I might even get him into a shop or two,' said Red. Now it was Helen's turn to look disappointed as I was whisked away before any more could be said. Helen was quite like my ex-wife, which could have been disturbing but at least she spoke to me; it was more than her and Toby seemed to be doing. I wondered if our raucousness was not to her taste, it certainly didn't impress my ex-wife.

The hire shop just gave us another tandem without any fuss, apparently there is no great bike smuggling ring on Guernsey and they were sure it would turn up. They included a bike lock this time though. We had a lovely day but never saw Toby and Helen all afternoon. However, it was Frank and Barbara that nearly went missing for good.

Back in the hotel I asked Red how she was getting on with the girls. I was really just checking she was okay when, inevitably, we divided up. It turned into an interesting discussion.

'I thought Nod was your new boy,' she said.

'I know, he looks old for a Junior Buck,' I answered.

'It's not that, talking to Linda you would think he's showing you the ropes.' Nod's wife Linda was attractive in a stern sort of way and she seemed more interested in my brothers than their partners.

'He's a good lad, a bit cheeky, but he doesn't over play his hand.'

'Oh, I think she has got big plans for Noddy. All the girls are lovely but I can't work out whether some of them are just naive to your real job or prefer to think all you do is lark about.'

'Well, we're terrible at sharing stuff about the job, it's probably just that.'

'You'll always tell me everything, won't you?' This took me completely off guard. We had been having a lot of fun together but I hadn't thought much about the future.

'Of course, I will.' I couldn't work out if this was a lie or a denial of a long-term relationship. Red moved on, I think she knew it wasn't time to push things.

'Yeah okay!' she laughed, knowingly, 'There's something more important anyway.' I must have looked worried. 'We've got an hour before dinner and I was thinking about finding you a shirt.'

The shirt event had become more than a memory.

When we got to the bar Toby was already there. 'Hiya Tobe, where's Helen?' I said.

'She's in the room, did you get another tandem?'

'Yeah, no problem, did you have a good ride?'

'It's a sore subject.'

'Oh no. Are you both alright?' Red asked, thinking they'd fallen off.

'We're fine, well Helen's great she's been dragging me around the shops. We bumped into Frankie.' The way he said Frankie made it sound as if he needn't say any more.

'Go on Tobe,' I said.

'The bastard done me up like a kipper, I should have known but I didn't think he'd pull a fast one with Barbara around.' I waited for further details. 'We were chatting away and the next thing I know is that they are borrowing the bike for a try out because they might get one themselves. Not seen them since, I hope he got a puncture.' By the time he got to the end of his story we were all in fits, it seemed so unreal.

'Are they not back yet? Dinner is in half an hour,' I said.

Twenty minutes later we were nearly all there, making another dent in The Cat, but Frankie and Barbara were still nowhere to be seen. Just then a squad car pulled into the hotel car park, we knew because it heralded its arrival with a blue light and a two-tone. The mood in the lounge became a mix of worry and muted excitement. Were they all about to be treated to a holiday livener? The whole hotel was nervously watching the door, a second barmaid arrived from nowhere and immediately started whispering to the first.

The anticipation was agonising, the other guests had joined the staffs mumbling as if the near silence would prevent whatever they imagined from happening. Barbara came in first, looked at our little crowd and made a beeline for the bar. Next came the policeman, casual, but in uniform and followed closely by Frankie.

'Hi guys, this is Pete, can we get him a drink,' said Frankie.

'Of course, what do you want Pete?' said Nod.

'No, not for me, I just wanted to say hello, it's not often we get a crowd of our boys from the Big Smoke all the way over here.'

'So how do you know Frankie and Barbara, Pete?' Granny asked.

'I arrested them this afternoon. Grand theft tandem.'

'Sorry, did you say arrested,' said Toby. He looked at me quizzically.

'Yes, all a mistake. We had a tandem stolen this morning and I knew we hadn't hired one to this unlikely pair, it's a family business you know. Well, I nabbed them.'

'Tell them how you solved the real crime Pete,' there was a subtle hint of sarcasm in Frankie's tone but it went right over this Bobby's head.

'Oh, we found the other bike, or rather it got left outside our shop this evening.'

'We got lucky apparently,' said Barbara who was now on her second Bacardi.

'Is that the dinner bell,' I said.

169

'Oh yes, thanks again for the lift Pete,' said Frankie. Pete shook everyone's hand before he finally left.

'Don't ever lend me your bike again Toby.' Toby was trying to object, with a few words Frankie had managed to make it his fault! Suddenly it all became irrelevant.

'Dead Ants,' shouted Eileen, everyone dived on the floor, masses of limbs waving in the air, I missed who was last, but I was starting to suspect Granny's wife of being slow on purpose.

Dinner took a while, probably because we spent most of it on our backs and not sitting at the table. I had to call a truce, the hotel staff were very friendly but they were starting to get a little miffed. We retired to the bar, where I was accosted by Eileen, Kate and Barbara. These three had become a little gang, they even looked alike with their shades of dark hair and deep brown eyes. They were lively, definitely not shy, and happy to get the beers in. Conversely their husbands couldn't have been more different.

'Bad Bunny, Tomato, Bad Bunny,' they all begged. It sounded like some sort of dodgy soup, I had no idea what they were talking about.

I handed over The Cat and said, 'You better get a round in as well.' It was obviously another drinking game so they needed a forfeit. 'What's Bad Bunny when it's at home then Gran?'

'Oh, that's a good one, Eileen always loves that,' he didn't reveal any details. The girls came back from the bar with what looked like a pint of lager that was going off. A monster was concealed at the bottom of the glass.

'What's that?' I asked.

'It's the penalty,' said Kate.

'Yeah, but what happened to it?'

'It's half a pint of lager, half a pint of cider, with a Pernod and Black depth charge,' said Barbara. Kate held it up to the light. You could just make out a shot glass inside the pint, already erupting, turning the concoction a milky purple.

'It shouldn't be mixing yet,' Eileen was disappointed with their creation, 'but it will do.'

'If that's a forfeit, haven't we got a few dead ants from the restaurant to go first?' As I asked everyone threw themselves on their backs around the bar.

'You first Tomato,' cried Bones.

'No, but that wasn't a shout, it's not my call.'

'I think you'll find that you called truce Tommy, and you just broke it,' said Noddy. For a punishment it actually wasn't bad, but by the time the slow ants were done it was a third gone. Eileen put the glass down in the middle of the table having taken a swig. The depth charge was looking imminently dangerous. We had decided to spend our last night in the hotel bar, apparently there was some live music booked. And of course, some side entertainment from our little entourage.

'Come on Eileen,' I said, 'what's a Bad Bunny?' It occurred to me to ask her whether she ever went on *Midnight Runs* but taking the piss out of the wives is out there with messing with your bedding or grub; it's just not done. Granny looked down at me, I'm sure he was reading my mind. Eileen took over, she certainly had plenty of energy.

'It's all about ears,' she started.

'You'll be alright Toby,' shouted Frankie.

'Get in a circle and I'll show you,' everyone shuffled around to Eileen's command. Chairs were moved and tables shifted out of the way. We ended up in a sort of ring:

	Kate	Eileen	
	Jules	Barbara	
Bones			Me
Julie			Red
Linda			Helen
	Noddy	Toby	
	Granny	Frankie	

It was a long lounge with a bar at one end. There were other guests around waiting for the band. We were about to give them some warmup entertainment.

Eileen put her hands up to the side of her head. 'I'm the Bad Bunny,' she said, 'Kate and Barbs, you have to put your closest hand only, like this,' she took one hand down to demonstrate. 'You're only a bit bad.' We were all engrossed, so were the rest of the bar. 'To transfer the Bad Bunny all I have to do is take my hands off of my head, point at someone and shout Bad Bunny.'

'That's easy, how do you get a drink then,' Jules asked. I thought *he should know better, he's the oldest one here*, he should know that nothing is ever that simple.

I'm sure I heard Helen mutter, *Bloody stupid*, I don't know if she meant Jules or the game. Eileen ignored them and shouted, 'We're on.' She started to sway around flapping her ears, almost pointing at everyone, Kate and Barbara joined in the rhythm. She stopped, looked directly at Jules and shouted, 'Bad Bunny.' He obediently threw his hands to the side of his head, creating a smug pair of ears, Bones even managed to raise a left ear. Kate didn't move.

'Gulpers, both of you,' Granny was pointing at Jules and Bones. I was confused, I wasn't alone.

'I've still got ears on,' said Eileen, 'my hands have to leave my head.' Jules was disappointed as he had been bragging that he'd never get caught.

'Oh, that's quite nice,' Jules took a large mouthful of the circumspect pint and handed Bones the glass.

'What me as well,' he didn't wait for a reply and took another hefty swig. Eileen and Gran were both shouting to be careful as the depth charge smashed into his front lip.

'I think I've bled into this you'll have to get a new reward, I'll look after this one.' He took another mouthful, this time being a bit more careful, 'This is lovely.'

'Shouldn't it be at least a little unpleasant,' I said, 'it's meant to be a punishment.'

'I'll go,' said Granny, 'I think the misses is going CEOF, shall I get a round in as well?'

'Yeah, I'll help. What do you mean *cough*?'

'C.E.O.F., *cough*, Cereal Enjoyment of Forfeit.'

'Shouldn't that be S. Serial?' I didn't like to correct Granny, he was the one with the grammar school education.

'No definitely C. The way she's going she'll have her head in her cornflakes tomorrow.' I couldn't help laughing but Gran was serious. 'She hates Crème de Menthe that should slow her down.' We came back with another depth charged pint. This one had more of an emerald tinge as he held it up to the light.

'I'm not drinking anything green,' said Jules.

He did.

So did Eileen.

The weekend was a blinding success probably because we'd been too busy playing silly games to even think about babies. Even the Hotel manager invited us back. I never did find out whether Pete knew we were firefighters; I got the distinct feeling Frankie might have somehow given him the impression we were officers of the law.

Apparently, Frankie and Bones hadn't been worried a bit, they both knew it would be okay! Which they only chose to mention now we were home. Luckily for all of us, no one had slipped up and mentioned babies. That subject had remained unspoken.

However, we'd been thrown straight back into the fray and I was trying, not very successfully, to comfort a victim. She'd been in the fire and so had her dog. She was wandering around outside when we found her, a little disorientated. There were signs of soot-stained snot on her top lip and her reddened eyes were still streaming, real tears, adding to the physical effects of the fire. She was about thirty I suppose, shoeless and still in her nightgown; it was about 10 am; there were no clear bedtimes in Lambeth.

An ambulance was on its way so I tried to calm her down. She had a vice like grip on the Standard Poodle that was almost as big as she was and had probably recovered a lot faster than her. I had managed to prop her against the garden wall to stop her wandering up and down, I was sure she might fall. This was Brixton's job and they were busy putting out what smelt like a kitchen pot left on the stove.

She was telling me how she had to wake up Mitzi, the poodle, to get her out of the flat when I could see Granny and the Ambulance crew on their way over. I was feeling quite pleased with myself, even after an uneasy start I seemed to have calmed her down; she was no longer the manic parading woman we had been confronted with on arrival.

'We're going to get the Ambulance people to make sure you're okay,' I said.

'I'm alright,' she mumbled. She was obviously traumatised but I was more worried that she'd inhaled too much smoke.

'Just let them look after you for a bit,' I said. She didn't answer but nodded and squeezed the poor dog a little tighter. It started to wriggle.

'You're going to have to put the dog down,' I said.

She went into convulsions of screaming panic, 'No! Nooo!' I couldn't understand the sudden change. All my smooth talking, shattered in a second, I thought *she must be afraid of doctors or hospitals or something.*

Fortunately, Granny was close by, 'He means put the dog on the floor while we check you over, what's her name, she's lovely, I'll look after her, we'll both come along with you.' She was instantly pacified, transfixed by Granny who managed to give me a stare of disbelief.

'What's the matter Tom?' Toby had come over to see what all the screaming was about. I didn't know how to tell him, honesty seemed the best approach.

'I just threatened to kill her dog.' This was going to live with me for a while, sometimes you just know when you're not going to get away with something.

It didn't take long.

We'd had the early morning to catch-up, I think those that had missed the trip were a little jealous. Now we were in full banter mode; the shrieks and laughter were getting pretty loud and so was the barking. It was morning stand-easy and I was beginning to regret my attempt at canine casualty handling. Out of the blue our Guv put his head around the door and said, 'Is there a dog in here?' I thought not him as well. The Guv didn't normally join in with the ribbing.

'No Guv,' I replied. There followed yelps, yaps, barks and all sorts of other dog related noises. That's when I made the classic mistake, 'Alright guys, that'll do, I must have really hurt her feelings.' It was like a cat had got into a kennel as the barking became even louder. I buried my head, took a deep breath and stood up to confront them all.

'Hooowwwll.'

From my bumbling beginning, we now had a dog, many dogs! Unlike other places in the world, dogs are definitely not meant to be part of station life, but for the next few weeks we had our very own hound. Toby is an excellent mimic, I have seen staff searching for a cat in a restaurant, until we couldn't contain ourselves any longer. We made Toby stop his meowing, but still the staff kept up the search. Now he had progressed to dog. Not just barking, he could do the low-pitched growling and whimpering as well; I knew it was him but still had to look around to check.

We didn't plan anything. It just developed, the odd bowl of water left on the floor and the odd yelp here and there. Someone also brought a lead and a rubber bone and we would leave them in different places around the station. Even the Southwark boys asked us where we had picked up the Mutt, the rumour was spreading around the division. The cleaners were convinced, I even heard them discussing what breed it was.

'It's a Bitsa, bits of this and bits of that,' said Pearl.

'I haven't seen it but I'm fed up trying to sweep up all the bloody hair from all over the place,' Josie was propping herself up with her major tools, the mop and bucket, whilst her trademark fag end was magically moving but stuck firmly between her lips.

'It's a bloody mongrel alright,' added Pearl with increased authority, 'when you getting rid of that pooch, Tommy?'

'What porch? Am I getting fat?' I kept walking, managing to hold back a grin until I'd left them behind. Pearl and Josie were like old hands, they were as much a part of the fire station as the fire engines and they could banter with the best of us. Most times they got the upper hand, they had easily heard and seen it all before. This was much to the surprise of Frankie who accidently let his towel drop coming out of the shower. He was a far too slow covering himself up, almost proud of his exposure and now has a burn mark for a memory.

It could have been a reflex action but it looked far too rehearsed. It was the only time I'd seen Josie's fag leave her lips and it was also the fastest thing I'd ever seen. If you'd blinked the fag never would have left her lips and you'd wonder why Frankie had become suddenly so shy and squeamish, holding onto his shrunken manhood whilst both knees were buckling.

The dog game was almost dying a natural death when it all blew up again. We had another unwelcome visit from our friendly lump of an ADO and somehow or another he cornered me in the same place as the leash.

LOUD BELL…
Distant bell, click, LOUD BELLS, lights come on.

The TL was on its way to somewhere in the East, C Division, Noddy and I were already on our way back up the stairs. 'What happened there Tom?'

'I don't know, the bells were all over the place, probably just a glitch. I'm going to clear up the Mess for Rodney.' We were on much better terms these days, and he was driving the TL.

'Alright, I'll be right down to help, just got to go to my locker.' Nod disappeared and I walked straight into ADO Fatty Farmer as I entered the Mess room. It dawned on me all at once, the first bell must have been him announcing his arrival on the station like all good Senior Officers should, but blimey he'd moved it to get his lardy figure up here that quickly. I had an image of him wobbling along the corridor all excited; he should have waited in the Watchroom for the Guv but that seemed to have passed him by.

'What's this then?' he said.

'What's what Guv?' I said innocently, pretending I hadn't seen the chain and leather handle.

'Don't give me all that, this on the table?'

Oops, I thought, *he sounds a bit upset*. It's a well-known fact that a lot of senior officers think firefighters are a bit dumb, I was good at playing that angle. Too good.

'That looks like a dog lead Guv. Have you got a dog?' My mouth was moving too fast for the self-preservation part of my brain to keep up.

'I know it's a dog lead,' he said, becoming more animated, 'now where's the bloody dog?'

'I don't know Guv, where did you see him last?' I said with my best hurt look in response to his outburst.

'I didn't see him, I haven't got a bloody dog!' he shrieked.

'What's the leash for then Guv?' I was starting to realise there was no good end to this charade, only a shout would help. I didn't believe it when it happened and looked around to see if Granny was casting a spell.

Distant bell, click, LOUD BELLS, lights come on.

I thought he would explode, his face was going purple and glistening saliva was running down all of his chins. I had gone too far. 'Got to go Guv,' I said and I ran for the pole house, wondering if we'd left a water bowl on the floor somewhere.

We were called to an Automatic Fire Alarm actuating on Westminster's ground. We looked at each other in the back cab, the memory of the Grand Hotel was still raw. Frankie threw a right and we stopped holding our breath, we were now going in the opposite direction than our recent adventure. It gave me plenty of time to quell any impulsiveness and tell my story; Frankie nearly crashed the machine into the Houses of Parliament before I'd even started.

'I think I might be in trouble Guv, he was pretty mad.'

'And who would that be Tom? No senior officer reported to me. There can't have been anyone on my station.' Our Guv was laughing as he added, 'Alright Guy's, time to cool it on this one.'

Toby howled like a wolf as I said, 'Aw Guv we were just getting going.' But that was it, we took the invisible hound to the dog's home. I wonder if Fatty found his bowl.

He hadn't but he'd left a far worse ultimatum. It was time for the lockers to go. This was a direct order from Divisional HQ. Apparently, we were getting a fitted carpet and they had to be gone before we finished this tour of duty. After much moaning we made a plan to empty them out over these two days and get rid of them over our night duties. It had been a long battle but I guess we all knew they would go eventually.

15

Still September 1984

A Bit on the Side

I hadn't even got to the dormitory when I met Toby, towel around his waist and on his way to the shower. 'They're staying,' he screamed, 'they, are, fucking, staying!'

'Who is?' I said.

'Not who, what. What else do we want to stay?'

'What, the lockers?' He couldn't be talking about anything else. 'Who said?'

'Look, look,' he couldn't contain himself, he was nearly dumb with excitement. He took my hand and pulled me from the corridor into the dormitory and onto a lovely new carpet. A new fitted carpet, fitted around our bays of now, not so temporary lockers. I looked at Toby, we grabbed each other and started dancing around; fortunately, his towel stayed up.

'Shit, no one told the fitters. They must have started early.' It felt like we'd pulled off a bank heist, I kept looking down, unable to believe my eyes.

'It's really there Tom, who imagined they'd give us a carpet.'

'We can't move them now Toby.'

'I know, it's brilliant. Come on we might even get a couple in, this has got to be worth a celebratory pint,' Toby couldn't stop grinning. Nor could I.

After a quicker than normal shower we rushed to The Windmill, Toby got the beers and we sat at the bar. It was quiet but it normally was, Del, the landlord, had opened early for us, as usual.

'How are you enjoying living with Bones,' he asked.

'Well, he doesn't stay, I'm on my own. I'm constantly having to change rooms, it's dusty, draughty and I love it.'

'No regrets then?' There was a joking look on his face.

'Hey Tobe, no I really appreciated your help…'

'Not me, the Misses.'

'Was I married? Am I still married?'

'And what about, *I'm on my own*, doesn't Red visit?' Toby was teasing.

'Well yeah…well, you know,' I played along as if we were good little boys.

'Yeah okay! Has he got you working?'

'Yep, I'm even learning some new skills, when Bones is around long enough to show me. He must have jobs all over, he tells me what he wants done and then disappears.'

'Bit trusting Tom. No disrespect but you've never done any building work before, have you?'

'None taken Tobe, I quite agree. He's got another bloke called Don who must be worse than me, he spends more time with him.'

'Have you seen the carpet?' Granny almost spat his words out before he even got to the bar. 'Someone's dropped a bollock.'

'Easy Gran, we're in company,' I said, his excitement allowing an unusual lapse in decorum. He looked around the empty bar. 'Well okay,' I shrugged. There was only the barmaid who was out of earshot and had somehow managed not to see Granny's entrance. At this time of night, the pub was just another room of the fire station. 'I think they've dropped more than one bollock. Wouldn't it be a shame if it was Fatty Farmer.'

We had another beer. It felt like we deserved to stay all night. Nod came in, 'Have you seen the carpet?'

'It's beautiful, ain't it,' I said.

'Well, it's going to look daft when we move the lockers tonight.' I don't know what had happened to Nod, he'd shown so much promise early on.

'You better have a beer Nod, it might knock some sense into you,' Toby looked nonplussed.

We would all be celebrating this little win. The *fait accompli* that now lay neatly around our redesigned dormitory might not rock everyone's world but to us it was the best gag we'd pulled for ages. Toby thought we should send the Brigade a thank-you card for our early Chrimbo present, of course we never did.

We got back to the station even more lively than normal. Frankie had taken the night off at the last minute, I'm not sure if it was to get out of moving the lockers again or if he had other, more surreptitious plans. Granny thought he was playing away, he'd seen him leave the station this morning all scrubbed up with his toothbrush sticking out of his back pocket. Apparently, to Frankie, that was as good as an overnight bag. Consequently, we needed a stand-by driver.

Somewhere down the line there must have been a communication breakdown and Staff sent in Basil to drive the Turntable Ladder, but we only needed a driver for the Pump Ladder. Basil wanted to stay to keep up his skills on the turntable so Rodney was now driving the Pump Ladder.

That was step one in the forthcoming debacle. There are those who say it could have all been different, that this stage was really down to Frankie, but I don't blame it on his toothbrush in the slightest.

Basil certainly had plenty of practice on the TL. He not only pitched it around our yard but drove it to many shouts. It was busier than normal; I wondered if he was regretting his decision to stay.

Distant bell, click, LOUD BELLS, lights come on.

'Bloody inconsiderates, what do they want a bonfire for tonight, surely it's warm enough?' said Granny. We were off to Mepham St, again. A cosy little den, a disused railway arch open at one end and ideal for a bonfire.

'Careful Granny, we could all be there one day,' I laughed.

'Can't we ever let them keep their bit of warmth? It's only going to get colder,' said Nod, who'd found some compassion from somewhere.

'What don't you need the practice putting them out anymore?' asked Toby.

'The smoke goes straight into *The Hole in the Wall*, that's probably where the call came from, the Landlord gets upset when his punters can't find the bar,' Granny was equally sympathetic but also practical. That didn't stop us being unpopular with the clients from this arch.

'Will they never learn, how many times have we told them to try somewhere else?' I said. Unfortunately, these drifters never answered, we could have been speaking Martian. Generally, they just bowed their heads and mumbled profanities, but occasionally they got a lot more animated.

'Yeah, like Southwark's ground,' said Toby. We took a jet straight off of the hydrant just in case we needed to retreat in a hurry; there could be quite a bunch huddled around the fire. Tonight, the dingy railway arch was deserted apart from the glowing embers of abandoned flames. The inhabitants were all more interested in a mobile soup kitchen that must have arrived shortly before us and was now being mobbed. It was a surprisingly similar scene to when our Canteen Wagon showed up on large jobs.

'Make sure it's out Nod and make sure everything's wet or we'll be straight back,' said Gran. This empty, disused arch is more of a meeting place than a doss. There was no mistaking it for anything else; it was always alight, it was always dark, charcoal stained, and we were always there. I'm sure some of its visitors must have been professional arsonists; they had an uncanny knowledge of how to set light to soaking wet trash. Spalling, even blacker bricks, pointed to the usual seat of fire, although there was debris everywhere, their collection of future fuel. The place was ingrained with soot and a decent topping of rotting detritus.

The unusual lack of *gentlemen of the street* had made us relaxed. We were kicking the brands, spreading the rubbish around to help Nod, when suddenly the fire screamed…

'Fuck off.'

We all froze for the briefest of moments and stared at the talking embers. The rubbish moved unnaturally in the dim light, gradually scattering the soot-stained refuse. Granny retracted his drawn back leg that would have been a blinding kick for goal. The merest human shape grew out of the ashes, unfurled itself from what we thought was the bonfire and stumbled into a crouch. There was a streetlight nearby but the arch held onto the night, making visibility monochrome at best. The creature attempted to stand, I imagined a dark wraith emerging from a smoky chrysalis but went to help anyway.

'You alright mate,' I said.

'Fuck off.' He grew, pulsing an unearthly blue tinge having been lit by our beacons, he staggered and made a line directly towards Noddy. We were suddenly awakened from his spell and moved to protect one of our own. It was unnecessary, he took a couple of side steps, muttered something under his breath and disappeared into the night.

Nod had come close to vagrant possession, 'Did he walk right through me?'

'What the fuck was that?' said Toby.

'He should be on fire,' said Nod, 'if he had breathed on it, we would have had to make them up.'

'He would have been well alight if you hadn't drowned him,' I said.

'What do you want it to go down as Nod, a rescue or a wash down?' said Gran. The Guv sent the stop for a rubbish fire.

Our machine had been quiet the rest of the night and I had gone to bed early, I'd being doing some work for Bones, mainly demolition and removing the mess I'd created. It started off like a good workout and ended up harder than anything I'd done before; I was shagged. My unusual bedtime was step two; anything out of sync with normality had to take some blame.

Distant bell, click, LOUD BELLS, lights come on.

I hadn't really woken up, I'd finished rigging whilst still half asleep and was now leaning back with closed eyes, full faith in Rodney for some unknown reason; that was definitely step three.

We were ordered to Brixton's ground, which really isn't that far. I was dreaming of being turned back and not having to leave my drowsiness. Every second, whilst still semi-comatosed, realising that I would have to come round soon. I allowed myself a little time to think of my days off; Red was still on leave and we'd planned another mini break to the Lake District. We aimed to get the 10.05 out of Euston, a little ambitious perhaps, but I hoped to get an early relief. A couple of the Green Watch were always in early.

When it came, I was somewhere on that train, cuddling up to Red, her long hair tickling my dozing cheeks. There was an awakening thud. I thought we'd hit the kerb but we were already at too high an angle, our nearside wheels were definitely airborne. I'd felt this before with Rodney, on one of the rare occasions I got to ride on the back of the TL. He'd managed then, to briefly fly the machine around a roundabout, miscalculating the speed to circumference ratio but quickly returning to *terra firma*. This seemed different, higher. We continued to tip, no one was breathing. We weren't coming down, not on our wheels anyway.

There is a moment, mathematically, where the appliance would have been perfectly balanced. We could have driven along that way, like a circus trick, but Granny's weight was too high. He was sitting next to what were now the upper windows. Any hope that he may have slowed our trip through equilibrium was vacant and fanciful. At some stage we went over my imaginary fulcrum and time slowed down, it might have already become protracted, I can't remember.

They say that moments before death your whole life flashes before you; that didn't happen. However, I was aware of every detail of every instant, every second lasting long minutes. There was no: nappy/school/first shag moment, just full awareness of each nanosecond. Our journey through ninety degrees took forever. I felt the weight shift slowly in my direction as we passed the point of no return, when whatever we had hit had won and lifted us further than we wanted to go.

This was the time when I realised, *we have definitely fucked up;* my mind was able to rationalise whilst also recording the details of our physical misfortune. Everything was exaggerated: I could see the hair on Rodney's ears, the streetlights beamed reflection through our oblique windscreen, the Guvnor's whitening knuckles, Toby's helmet sliding along the shelf between the front and back cabs. It could have been traveling backwards as it was losing the race to keep up with the appliance. The machine strained, different parts fought with each other, yelling war cries at the other factions, some pulling, some squashing in indecision. I was convinced it was ripping itself apart.

The guys were speaking, screaming, but I couldn't make out their howls. The appliance angles were now all wrong, it had become a variable diamond. The gradual arc of sideways travel had also sent my own stabilisers out of their comfort zone. The machine was fighting back, battling the dance between the chassis and the superstructure.

The machine was losing.

The Tarmac reached through my open window trying to grab anything it could. There was another thud, a smack, louder, more final, a shattering and scraping encounter. The second ninety degrees had happened a lot faster. Gran landed on Toby, Toby landed on Nod, they all landed on me, several loose bits of kit joined in. We hadn't stopped moving, forward momentum was still in loose control. Quickly the friction of the gravely roadway bit into our red metalwork.

We stopped.

After an elapse of silence which heralded a few moans, the Guvnor asked, 'Everyone okay?'

'Yes Guv,' said Nod.

'Yes,' said Granny.

'Yep,' said Toby.

'Fucking 'ell,' said Rodney.

'Jees, you're fucking heavy Gran,' I added.

'I'm asking again, can everyone move, any blood and guts where they shouldn't be?' said the Guv.

'Where the fuck did he come from?' said Rodney. I couldn't see the Guv or Rodney now, I was being squashed between, forty odd stone of London's finest above, and the wrong bit of fire engine below. Everyone grunted an okay, including me.

I could hear the Guv sending a priority message, '…bravo, two, two, one, unable to proceed to…*wherever we should have been going*, request full RTA attendance to…*wherever we were now.*' He was calmer than usual, if that was possible. As he spoke, I imagined the other end of the radio, the ethereal place that existed behind the clipped language that was Brigade Radio Procedure, the human part. A windowless Control Room, separated across the space of London, connected by waves, separated now, by silence. Our Guv's message carved through operational procedure in that room and added a practiced alert. The wait grew, seeping into every corner, into the carpet, into the ceiling tiles. The merest hint of perspiration shone like a jewel atop the crisp troubled uniform of the radio operator.

'Bravo, two, two, one, will you be forming part of the required attendance to the road traffic accident?' she said.

'Answer…' The Guv dropped the bloody radio handset. 'Fuck,' he said, to no one, as he scrambled for its retrieval. His new, unwanted riding position showing signs of beating his composure. A murmur returned to the Control Room as staff who had been away on breaks and such, slipped into the silence, only broken by the bleep of the Busy Signal. The Officer of the Watch stood, it was all the authority she needed and an air of command cosseted the Room.

The quiet was broken as an inattentive appliance, somewhere else in our part of London, tried to contact Control. 'All stations wait, please observe the busy signal.' The radio operator enforced her command of the air waves.

Hand over hand the Guvnor regained the radio handset, 'From Bravo 2 2 1, answer no. Further traffic over.' Dread filled the Room, knowledge giving way to emotion, as whispers hung on demons souls.

'Go ahead with further traffic, over.' She was echoing the training of the whole room saying what they knew she should say, what they would say if it had been their turn as radio operator, mouthing the words into the worried breath from her lips.

'Make ambulances two, over.' That clinched it for me and them. They knew something had gone seriously wrong and could now only dispatch help and wait.

I thought to myself, '*I might be going off duty early after all.*'

'Can you climb out boys?' The Guv was still in control. Everyone seemed okay, plenty of groans but no real injuries. Toby squeezed himself from our knot of firefighters, climbed up the BA brackets and somehow managed to open the cab door onto our new roof. Out he went, Gran followed and managed to only stand on me and Nod a couple of times. I heard the Guv telling Toby to go and check on the car driver. Rod was the last to go except me.

'Sure you are okay Tom?' he said.

'No worries Rod, after you.' It was genuine concern, I really had misjudged Rodney. As I stood up a sharp pain shot through my back and I screamed the bravest, involuntarily cry I could manage. The Guv and Gran looked back down into my pit, wide eyed.

'Shit Tom, what's up, you sound like you trod on a cat,' said Gran.

'Naw, just another one leaving. I'm not sure how many I've got left?' I said, 'I'm going to have trouble climbing out Guv.' I wanted to sit back down but the seats were now wall furnishings. Before I knew it, a piece from the short extension ladder was being lowered into the cab.

'Give that a go Tom, or we'll have to rig something up,' said the Guv. I managed the short climb one handed, I'd done something to my left hand as well as my back, but I was moving.

I emerged into the quiet of the post apocalypse, a time before we would normally arrive, into the vague, eerie silence, when the crunching and breaking of an accident were complete and resting. There was an unwarranted calm of a whispered recovery, that would emerge under the neon like streetlights, punctuated by the distant traffic signals. Voices started to replace the shocked silence, questioning and worried. Westminster's blue lights heralded my climb to the near side roof. I never imagined that this morning we would be the ones needing the assistance of the fire brigade. They took over and we allowed ourselves to become the helped, not the helpers.

'You boys are so brave,' I told them as they took me to the ambulance. Gran came along, if Frankie had been there, it would have been him; the ambulance driver was gorgeous.

'What happened then Gran,' I asked.

'I didn't see it, I was asleep, the Guvnor said a car ran the red light, Rodney didn't stand a chance, he came speeding out of nowhere and we drove right over his bonnet.'

'Shit Gran, is he okay? We could have killed him.'

'Shit Tom, he nearly killed us! He walked away.'

'But a few seconds difference and we could have driven over him.'

185

By the time we got back from hospital our lopsided machine was already standing forlorn in the yard. My treatment at St Thomas was excellent but still our misshaped fire engine had beaten me home.

I'd broken a couple of ribs and a small hand bone, but I was already feeling better. I wasn't even going to be late for my weekend date. I limped back into the office even though there was nothing wrong with my legs, my arm in a sling and my best, *I'm in so much pain*, expression.

'I've had a bit of a near miss,' I said to the guys and a couple of the Green Watch who were in early, 'I didn't see a thing but I've since become swollen and painful.'

'Piss off Tommy, nice to see there's not much wrong with you,' the Guv was being extra nice, 'Do you want to fill in the accident book now?'

'Best not Guv, I might get flash backs. I'll send in my certificate, I've got a train to catch.'

16

Late October 1984
Make and Mend

I'd managed to eke out my sick leave to three weeks and I probably could have stretched it further but I was sure Bones needed my help. I couldn't do any work on my temporary accommodation whilst certificated and I felt guilty because it seemed like I wasn't paying my rent.

It was my first day back and the Guv had decided we could stand down for the watch. *Make and Mend* he called it.

Nod was confused, 'What's that then?' he asked.

'It means we go to Shouts only, the rest of the day is ours,' I said.

'It's an old Navy term,' said Granny, 'sailors would be stood down to mend their uniforms.'

'We don't have to mend ours, do we?' said Noddy.

'No Nod,' I said. There was a strong rumour Nod had applied for promotion. I was beginning to think he had all the makings of a Senior Officer.

Our Sub Officer caught me and Nod in the corridor, not that we were doing anything wrong other than being there at the same time as he was. 'You'll do, in the office now, Bones has got a job for you,' he said. He walked right by us, off over to the river for the day. I was immediately upset, his harsh approach had made me wish I'd stayed in the Mess just that little bit longer, apart from that I was sure the Guvnor had said we were standing down.

'Ah, can you do us a favour guys?' said Bones as we entered the office.

'Of course we can Bones, anything for you,' I said. I hadn't really noticed our new cook hovering, bouncing from foot to foot. Charlie was temporary and had only been with us a couple of weeks, two weeks too long as far as we were concerned. He needed help.

When we first met him, things didn't start well. 'My name is Charles but you can call me Chas, just don't call me Charlie, I hate that.' He obviously hadn't done his research.

'Okay Charlie,' said Frankie. Charlie had definitely eaten all the pies, he was round, and he looked like a greasy version of the Pillsbury Doughboy. He also came with the props: dogtooth trousers and white jacket, complete with his past recipes, all down the front.

'Where's your white hat?' asked Rodney.

'My Toque, I didn't think it was necessary,' said Charlie; he would only ever be Charlie. I thought *that funny hat that chefs wear must be a Toque*, and wondered if I was the only one not going to let on that I didn't know what it was called.

'Blimey, no Toque Blanche, on your first day as well, that's a bit slack Charlie,' Granny obviously knew its name, I should have guessed. Charlie was an agency cook, although he assured us he was a chef. We didn't even want him to do the washing up, which he thought was a matter of dunking everything in soapy water and hoping the food waste would mysteriously evaporate.

Our real cook Abby had recently retired, she didn't want to and we didn't want her to go, but the Brigade decided that she had reached compulsory retirement age. Probably implemented by the same bright spark who hadn't organised a replacement and believed this agency provided cooks! Now Abby even had style when she washed-up. She would put her orange peel in the water; she caught me fishing it out once, 'Leave it now, it make dem cup, dem smell nice,' she said in her Jamaican accent.

Today Charlie had a real blinder for us all. 'Charlie haf loft is forth eef,' said Bones.

'What?' I said.

'Itf not bunny,' Charlie followed behind Bones as we all moved back out to the corridor.

'Where did you have them last?' Nod asked, who had obviously understood.

'On da buf, day waff urtin, fo I ook em out,' gabbled Charlie.

'On the bus? So where did you put em…them?' I said.

'Im me yacket ocket, af ufual.'

'We've been through all this,' said Bones, 'can you help him look for them?' I was starting to get a clammy feeling. We hadn't eaten yet today but the White's had, I remembered the Nurses Easter Ball and chuckled to myself maliciously.

Then it came to me, quite wrongly actually, but I could imagine the Whites hiding them, I could quite clearly see Patty sneaking about, teeth in hand. My mind raced on to our impending search, the thought of putting my hand somewhere and finding Charlie's choppers was making me quiver.

'Where else could they be Charlie?' Nod asked. Charlie looked thoughtful, which was difficult because his empty mouth wouldn't stop flapping up and down. He was miming taking his teeth out and putting them in his pocket and I was reminding myself that he was never going to get anywhere near my food.

'Yef, da buf, da buf waf cwouded, I was fwitting on da bwench.' He put his hand up and scratched the top of his head, it was becoming very surreal. There was a definite Oliver Hardy likeness, he was even dressed in black and white.

'You have checked your pockets, Charlie?' I said.

'Yef, bup I wemember now, ip waf a fwuggle.' A big smile spread across his face, one of realisation. 'Day muff be in da blowks ocket oo waf fittin nexf ta me.' He seemed quite happy to have solved his little mystery and wobbled back towards the mess. It took us a while to process the whole conversation.

'You've loft dem den,' I shouted after him.

'I'vf dot me fpwares,' he was giggling silently to himself. A yoyo of agitation, enveloping his arms and shoulders rolled down his vast barrel of a back.

'When are we getting a new cook?' I asked Bones. I was really feeling quite relieved, suddenly I could see giant sets of false teeth all over the station.

'What? I was just thinking about the man sitting next to Charlie on the Bus this morning,' said Bones.

'I wonder if he's found them yet?' said Nod.

'I wonder if he'll work out how they got there.' I said.

'Poor bastard,' said Bones, shaking his head.

As usual when we had a rest day, we didn't stop. We had been in and out all morning. A couple of shut in lifts, a skip alight and quite a few over the river. The drivers were the only ones really working as a lot of the time we were turned back before we arrived. I just looked at it as a nice ride around the West End. There always seemed to be plenty of scenery walking around that kept us extra amused.

'What happened to Fm Ted, Nod? I haven't seen him for ages. He'd love it over here,' asked Toby.

'He's standing down himself, I suppose,' I offered an explanation.

189

'No, he's in my locker,' said Nod, we really needed to liven him up. Gran was quiet as well.

'Didn't you have a game today, Gran?' I asked.

'Yeah, but I've no leave left.' That was the sort of thing that upset Gran but I was sure something else was up.

'You okay Gran?' I enquired when I thought everyone else was distracted by an attractive group of passers-by.

'Yeah, I just feel a bit out of sorts, like something is about to happen.'

'We better come off the run and lay in our pits then, something is always going to happen, that's our job,' Toby was laughing and Gran joined in but he still looked a little distracted.

I'm not sure everyone else really appreciated Gran's intuition, it was more of a joke to most of the watch, part of the banter. Gran didn't normally acknowledge it himself.

When we got back, we made Nod get Fm Ted out of semi-retirement and put him on the run. It worked as far as our stand down was concerned; we didn't turn another wheel. That wasn't all we spied in Nod's locker.

'What's that?' Toby's hand was already traveling towards what can only have been fireworks.

'Toby!' I yelled, 'Behave.' It shouldn't really come as a surprise that firefighters love fire, Toby often admitted a love of arson in his youth. Our love of fireworks however went a little way beyond acceptable.

Noddy showed us his stash, a pile of bangers and super bangers, as he called them, they were actually crow scarers. He'd managed to separate them from the timed strip that they should be on and they could now be used individually.

'Bloody hell, that's an arsenal. What are you going to do with them,' said an excited Toby.

'I've been asked to help out at my football club's bonfire party, I'm in charge of the fireworks,' said Nod, 'I thought I'd bring some in to try out.'

'Hold on, is this another part-time number you haven't told us about?' I asked.

'Naw, but that's a good idea, I just got roped in because I'm a fireman. These are some of the bangers.'

'You could start a war with that lot,' Toby made a grab for the bag to have a closer look.

'We should give them a go,' I said. We were still on stand down.

'Come on Nod, let's go downstairs, it's the weekend there'll be no one about,' said Toby, he had taken on the role of naughty schoolboy.

'Well, they might make a bit of a racket,' said Nod. He was dying to have a play but was having second thoughts, probably brought about by Toby's level of enthusiasm. 'We'll need something to muffle the noise, they were bloody loud in the sports ground,' he said. We were just about to light one anyway when I had a bright idea.

'I know just the thing, I bet Rodney still has some small bags of flour that Abby used for her pies, he won't miss one, will he?'

'What, put it in the flour?' said Nod.

'Yeah, it'll muffle the noise,' I said. I didn't wait for an answer and off we went to the Mess, Rodney was there. 'What's he doing here,' I whispered as we piled through the double doors. It was the afternoon and the Mess should have been deserted, Charlie would have gone home ages ago and I thought Rodney would be on his bed.

'I'm doing me shopping list. What are you doing here?' He answered with his head in our Mess cupboard. His ears obviously worked better with his hair tied out of the way.

'Sorry Rod, I thought you'd be having a lie down. Can we make a pot of tea?' I decided that I couldn't come straight out and ask for a bag of flour, it would take far too much explaining. I always work on the principle that if you ask you might get a no, so it's much better to go ahead without involving anyone else in the decision-making.

'I was going to do that when I finished my list but go on put the kettle on then.' He left his rummaging, turned and stood at the servery, his head down studying his list.

'What we having then?' Nod engaged him in conversation while Toby gave me a secret slide of his eyes towards the Mess cupboard. I put the kettle on the stove and tiptoed over.

'I was thinking Chilli one night, is there enough rice in there for you as well Tom?' We were never going to get away with this, Rodney seemed to have developed a sixth sense as well as elephant ears. He hadn't taken his head up from the list and was now chewing his pencil, I looked over; there was nothing miraculous about his lugholes. I also couldn't find any flour. 'Bottom shelf on the left.'

'What!' I said, I could see Nod's disbelief and thought if Rodney looks up now, we'll definitely be rumbled.

'You must be looking for matches, you haven't lit the gas yet,' said Rod, having misunderstood my surprise.

'Oh yeah, got them,' I was sure my nervousness must have been showing in my voice. However, I'd found the flour and thought I'd take some matches as well. I threw another box to Toby, 'Do the honours Tobe, I've got an EP coming.' I scuttled away doing my best to hide the flour.

'Fucking Veggies, get out of my Mess if you've got an *emergency poo…*' Rodney went on but I was already through the Mess doors. Toby and Nod weren't far behind, they'd abandoned Rodney to his list and kettle and we descended to the covered wash behind the appliance bays.

'Light blue touch paper and retreat,' I said, helpfully.

'I know but I've pushed it in too far and now there's flour on the tip,' said Nod.

'Gis it 'ere,' Toby took over with much more success, much more. There was an unremarkable bang, it was loud but muffled; the flour had worked.

Then, just as I was noticing that the bag of flour had disappeared and created a vast cloud of dust, there was a second bang.

An almighty crescendo rocked our little theatre, it wasn't a banger it was an explosion. My ears had momentarily given up all thought of being able to hear, I'm sure we all swore. We looked at each other and quickly decided to do the honourable thing; we ran away. I took the external stair up to the first floor but stopped as I heard the Guvnor and Bones come out of the office onto the balcony.

'I can't see anything, maybe it was out the front,' said Bones.

'I'll be surprised if we aren't called out, it sounded like we were right on top of it,' added the Guvnor.

I skulked away, out of earshot and back down to the Watchroom where I found Toby and Nod. 'Wow that was something else, what on earth was it?' I asked. Nod was hitting his ears with the palm of his hand.

'I don't know, what was the second bang?' Nod said, now smacking the other ear.

'I reckon that must have been a dust explosion, a good bit of station training.' I started massaging my ears, watching Nod was infectious.

'I've got a bit of a confession to make,' Toby had been quiet so far.

'Go on then,' we both waited for a revelation.

'I reckon you're right about the dust Tom but I did use a second banger.'

'Shit Tobe,' I said, 'you didn't leave the stash open Nod, you need to know he's a bloody arsonist at heart.'

'I haven't got them,' Nod patted his pockets even though they would never have fitted. Toby slowly raised the tatty bag of destruction in front of his villainous face, he had *let's do it again* written all over him. Toby had become possessed.

'Come on, let's blow up the floaties while we've still got a chance.' The fireboat was going to become a separate station but I didn't think that was a good enough reason to give them all a heart attack.

'Let's go and check out the wash, it might be messy.' We hadn't stopped to see what sort of devastation we might have caused to our first scene of operations. There was no evidence whatsoever, not even a bit of flour packaging. It was almost upsetting but it engendered more devilry, I could feel Toby's excited energy.

We returned to our locker room via the south staircase, just to avoid the office. To Tobe's disappointment Nod had reclaimed his lethal weapons. 'I think you should put those to bed Nod,' I said as we entered the dormitory; it was never going to happen.

Granny was laying on his bed, eyes closed, obviously thinking about what bit of kit he would mend next. Toby went into stealth mode, 'Give us a little one,' he whispered. I just couldn't think of an excuse not to, he was too inciting a target. Nod and Toby went through a great deal of paper rustling, punctuated by the odd murmur that took forever. I was just about to hurry them up when a classic banger came out of the bag, was lit and thrown under Gran's bed with an almost expert swiftness.

A lesser man might have died, a lesser man might have risen even further off of the mattress; I'm sure Granny levitated. We sat around on the lockers doing our best impression of innocence. I thought that's the end the Guv must have heard that. Gran came round but didn't get up, looked from side to side, he must have been making sure all his bits were still there. 'What the fuck,' he looked at us but was still confused or perhaps concussed. We couldn't contain ourselves any longer. I thought Nod was going to have a seizure, kneeling on the floor slapping the new carpet much harder than he had his ears.

The far door opened, I thought *here we go, curtains for sure*. Bones walked in with a tray of tea. 'What's so funny?' he looked down at the array of cups.

'Me and the Guv have made a pot of tea,' he said rather proudly, as if they'd performed some sort of intricate experiment.

'Cheers Bones,' I said grabbing for a cup, 'you and the Guv have been down in the Mess, you better not let Rodney catch you.' The mess was probably just far away enough to be out of earshot. We'd got away with another one.

'Can you smell burning? 'Bones was sniffing the air. There was much shaking of heads and a *no*, here and there, he went back out with an empty tray.

Gran said, once we were sure Bones had gone, 'I can smell burning actually.' We all looked over at his prostrate form, he still hadn't risked elevation.

'It's you,' I shouted.

'Wah, your heads on fire screamed Toby.' Wisps of smoke, previously hidden, were coming from behind Gran's head, fine plumes of potential eruption. Gran now leapt into action, once vertical we could see that it was actually his towel smouldering nicely. It went from hanging over the bed head to being flapped around in Gran's huge hands in fractions of moments. This professional manoeuvre, born from years of firefighting experience had the opposite result to the desired extinguishment. It was like an incendiary magic trick, quickly followed by fire walking in Brigade socks, I'd never heard Granny swear so much. He'd managed to fan the fire to really get it going and was now doing some sort of rain dance over the flaming towel.

'Help then,' he pleaded.

We couldn't, we couldn't even breathe.

I often wondered what we might get up to if we weren't so busy. The odd firecall kept us in check, slowed down our ability to amuse ourselves. These interludes had much greater value than we ever realised, they were like group counselling sessions. We certainly had no trouble relaxing at work; while we were together, we felt untouchable. Every now and then a job came along that would test our ability to shrug off the trauma. Gran was right, one of those incidents wasn't far away.

17

November 1984
A Late Night

Noddy was having a little whine about the paperwork that goes with the Leading Fireman's job. He was doing a bit of acting-up but still hadn't got used to the typewriter. 'I can't believe it all has to be in triplicate and then I have to file them,' he said.

'I know, miles of paper that no one will ever read,' I said. The station office was full of files, going back years, records of our every job, every tragedy.

'And bloody typing, I can't get my fingers around that,' said Noddy.

'You'll pick it up Nod,' said Granny, we weren't really that interested. Nod had been with us for eighteen months and had already applied for promotion. Most of us thought it was too soon, but apparently, according to rumour, the Guv had recommended him. I'd be sorry to see him go, but most people have to try a couple of times before they get made; the odds were that he'd be around for a while. He certainly would need to brush up on his typing skills. Granny and I were dangerously unoccupied so the office wasn't the best place to mill around, even at this late hour. We could be asked to do something any minute or we could invent something ourselves.

Distant bell, click, LOUD BELLS, lights come on.

The TL flew off over the river with Noddy in charge. 'He's loving it really,' I said to Gran as we were walking back up the stairs.

'Yeah, shall we help him with some typing?' I was on to Gran straight away and now there was no stopping us.

'Be rude not to,' I said. I slipped Noddy's report of our last rubbish fire out of the typewriter and flipped one of the sheets of carbon paper. 'He hasn't even started typing yet.'

'Well, he'll get plenty of practice when he has to do that one again,' Granny was giggling, finding this greatly amusing. Sometimes the thrill is more in creating the mischief than the outcome.

When Noddy got back we slipped into the office casually, we didn't want to miss out on our finale. The speed of Nod's typing meant we were excruciatingly early as he raised a finger to find another elusive key.

'It's too cruel to watch Granny,' I said. I was having regrets, I hadn't realised Nod was such a novice typist. Another tap echoed around the nervous office.

'You're quiet boys,' said Noddy innocently, his head was scanning from side to side whilst he was holding his finger up in anticipation.

'Oh, stop him Tom,' said Gran, 'it's too painful.'

'All done,' he added a nod, 'I'm getting the hang of this.' He unfurled his work and laid out three perfect copies. Gran and I looked at the report and then at each other.

'That's amazing,' said Gran, giving me a wide-eyed look.

'It is really,' said Nod, 'I normally manage to get the carbon paper the wrong way around and type all over the backs and stuff.'

'I know, I checked it for you while you were out,' I said.

'Tomato, you're useless,' said Gran. Noddy just looked at us quizzically.

'Well how was I to know he'd already got it round the wrong way?' I said.

'Thanks Tom, you're always a help,' said Nod, I'm still not sure if he had caught on to our failed wheeze.

'Come on, I'll buy you a beer in the Chummery,' I said, feeling unnecessarily guilty.

'Bet you can't ring the bell,' I said.

'I'm not finished yet,' said Toby.

'It would have to be a bigger bell for you to hit it Tobe,' goaded Frankie. The TL had been in and out all night; we had been busy but only with false alarms and a bit of rubbish. We had been quiet for over an hour and were getting restless. Supper had been mince D, hot and loads of it, the guys were never full though. I'd joined in with my own version of D, a chilli con veggie.

'It was never this quiet when I was in the A division,' said Rodney. I thought, *where has he been all night,* he was driving the TL and they hadn't stopped all evening.

'Oh, here he goes again,' Granny spoke up, I'd forgotten he was here.

'I bet there were nights when you didn't even get back to the station,' Frankie was winding him up now, but he carried on anyway.

'There was actually, did I ever tell you about the time when...'

'You won't be able to stop him now,' I groaned. Toby and I were grinning but Noddy was sucked right in. Actually, we learnt a lot when the older hands started to reminisce, as long as you could sort the reality from the embellishments.

'Haven't you heard this one yet Nod,' I said, 'perhaps Rodney will tell you the full version on the way to your next shout.'

'Oy, oy, have some respect,' said Frankie as he got up and sneaked out, hoping we'd be left with Rod's drone. Suddenly there was a dull thud as Toby's can hit the wall just below the call out bell. The fire call bells were located in just the wrong place for casually slurping firefighters and had become a target for empty cans.

'Rubbish,' said Granny.

'Go on then, show us how it's done,' said Toby. He didn't need encouraging, his arm was already drawn back in an arc.

'No Gran,' I screamed, but it was too late, Granny's mug shattered in the same spot as Toby's tinny, and it wasn't even empty.

'You wanker,' cried Rodney, well it was his bedroom. Through the laughter I couldn't tell whether Granny had meant it or just forgotten that he wasn't drinking beer. He never did say. He still acting unusually and this latest bit of vandalism was extremely out of character.

Distant bell, click, LOUD BELLS, lights come on.

The bell rang on its own. 'Don't forget you've got some clearing up to do,' shouted Rodney as we ran for the pole. The TL went out somewhere over the river, we weren't invited, again.

It was the early hours of the morning and we still hadn't turned in, 'Aren't you two going to piss off to bed?'

'Sorry Rodders, you should have said,' Toby replied.

'He just did,' I said. Rodney, our resident night owl never seemed to turn in. It was well gone four and the bells had nearly worn themselves out since Rodney's spurious claim of quietness. It seemed to have calmed down now and the rest of the watch were *soundo*. Toby and I got up, left Rodney to his pit in the Chummery and crept into the main dormitory. My duvet was already laid out, I'd long ago abandoned the itchy grey blankets that were Brigade issue. I stripped right off, many of the guys would sleep in various states of half dress just to get to the machine quickly; I would still be there before them, albeit without socks. I laid down and the bells rang again.

Distant bell, click, LOUD BELLS, lights come on.

'How many's that?' Toby shouted, 'I bet it's the TL again,' any pretence at being quiet was now a waste of time.

'It's Rodney's fault for sending us to bed,' I said. It was always quite amusing watching the sleeping crew come round when you were already fully awake. Nod was busy hopping around, trying to run to the pole house and put his trousers on at the same time.

'Easy Nod,' cried Toby as he gave him an arm to stop him falling over.

'What's it like being awake yourself Tobe?' I grinned.

'I can smell it,' called Frankie as we pulled out, blue lights flashing into the vacant Sunday morning. I couldn't smell it, not yet, we were busy rigging and the rear cab smelt even more of smoky tunics than usual.

The Guv, almost too calmly, turned his head, 'Clapham's made it Four, Persons.' If he could have found a shorter way to tell us, I'm sure he would have. We were all awake now.

'Useless bloody things,' the Guvnor was trying to listen to local traffic on his personal radio as we hared along Nine Elms Lane. He'd heard something and lent back again, 'Crew of three.' Gran quickly slipped into his set to join me and Toby. We turned into a relatively new estate just a short distance onto Claphams ground. There was smoke everywhere, streets of it, uncleared by the lack of any breeze, menacing and confusing.

We were out of the machine as Frankie was applying the brakes, he'd only paused momentarily to manoeuvre safely through the murkiness and had easily found the incident. The atmosphere was different, a tragic peace invaded the dense, fiery smog that filled the whole street. Our enthusiasm was at once quelled, it had become a rudeness we didn't at first understand. There was a pump running, feeding a snaking hose strewn over the pavement, but even that had a hush. A clunk of a dropped hose coupling momentarily broke the silence. The normal firefighters' shouts were absent.

Toby and I looked up at Gran, his stare wore an uneasiness; it was another indicator that this was no ordinary job. Something had passed between us, something left by the first crews that hung in the smoke, something we didn't understand.

Clapham's Guvnor was standing in the middle of it all, an island of rock commanding the surrounding hazy ocean. He waved us straight towards the open door, 'Go on boys, in you go, see what you can find.' He then turned to talk to our Guv and in that action, the address of a contemporary, his battle waned and I saw his strength falter.

Toby was starting up as we made the front door. 'Stay together boys,' he said, as the mask covered his face. It was a subtle reminder for me that we had Granny with us; Toby and I are used to working as a pair. It was hard to make out but we were about to enter a mid-terrace house. There was no clean, fresh air to stand in to start our sets so we made do with a purge from the cylinder.

As far as I could make out from the door, an internal staircase was in front of us and the ground floor was off to the right.

'Last crew went up and straight on. You go up and right,' Clapham's Leading Hand took our tallies and handed them to BA control.

'It all seems a bit urgent,' I said, 'what we got?'

'Young family, four or five missing, go get 'em.'

We were in, following the line of hose that went up. It was far too hot, but that realisation was not getting through, not yet. Our eagerness to rescue a child had supressed the experience and knowledge that no one wanted to admit. At the top of the stair, vision went completely and we had to slow down. We turned back along a landing towards what should be the front of the house. I was last, following Granny's massive heels. I swung around the banister, slipped and landed hard on my spine.

No one had seen, it was still too smoky, they hadn't heard either and I temporarily lost Toby and Gran. There are many advantages to having three in a crew, especially if you have to pull someone out. While two of you do the carrying the third can lead the way through the blind obstacle course that is a burning building. We just didn't normally have enough personnel for that sort of luxury. There are disadvantages too; it's harder to keep tabs on two buddies, so by the time Gran knew I was missing and had told Toby, they were already further along the landing. There wasn't far for them to go.

My unwanted seat was confused, piles of debris soaked my hands. There was stuff everywhere, I couldn't make out what anything really was. This was mostly due to trying to see by touch, but also because everything was covered with a layer of hot soggy plaster. The first crew must have fought the fire as they climbed the stair. It was dawning on me that we weren't going to find anyone alive in here, not if the fire had taken that much of a hold that the ceiling was now on the floor.

The fire must have been flashing and that would be far too hot for anyone to survive, especially kids. I turned over onto my hands and knees, gave the banister a good shake and then used it to help me stand back up. There was no one to see me but I still acted nonchalantly, as if nothing had happened: I rubbed my hands down my tunic to get rid of most of the crap, got over my self-consciousness, pretended I hadn't tripped up, and made my way forwards. Granny was shouting something, probably wondering what had happened to the missing Tomato. I caught up easily, not bothering to repeat their search of the corridor. They were waiting to enter the front bedroom.

'What have you been up to Tom?' Toby asked.

'Just having a close look around Tobe,' I answered, still brushing myself down. The door was ajar, we stooped, crouched and crawled between the bedroom wall and a double bed, a murmuration of firefighters creating a six-armed rasping monster. This had every indication of an adult bedroom, the silky bedding and several pairs of ladies' shoes, strewn by the doorway being the biggest clues. Toby was leading, testing the obscurity ahead while we brushed along the wall. As Granny was reaching over the bed I got back on my knees and checked underneath.

We hadn't discussed this, I couldn't see Toby but I knew he would be focusing ahead, ensuring a safe route, just as he knew we would be extending the search as far as possible in his wake. It hadn't taken long but we had morphed into a single three person groping entity. Our path was crowded, a small channel into what may have been the main bedroom. There was nothing behind the door.

Out of nowhere came a shrill that was Gran's shocked cry, 'On the bed!' A bleak exclamation but all that was allowed through his speech diaphragm. His hand snapped back to his side. *Not again*, I thought, mentally preparing myself. Toby opened the front windows, and the smoke cleared fast, too fast, I wanted to seal them up and return to our former seclusion. We stared; the horror slowly filled my body like someone was topping me up with a warm kettle.

I felt sick, sick and clammy, my fire-helmet had become too tight but it was the only thing holding my head together. I saw a frightened child, a scared and lonely baby. A wisp in the middle of a vast cot, framed by his mother's shroud. He was stiff. His small limbs locked in a struggle with an invisible monster. One arm stretched up into his, and now our darkness. I let my mind wander: *The fire's evil gasses had worried him, scared his brief soul and overcome the terror of being found playing with matches. Now he desperately needed a comfort zone. In the complete terror that can easily envelope the young, he sort out his mother. She was errant. He had managed the choking climb, as he had before in other circumstances, seeking her protection. She might be here, in the strange mist, out of his short reach. But there was no Mummy. He rolled over to stare into the darkness, the heat, now much stronger than her embrace, reached down his tiny throat and without compassion, extinguished his shy life.*

'He's about the same age as my nephew,' Granny was the first to speak. He could only have been about three years old, his hand out-stretched in a vacant cry.

'Who's he reaching for?' Toby said, not really wanting an answer.

'For his Mum I suppose,' said Gran. I could only look at his burnt mouth, the fire had left its mark. A last gasp of burning fumes. He had been dead a while. It didn't make it any easier, we had still come too late.

'We haven't finished our search,' Gran was the first to stop staring. I no longer wanted to be a witness to what felt like torture. We continued our job, now a hunt for more victims. I had one eye on the perpetually sleeping child, just in case he might wake. There wasn't much left in the room, there wasn't going to be anything we wanted to find. Toby gingerly opened the double wardrobe; another great hiding place for toddlers, it was just clothes. Granny lifted some loose bedding and it erupted, feathers filled the unwelcome tomb. They flew about in the draught that had helped ventilate, and started to stick where they landed, most of them on me. Any other day it would have been funny.

The smoke had virtually cleared as we came out of the front bedroom, there were firefighters everywhere. 'Let's get out of here,' I said, 'no one's in BA anyway.' Toby and Gran didn't need to be asked twice. There were some other firefighters at the top of the stair, just about where I had fallen. I was asked to stop.

'What's up?' I asked.

'Easy mate there's a dead kid here, let me place your feet,' said the guard. I wasn't sure I'd heard correctly but before I could ask again, he grabbed my ankles and guided my feet forward one by one. I felt like he had punched me in the chest, I ripped off my helmet and mask. 'Oh, hi Tom, I didn't recognise you with your clothes on,' it was one of Clapham's boys. I didn't envy him his task and wasn't surprised at his poor attempt at humour. The fire was at its wispy stage, extinguished and ventilated enough to see, but still steamy. He saw me trying to make out the child, 'Under the debris,' he tried to clarify. I still couldn't see anything, I decided I didn't want to and ran down the stairs.

I was filled with a killer's dread, surely, she wasn't alive when we got here? Surely, she wasn't alive when I blundered around that newel post and fell right where my foot had just been stopped from treading, when I landed on her now broken and previously hidden body? The consuming vision of the little boy on the bed was replaced by this new blurred insanity. Toby and Gran followed me out, they had seen me rip off my facemask. I was waiting by the front door and BA control.

'Shit, we must have walked right over her,' said Gran, how did we know she was a girl, I couldn't tell. All I could think was that I must have fallen right on her, I just couldn't bring myself to say anything.

We slowly walked over to Clapham's Guvnor, 'We found a little boy, on the bed in the front room upstairs Guv,' said Toby.

He looked quite vacant, 'That's four then.'

'Where were the other two Guv?' asked Toby.

'Yours, top of stairs, and two in the wardrobe in the back room.' Toby had gulped in the middle of his sentence, for the slightest moment he thought we'd missed them when we searched the front bedroom. I gulped too; we had missed the baby at the top of the stair. I tried to console myself with the fact that I still couldn't see her when the smoke was clearing and that we came too late for the whole family. It didn't help much. 'I'm a bit busy Guys, but thanks. Tough one, eh,' the Guv returned to his duty.

'That's where I fell,' I said quietly. I wiped my eyes, mixing soot and feathers with the tears I was trying to hide.

'We didn't see her either Tom, no one did,' said Toby.

It was Gran's turn to be quiet, he was looking distant. Then he spoke, 'It's not over.'

'We might not get caught up for too long Gran,' said Toby. I had an idea that wasn't what Gran meant.

The fireground was even more eerily quiet as dawn threatened the bitter street. A few neighbours were standing around, it was still very early and they were whispering respectfully. They couldn't have known anything but they suspected everything. Only the pump murmured as firefighters were exchanging agitated glances or not even that, afraid of showing a dampened cheek.

Then it came, incongruous to our graciousness, a scream.

'MY BABIES!'

A high pitched shrill that suddenly filled the whole estate and then wasn't there. From nowhere she screamed again,

'MY BABIES.'

All eyes turned as the appliance lights reflected off her gaudy earrings. She staggered into the middle of the street, shoeless. Two police officers moved to intercept, but her energy failed and she crumpled into a blubbering, red satin heap. The firefighters had all frozen as the neighbours exchanged sullen glances. She was an assault on our grief, I stood, shocked, feeling only disbelief. A collective refusal to accept this newly painted scene hung from every heart. I couldn't work out what to feel about this truant mother; I was overcome with a tiredness that could no longer find a hero.

I thought *someone will say something*, emotions were high. No one did. The early morning sun shimmered, incongruently, on the stained creases of her spent frock; like glowing embers of forfeited pity, her frivolity had been replaced by the fire.

I thought I could see Granny trembling, he watched her momentarily, was he realising a prophecy? He slowly turned his head away. 'Come on Guys, let's get these sets off,' said Toby. I closed my eyes, all I could still see was a boy's pleading arm, the sibling of the baby that no one saw. I will never forget that child. He reached out and we came too late.

Everyone helped doing the sets, they normally do but it was more special this morning. We were supporting each other subconsciously, but it was still very quiet. I spoke loudly, I wanted everyone to hear, 'Thanks Guys, glad you were there this morning.'

Toby put a hand on my shoulder, 'Someone had to stop you and Gran having that pillow fight,' he said. Suddenly we were all chatting again.

Frankie shouted, 'Where's the fucking Rosie?' A cup of tea, yes, now that would put everything right. Nod walked in with a tray.

Red was at my home when I finally got off my bike and ended that awful morning. I can't remember why she was there but it had seemed like a good idea at the time.

I also don't know why it hit me then. I guess I'd had to deal with the traffic although I couldn't remember the cycle home. I propped my bike up against the side wall, no one was around. This was normal, I had to go through the house to open the back gate and it was secluded enough to leave my bike for a few moments. I started to take my gloves and headphones off and just collapsed into a torrent of tears. Real sobs, shuddering sobs; I felt a release of the suppression that I'd been holding back and suddenly, I lost control. Falling from my bike, I took a few moments and let it flow, I couldn't stop it anyway, then a deep breath, and another, and then recovery, of a sort.

At that point I wished I didn't have a visitor, but I'd regained my composure and was sure my face could be excused as cycling exertion.

She knew, 'Oh Tommy, what's wrong?' I'd only just walked through the door. I slumped into the dusty old armchair; at first, I couldn't bring myself to say it but I knew I was not going to hide this one much longer. My eyes began to leak again, lines of misery.

'Kids,' was all I managed to say. She held me and we both wept. I changed my mind, I was glad she was there.

18

January 1985
A Chrimbo Party

After a few months room hopping and trying to keep the dust out of my compact disc player, Bones' project was nearly finished. This was great news for Bones and sad news for me. I was going to have to get around to finding some permanent digs and even sadder, paying some rent. I quite liked the almost bohemian aspect of my current domestic arrangements; it was also cheaper than cheap. Bones had converted this old terrace house, with not too much hindrance from my practical help, into two lovely flats. So now it was time for me and my now extended CD collection to move along. Red and I had been spending a lot of quality time together but we weren't ready to make it any more serious; I would be looking for a bachelor pad.

At least station life was settled, if you didn't count Nod's promotion. It was the last night of a very quiet tour and we were all looking forward to our Chrimbo meal out in two days' time. As usual it is nearly the end of January, a much easier time to organise a Christmas party than December when so much else is going on. This year we are taking our wives and girlfriends to a Cockney Night: meal, music and dancing, what could go wrong? Red was dying to know whether Frankie was going to bring his wife or his girlfriend. She was also keen to catch up with the other girls that she hadn't seen since our Guernsey weekend.

We were sitting around the Mess table, Chinas at the ready, it couldn't stay this quiet for long. We hadn't had a shout all evening and were now convinced our supper would soon be ruined. Most of us were still eating, which gave the Mess a rare quietness, then he just blurted it out without any warmup or warning. 'I'm going to do the new fireboat course,' said Granny, he took another shovel of mince, as if nothing important had been announced. I was stunned, we all were.

'You're leaving too, then,' said Nod, who was only awaiting his posting. It seems that he had other plans all along, he didn't rate the promotion opportunities in the post office and was planning big things in the Brigade.

'I'll still be here though,' said Granny.

'Yeah, but it's going to be a completely separate station and you'll probably have to change watch.' Granny obviously knew this but Toby pointed it out anyway.

I looked at Granny, he can't have known but I was screaming inside, *don't you bloody go*. That was unfair on all levels, unfair because I was leaving myself. Suddenly, what had only been musings turned into a rage and accelerated towards me, my head began to swim in dithering selfishness. I just hadn't done anything about it, I hadn't even mentioned it to Red. I'd thought about it quite often lately and wondered if I'd be better off doing something completely different. I suppose I hadn't been able to get past that; what on earth would I do?

It had been a bad year, our watch had picked up some nasty jobs and I couldn't stop thinking about all the stiffs. Nod, and now Gran leaving, had got me confused. It was like they had beaten me to the finish line and now I could never end the race. I felt ashamed for not being able to cope, but I wasn't even sure that was the case. Most of all I was conflicted, I didn't want to leave my brothers but I didn't want to play with any more dead people. Losing two of the watch made me feel guilty for even thinking I'd become the third and that's not including all the floaties. I looked straight across the table into the faces of Toby and Frankie, I was convinced they knew what I was thinking.

'You still with us Tom?' Gran asked.

'I'm not going anywhere!' I said, but Gran was showing me a concerned visage that went deeper than his own news. I realised that I'd just contradicted my inner self.

'Have you applied Gran or just thinking about it?' I asked. I should have known the answer, the announcement was a definite statement of intent.

'Applied and accepted,' Bones answered for him, he had probably been in the know from the application stage, and felt it was now okay to give his confirmation. I felt a bit betrayed, neither had said a word. It's not as if it was gossip, this was family business.

'You kept that quiet,' said Frankie.

'Well, I hadn't really decided until I got the offer tonight, and I like the idea of the new Marine Qualification.' I could tell his mind was made up, I was missing him already.

'Bloody hell, it's me cooking, you should have said, the watch is falling apart around me,' that was almost a speech for Rodney, but the watch was going to look very different and soon.

'And you've got such a way with dead animals,' I said, which brought on the expected barrage of veggie attacks, even though we were all still in shock.

The Brigade had decided that it was time to upgrade the river response and that meant big changes for everyone at Lambeth; there was to be a separate, new River Station. There was even talk of a second floating station further out to the east. Most of the floaties had already signed up, I had no idea that Granny was that interested in the river. I had a brief flashback to the fire that had taken the lives of the four small children; if we ever mentioned it, we referred to it as the *Kids Job*. We didn't really talk about that morning; Granny never did.

I was worried about him then but there were some incidents we just couldn't help each other with; we just shared the demons introspectively.

The A & B rang and Frankie went off for his nightly ear bashing. I don't know whether it was his wife or his girlfriend but he was getting aggravation from both parties and knowing Frankie, probably from elsewhere as well. He came strolling back into the mess, 'It's for you Toby.'

'Ooooh,' went the joint harmony. Toby never had phone calls at work. He caught my eye as he heard his name and I raised my eyebrows discretely. We both knew who was on the line.

'How about that,' I said, 'let me show you where the sink is Frankie, it's where the rest of us do the washing up.'

'Alright, alright. Hey Toby!' he looked around as Tobe was on his way, managing to gain everyone's attention with a dramatic pause, 'she sounds lovely.' He gave a sort of knowing nod and turned back to us grinning. I knew more; Red had set him up with her flatmate.

'So, you're going to be a floaty Gran, I'll still talk to you,' I picked up another plate and attempted to dry it with my wet tea towel. My recent internal conflict now re-hidden.

'That's good of you Tom,' said Gran.

Distant bell, click, LOUD BELLS, lights come on.

The TL took off over the river somewhere and we were walking back up the stairs. Frankie said, 'So what one are you having Tom?' I was puzzled.

'You've not had more kittens, have you?'

'No, the flats, are you going up or down?' I was still puzzled but starting to have an idea what he was talking about.

'Do you mean Bones' place?'

'Yeah, aren't you having one?' it really hadn't occurred to me, but it did now.

'I don't know.'

'Go ground and get the garden, you love that stuff.'

'Don't you think Bones and I should talk about it?' He was out on the TL, I suddenly thought I needed an urgent chat.

'I already did,' said Frankie.

'Aww, you're leaving the misses then Frank, that's sad.'

'No, no way, we're not splitting Tommy.'

'You're not making sense again, I know I'm a bit slow but...'

'No Julie was just mucking me about.' Frankie looked hard done by.

'Fancy that Frankie, someone mucking you about,' he either ignored my sarcasm or it went straight over his head. 'The ground floor is two-bed Frankie, but you seem to know a lot about it already.'

'Well, I've been consulting with Bones, you know baby stuff.' He made it sound as if Bones had been asking his advice, typical of Frankie to turn it all about face.

I was interested in the flat, but the upstairs, single bedroom, was probably more in my price range. As soon as the TL returned, Bones and I talked business.

The rest of the night passed pretty slowly but the morning had quite a surprise in store. When we talked about it after the event some things made more sense, to everyone else at least. I was still surprised at my ignorance of Rod's dubious part-time hobby. Apparently if you said you needed something, he managed to have it for sale the next week, normally from the boot of his car. We still don't know what is in his spare lockers; officially he only had one. None of us were brave enough to go anywhere near the others for fear of collaboration. The initial confusion involved me more than anyone else, even Rod.

There was a strange phone call. 'Do you have a Thomas Reef on duty today?'

They didn't announce themselves and I, not understanding the question, didn't ask straight away. I'm the only Tom on the station but I've never been a Thomas, and Fm Reef, is Bill Reef, is Rodney. It took me a while to work this all out.

'We've got a William Reef, if that's who you want, I can get him?' I thought it can't really be anyone else, so I continued, 'Who wants him?' The line went dead and I just thought it was a wrong number, not a very polite one, but already fading from my memory. I did think to myself, *I must tell Rod later*, and that was it, lost in the jumble of the synapses that are meant to be my brain.

About twenty minutes or so later, just as I was settling down to my dutyman incarceration, with crossword under my arm and a cup of tea in hand, two smart gents in suits and ties, walked into the Watchroom. I wondered what they could be selling.

'Can we see the Officer in Charge please?' said the first plain clothes policeman from behind a warrant card. He was overly confident, but perhaps a little short for a Copper; the second was tall enough to stare over his shoulder. Apart from their height, they could have been twins.

'Sure, I'll get him, what's he done?' My attempt at humour caused a surreptitious glance between them as they both entered the Box. It seemed as if they were recalculating a previously rehearsed plan. Perhaps the Boss was in trouble.

'Oh, hi, how are you?' said number two, quite informally as if he actually knew me.

'Can you just give your Guvnor a call?' the first officer was a tad abrupt, like he hadn't heard of the word, *patience*. I had put down my tea already and picked up the phone.

'How's Maria?' the taller more relaxed Officer asked. He'd recognised me through my wife, but he obviously didn't know her well enough to know we were history.

'I don't know,' I said without explanation.

There was no answer from our office. I was just about to try the Mess when officer two piped up, 'Can't you just ring the bells or something?'

'Is there a fire?' I said, I was starting to get annoyed at their attitude. Before they could answer I said, 'Come on, I'll take you up.' We made it up the centre stair and into our main corridor when the bells dropped. Number two hadn't given up his questions about my soon to be ex-wife; I didn't recognise him at all but I didn't even try to remember. Number one was put out by his colleague's relaxed attitude, disappointed that his lead had been stolen.

Distant bell, click, LOUD BELLS, lights come on.

'Sorry, got to go,' I turned and ran for the pole house without waiting for a reply or worrying about leaving them stranded.

As we pulled out of the doors to a dust chute alight, I noticed the first officer lying on the floor at the bottom of the pole house, clutching his hands. I didn't say anything, his mate was there to help, somewhere. Probably walking down, the stairs without burning his hands or breaking his ankles.

'Who were they Tom?' asked the Guvnor.

'Old Bill, they wanted to see you Guv, been robbing banks again?' It was getting near the end of the shift and the guys quickly forgot about the two blokes in the corridor. We were much more interested in the exciting prospect of overtime. That's everyone accept Rodney, although we were unaware at the time.

'What do ya reckon, bit of O.T.?' said Toby.

'It's a bit early,' said Gran.

'Better not wing it, we could get our collars felt when we get back,' I said.

'What's that all about, Tom?' asked Gran, he'd raised his voice, as if he wanted everyone to hear.

'They wouldn't tell me Gran, well above my pay grade.' Unfortunately, it was a false alarm and we were back at the station with another half an hour of our tour to go.

The machine had hardly pulled into the bay as Rodney shouted to me, 'Book Curly for me Tom, I've got to get away,' and in the same breath, 'is that okay Guv?'

'Is he here?' asked the Guv, as Rodney leapt from the Machine.

'Yeah,' came the distant reply as he virtually sprinted towards his car.

'William Reef?' came the call from the Watchroom, the Old Bill was still around but Rodney had a flying start. He jumped in his car as the two officers almost tripped over each other, both trying get out of the Box at the same time. The shorter of them was limping and flapping his hands, and much to number two's frustration, blocking the Watchroom door.

'They'll never get him,' I said, as we all shuffled, in various states of taking off our boots and leggings, to try and get a better view.

'This is better than the Sweeney,' said Gran. Rodney's car door slammed shut as the old bill were still negotiating the rear of the appliance bay. They ran into the morning glare from the darkness of the appliance bay, their Savile Row appearance doing nothing to aid the chase. Rodney had a usual parking place that he was obsessive about, he would move his car at any time of day to reclaim his small piece of territory, directly facing the open rear gates. I wondered if he had his passport secreted in the glovebox. Escape beckoned to him in the shape of Lambeth High Street.

'Go Rodders,' I shouted. We held our breath for his old Escort Estate to roar out of the rear gate into the sunrise, and away from his hapless pursuers. Luckily, the normally crowded yard had yielded Rod a direct run for freedom. The twins raced around other parked obstacles, Number Two using his long reach and the rear light of a Staff Car to help propel himself forwards.

We waited. Nothing happened.

'He's had a change of heart,' said Gran. The two police officers, sensing a possible victory, made a last Keystone dash. The first had decided to go for their car, expecting a Blues Brothers moment, the second went straight for Rod and tripped over the first.

'I bet that's ruined their *Whistles*,' said Frankie.

'Who's got the camera rolling?' Toby said, as they danced in the yard in an attempt to pick each other up.

'What's he doing?' I wondered aloud.

Rodney, unaware of the pantomime, got out of his car. 'He's going to *Hill Street Blues* it across the car roofs,' suggested Toby, who like all of us was getting over excited about the show. Rod had enough time to kick the car door before he was grabbed, he would have had enough time for a pint if they were open.

He was cuffed. As they limped to the squad car, Toby shouted, 'What happened Rod? Fail to start?'

'Keys are in me fucking locker,' was all he said.

'Take us off the run Tom,' the Guvnor had joined our viewing gallery.

That brought our tour of duty to an abrupt end and we were now getting ready for another watch outing. Toby and I had a quick pint before we went to pick up the girls, two days had passed since Rod's demise and we had no idea how he was getting on. Vanessa answered the door, she had poured herself into a slinky number and she looked gorgeous.

Toby obviously approved, they just stared at each other, even on the doorstep I felt in the way. I had to have a look at Toby, to check, but all I could see were his big ears, even if they were mostly hidden by his golden locks; Vanessa obviously saw something I'd missed. I caught a glimpse of Red entering the kitchen, and made a bid for entry.

'Come in for a quickie, the cabs not due yet,' said Vanessa.

'I don't think we've got time for that, but maybe a drink,' I said.

'Cheeky,' she answered. This was their second date, we had set them up for tonight but they didn't want to meet at our Chrimbo party so they had already been out together. Toby had split with his long-term girlfriend shortly after our Guernsey trip. He'd had a few dates since then but nothing that serious.

'Wow, you girls look gorgeous, are you going somewhere?' I said. Red gave me a hello peck on the cheek, her perfume went straight to my head as I absorbed her cute, blood red, sultry outfit; she would certainly be turning some heads tonight.

We met the rest of the watch in a pub local to the venue, I was at the bar holding the kitty, as usual. The main discussion had, of course, been about Rod's unusual way of going off duty, but we hadn't forgotten our speculations on who would be with Frankie. Toby reckoned he would turn up with his girlfriend.

'My money's on his wife,' I said.

'You've got it Tobe,' Granny was staring over everyone's heads. Frankie came into view, talking and walking with a very attractive girl. Not what I'd expected though, she was quite short, making Frankie stoop, and obviously a little on the pregnant side. I wondered if I'd misunderstood our earlier conversation. Equally, Frankie's tales of his exploits had always involved tall, skinny creatures. He began the introductions, I'm sure he didn't call her Julie but I was distracted by his wife approaching from the Ladies. I thought *bloody hell, he's brought them both.* Red gave me a funny look, as only a nurse could; I'd gone into a cold sweat, as if I was the culprit. Then Bones turned up from the Gents and put his arm around the newcomer's low shoulders. They made a more likely pair, but the shock caught us all off guard.

'You've met everyone,' he said.

'That's not his wife,' I tried to whisper into Red's ear, forgetting that she had met Julie. She heard but now everyone had crowded together and it was too intimate for discrete discussion. We had gone into that polite mode, accepting this new girl into our midst as if it wasn't unusual in the slightest. This was totally the opposite of our station behaviour, I couldn't wait to get around the Mess table to get to the bottom of this development.

Frankie came over and made a fuss of meeting Vanessa and Red, he kissed their hands and gave them all sorts of compliments. His wife just raised her eyebrows and asked for a Laurel & Hardy with coke, it was the sort of thing Frankie would say.

'Bacardi,' I told the confused young barman. Frankie sidled up to Toby.

'Punching above your weight there Tobe, she's a bit of alright,' and then straight into the gossip, 'What about Bones' girlfriend, eh, imagine bringing her tonight. Does she look pregnant to you?' he stopped for breath.

'Just a bit' I said, sarcasm dripping from my tongue.

'Yeah, I thought you knew, working with him and all that.' I was still trying to work out the process of telling Red what was going on. Frankie was off and mingling, totally oblivious to his wife who didn't really seem to care.

I took my chance at clarification, 'I guess it's a bit confusing,' I started.

She politely interrupted, 'Well that's Donna, she's five months gone and she's going to be your new neighbour, you know the rest.' I stared at her, my astonishment quickly changing to a broad grin.

'I guess you can fill me in with the details later,' I said.

'Oh, I can think of better things to do later,' I could feel her hot breath unbalancing the side of my face.

We were all there to my reckoning, and I was about to suggest we made our way to our themed evening. Suddenly Granny said, 'Isn't that Ruth, Rod's misses?'

'Is she coming on her own?' I innocently asked Toby. She was dressed up for a party but I think she had other things on her mind.

'Hi Ruth, is Rod with you?' Frankie's wife asked.

'He's still fucking banged up, ain't he,' she was slurring her words and speaking just loud enough to turn a few heads. 'Where is he? And where's that fucking bitch wife?' She'd gone up an octave and now the whole pub must have been aware something was about to kick off. People sidled away, but not completely. They wanted to ensure a good view, some even stood up to claim a better vantage point. I had no idea she was talking about me, I was the only one who didn't.

'She's after you,' Red clenched my arm.

'I don't know why.' I was thinking *my wife's in Counter Terrorism, what's Ruth got to do with that?*

'She is a policewoman, isn't she?' Red pointed out, it was a simple statement but it explained so much. I had a long overdue epiphany; no matter how I saw my wife, to everyone else she was plain and simple, Old Bill. Memories of all those unexplained *Rodney moments* flooded my subconscious; these were just as quickly replaced by Ruth. A wild vision, a Ruth seeking vengeance.

'Tommy,' she screamed, it was piercing, not quite worthy of a Western Saloon Door moment, but she managed a definite barroom hush. An obscure David Bowie song could now be heard on the Jukebox, as the rest of the lull waited for her next move. With all the purpose she could muster, she staggered forwards, wide eyes glaring. I could feel a wave of sad anger rolling ahead of her pink stilettos and strewn party frock.

She looked directly at me as Red clasped my arm even tighter and the first sign of confusion fell onto her face. Her eyes betrayed her uncertainty; she was hunting a tall blond and her prey wore a short red disguise.

As I was thinking *Rod can't have told her about my marital status*, she allowed her anger an outing. 'Who the fuck are you?' she didn't really finish the sentence. The height of her shoes gave up the battle with her ankles and she took a dive to the swirling wooden floor. Bowie managed to sing, 'God knows I'm good,' before the supressed hubbub excitedly returned.

Red and Vanessa ran to her rescue. I'm sure she was already crying as she hit the deck. She tried to jump back up, so as to pretend she hadn't in fact fallen at all. A gaggle of wives took her to the ladies.

'Shall I ask for the accident book?' Granny said.

She was ushered into a taxi home, but not before I was forgiven for being mistaken as a conspirator in Rodney's recent incarceration.

All this drama had made us late and they were already serving the meal when we eventually got to the venue. We were escorted to the last long table near the stage by waiting staff doing mad versions of the Lambeth Walk. As usual my request for vegetarian food hadn't got through the intricate process of informing the chef and I was fobbed off with a bit of melon to start and a hastily defrosted cardboard Lasagne for a main. Not quite the pie mash and liquor being demolished by the watch and played with by their partners.

As I looked up and down the table, I realised that I could never leave this bunch, they were a part of my soul. When Ruth came into the pub earlier the boys had all stepped up. Not to protect me but to help one of our own in her husband's absence. I lost all memory of wanting to leave; wrapped in the warmth of my family, and a little alcohol.

The cabaret started as we were still eating our traditional Cockney dessert of…Black Forrest Gateaux.

'And vere are you from,' the host asked the furthest table.

A loud, 'Deutschland,' was roared above the inattentive crowd.

'Gutten Abend,' cried the host in a superb German accent.

'He's no bloody Cockney,' cried out Frankie, who is actually from Sydenham but reckoned he could hear Bow Bells from his cot. His cry was loud enough to be heard over the general din but I don't think anyone understood anyway.

The next table were from Spain, then Sweden and as more people devoured their gateau the decibel level grew higher. I hadn't heard one local group yet and was realising we might have miss judged our choice of venue. He finally reached our table and we were ready. Before his poor Cockney accent had finished the question, we let go with a brilliant.

'Lambeth!'

'No, vere really?' he said, adding a little Tommy Steel stroll, 'Vere?'

'FUCKING LAMBETH,' I'm sure the cockney host understood.

'He's never going to believe us,' said Toby.

'Who would?' I said, 'Who would?'

'I would if you're asking,' said Red.

'What?' I replied.

'Were you reminiscing again?'

'What time is it?'

'It must be beer o'clock.'

'You should have said.' I looked down at the now blotchy fire engine red of the different parts of my sun-drenched body; it was definitely time to cover up.

'And don't get sand in your knickers, come on, last one there buys the first round.'

Glossary

45mm hose	Small low-pressure hose
70mm hose	Large low-pressure hose

A

A & B	Early pay phone system
Act-up	Temporarily take on the role of a higher rank
AFA	Automatic Fire Alarm
Akip	Asleep
Appliance	Fire Engine
Appliance Bay	Place where Fire Engines are parked

B

B.A.	Breathing Apparatus
B.A. board	Board where tallies of working firefighters are kept.
B.A. Tally	Detachable tag used to record a firefighter's details
Backdraft	Explosive increase in fire due to air entrainment
Banged up	In prison
Bells drop	Bells ring for a call out
Big Smoke	London
Bight	Large loop of hose or line
Bin Room	Room at bottom of dust chute, where bins are kept
Blues and Twos	Blue flashing lights and two-tone sirens
Box	see Watchroom
Boys in blue	Police
Branch	Nozzle attached to the end of hose
Bravo twenty-two	Lambeth radio call sign
Bridge	Make a safe route over a gap, normally with a ladder
Bridge Head	Control point for high rise fire

C

Call out	Call to a fire or other incident
Call slip	Paper slip with incident details
Chinagraph Pencil	A cross between a crayon and a pencil
Chuck up	Vomit or smell bad
Collar felt	Arrested
Con. Off.	Control Staff
Copper	Police Officer
CPR	Cardiopulmonary Resuscitation

D

Drills	Practical training
Dry Riser	Fire service pipe installed within tall buildings
Dust chute	Shute for garbage in flats
Dust, The	Refuse collection
Dutyman	Firefighter in charge of receiving calls
Duty-slut	see Dutyman

E

E.P.	Emergency poo
Escape	A fifty-foot wheeled ladder

F

Face mask	Transparent part of B.A. set that houses breathing valve
Ff	Firefighter
Fire Gear	Firefighters uniform to wear fighting fires
Fire-stopping	Protective building work to prevent fire spread.
Flashover	Sudden increase in fire due to heat build-up
Float	Fireboat
Floaties	Fireboat crew
Fm	Fireman, old gender specific term for Firefighter

G

Get to work (1)	Fight a fire
Get to work (2)	Order to commence with the orders given
Goer	A fire that is well alight

Gofer	Person who does menial tasks, such as fetch and carry
Guv	see Guvnor
Guvnor	Station Officer and above

H

Hand	Firefighter
Hooky	Crooked
Hose-Reel	25m lengths of high-pressure hose wound onto a drum
Hydrant	Water main outlet for fire service use
Hydrant gear	Equipment used to connect hose to a hydrant

J

JB	see Junior Buck
Jekyll's	Jekyll & Hyde's, Strides – Trousers (cockney rhyming slang)
Joanna	Piano (cockney rhyming slang)
Job	An incident, normally a fire
Junior Buck	Newest member of the watch

K

Kicks	Underpants
Knock off	Stop whatever you are doing

L

L Ff	see Leading Firefighter
Lambeth High St.	A High St that no longer has any shops.
Landlubber	Not a good seaman
Large Applicator	Long branch with Rose nozzle
Leading Firefighter	Rank between Firefighter and Sub Officer
Leading Hand	see Leading Firefighter
Length of hose	One piece of hose, 20 m long
Line	Length of rope
Line of hose	More than one length of hose joined together

M

Machine	Fire Engine
Make and Mend	Stand down period
Make up (1)	Clear up and put away all fire equipment
Make up (2)	Fire with increased attendance
Mess	Kitchen and dining area
Mess Manager	Firefighter who runs the Mess
Met, The	The Metropolitan Police Service
Moon	The display of one's buttocks
Mullered	Very drunk, Overdone

O

O.T.	Overtime
Off the run	Not working
Old Bill	Police
On the bell	Travelling to an incident with sirens sounding
Out duty	Spend the day/night at another Fire Station

P

Parade	see Roll Call
Pearl Diver	Fiver, five pounds sterling (cockney rhyming slang)
Pick up a job	Attend a fire or other incident
Pit	Narrow bed on fire station
Pole House	The vertical shaft housing the fireman's pole
Power take off	Appliance gear selection to enable fire pump to work
Pump	Fire Engine or water pump
Pump Ladder	Fire Engine with an Escape Ladder

R

Real Job	Large fire, not rubbish alight
Restow	To put equipment onto another fire appliance
Resus. pack (resuscitation)	Pouch containing face shield, plastic gloves
Riding	Having a place on the fire engine
Roll Call	Designation of attendees and the riding positions
Rose Nozzle	Branch that produces a wide spray

Rosie	see Rosie Lea
Rosie Lea	Cup of tea (cockney rhyming slang)
Routemaster	A type of London double-decker bus.

S

Set	Breathing Apparatus
Shout	Call to an incident
Slip (1)	Release the mechanism that retains the ladder
Slip (2)	see Call slip
Soundo	Sound asleep
Soup Kitchen	Mobile food canteen for the homeless
Spalling	Chipping away of stone/rock/brick
Stand by	see Out duty
Stand-easy	Normally morning tea-break with sandwiches
Start up	Start to use a BA set
Stn O	Station Officer (Guv)
STOP	A message to Control that the fire is out
Sub O	Sub Officer, rank below Stn O
Subby	see Sub O
Suzzies	Suspender belts
Swing the lamp	Tell stories, often exaggerated.

T

Tele-printer	Device in the Watchroom that prints out messages
Toby Jug	Ear, lughole (cockney rhyming slang)
Tour	Four days on duty
Trunnion bar	Part of fixing on fire engine for a wheeled escape.
Turn a Wheel	Go out on a Shout
Turntable Ladder	Fire Appliance with 100ft/30m ladder
Two-tones	Fire Engine sirens

W

Watch	Period of time on duty
Watch, The	On duty crews
Watchroom	Place where fire calls are received
Whistle and Flute	Suit (cockney rhyming slang)

| Workwear | Uniform worn around the station |

Z

| Zed | Snore |